SEXUAL DIVERSITY IN AFRICA

Sexual Diversity in Africa

Politics, Theory, and Citizenship

Edited by

S.N. NYECK AND MARC EPPRECHT

McGill-Queen's University Press
Montreal & Kingston • London • Ithaca

© McGill-Queen's University Press 2013

ISBN 978-0-7735-4187-0 (cloth)
ISBN 978-0-7735-4188-7 (paper)
ISBN 978-0-7735-8975-9 (ePDF)
ISBN 978-0-7735-8976-6 (ePUB)

Legal deposit fourth quarter 2013
Bibliothèque nationale du Québec

Printed in Canada on acid-free paper that is 100% ancient forest free
(100% post-consumer recycled), processed chlorine free

McGill-Queen's University Press acknowledges the support of the
Canada Council for the Arts for our publishing program. We also
acknowledge the financial support of the Government of Canada
through the Canada Book Fund for our publishing activities.

Library and Archives Canada Cataloguing in Publication

Sexual diversity in Africa: politics, theory, and citizenship / edited
by S.N. Nyeck and Marc Epprecht.

Includes bibliographical references and index.
Issued in print and electronic formats.
ISBN 978-0-7735-4187-0 (bound). – ISBN 978-0-7735-4188-7 (pbk.). –
ISBN 978-0-7735-8975-9 (ePDF). – ISBN 978-0-7735-8976-6 (ePUB)

1. Sexual minorities – Africa. 2. Sex – Africa. 3. Gender identity – Africa.
4. Queer theory – Africa. I. Epprecht, Marc, 1957–, editor of compilation
II. Nyeck, S. N., 1977–, editor of compilation

HQ73.3.A37S49 2013   306.7096   C2013-902846-3
                                              C2013-902847-1

This book was typeset by Interscript in 10.5/13 Sabon.

Contents

Acknowledgments

This project was made possible through the generous funding of the Ford Foundation and the Social Sciences and Humanities Research Council (Canada). We thank Deborah Amory, Paisley Currah, Barbara Klugman, and Cary Alan Johnson for their role in launching IRN-Africa, and Mark Blasius for his co-editorship during the first phase of preparing the manuscript, as well as his insightful comments on the introductory essay. Molly Egerdie and Adriane Epprecht did stellar work on the works cited and index, respectively, while Jacqueline Mason, Carolyn Yates, and the team at McGill-Queen's University Press earned our deep gratitude for their confidence in the project and their professionalism.

Several chapters are revised forms of articles published here with permission. Chapter 3 appeared as "The Making of 'African Sexuality': Early Sources, Current Debates" (2010) in *History Compass* 8 (8): 768–79; chapter 7 appeared as "(In)Justice in Sport: The Treatment of South African Track Star Caster Semenya" (2013) in *Feminist Studies* 39(1): 40–69; and chapter 9 appeared as "'The One Who First Says I Love You': Love, Seniority and Relational Gender in Postcolonial Ghana" (2011) in *Ghana Studies* 14.

Abbreviations

ANC	African National Congress
CAL	Coalition of African Lesbians
FGC	female genital cutting
GALA	Gay and Lesbian Memory in Action
HHRP	Health and Human Rights Project
HRM	Healing Revelation Ministries
IAAF	International Association of Athletics Federation
IGLHRC	International Gay and Lesbian Human Rights Commission
ILGA	International Lesbian and Gay Association
IRB	Immigration Refugee Board
LGBTI	lesbian, gay, bisexual, transgender, intersex
MDG	Millennium Development Goals
MSM	men who have sex with men
NGO	non-government organization
NIA	National Intelligence Agency
SADF	South African Defence Force
SAMS	South African Medical Service
SANDF	South African National Defence Force
TRC	Truth and Reconciliation Commission
UDHR	Universal Declaration of Human Rights
UN	United Nations
WHO	World Health Organization
WSM	women who have sex with women

SEXUAL DIVERSITY IN AFRICA

Introduction

S.N. NYECK AND MARC EPPRECHT

This book has its origins in the launch of the International Resource Network for Africa (IRN-Africa) in 2007 in Saly, Senegal. At its launch, IRN-Africa became the final regional component of the larger International Resource Network (IRN), which was founded in 2002 by the Center for Lesbian and Gay Studies at the City University of New York (CLAGS). CLAGS is a clearing house for information sharing and collaboration among researchers, activists and policy advocates, artists, and teachers who address diverse sexualities and gender identities throughout the world. A shared website for the autonomously governed IRN regions links visitors to a wide range of support groups, breaking news, and announcements of activist campaigns, publications, videos, and public events.

For the launch of IRN-Africa, a core group of academicians and activists that included Deborah Amory (Empire State College of the State University of New York), Paisley Currah (the then director of CLAGS), Cary Alan Johnson (International Gay and Lesbian Human Rights Commission), and S.N. Nyeck (University of California, Los Angeles) brought together about two dozen other activists and scholars from around the African continent and North America who were interested in the potentially transforming roles of sexuality, sexual discourse, and images. A particular concern of the workshop was to investigate and theorize non-normative sexualities and gender variance in the African context, and hence begin to unravel silences and stereotypes about Africa as a place where highly restrictive and oppressive ideologies of heterosexual masculinity and femininity are often held up as state policy or immutable culture. While the group shared excitement about emerging scholarship and optimism about new sexual rights networks and activist achievements around the continent, in the background was an abiding anxiety about the rise of explicit forms of homophobia and an acute health crisis that especially affects men who have sex with men.

Prior to the formation of IRN-Africa, a number of activist groups promoting the idea of sexual rights as human rights were active on the continent, often supported by Western donors and solidarity groups.[1] Academics, mostly from the West, have also helped to conduct high-quality empirical research and theorize gender and non-normative sexuality in Africa for many years. The newly launched network was not intended to duplicate or supplant these efforts. Rather, its founders conceptualized it as a platform to promote further comparative, intellectual, and critical understandings of the often-hidden roles that sexuality plays in shaping ideas and sociopolitical and legal structures in Africa. They prioritized the need to foster the development of a new generation of African scholarly researchers who have begun to engage the topic. IRN-Africa's purpose was thus to link people doing research (both academic and community based) in areas related to gender and sexuality in Africa, promote international communication and exchange through scholarship, expand knowledge building, foster comparative and collaborative projects among researchers, advance curricular and course development, and widen the availability of shared scholarly resources within Africa. At the end of the workshop, the organization formed a board of members from Africa and elected S.N. Nyeck as its coordinator.

After two years of active writing through a series of publications online, a follow-up conference titled Genders & Sexualities in Africa: Opportunities and Challenges in the 21st Century convened at Empire State College in Syracuse, New York, in 2009. The conference sought to explore questions and partnerships arising from new scholarship on gender and sexualities in Africa, including the diverse experiences of the African diaspora. Presenters included public intellectuals, artists, and scholars from a wide range of disciplines using interdisciplinary approaches. Essays in this volume represent a cumulated effort by members of IRN-Africa and other concerned scholars to critically engage with the debates about sexuality and gender identity in Africa today, as well as with contentious issues around methodology, epistemology, ethics, and pedagogy.

This is not the first publication on gender variance and non-normative sexuality in Africa, and the contributors all generously acknowledge their debts to research pioneers. However, this book showcases emerging African scholars and allows them to compare notes with other senior scholars. By so doing, it immediately challenges one of those stereotypes about non-normative sexualities in Africa that opponents of sexual rights often cite: that non-normative sexualities are not a topic of particular interest to African intellectuals or a serious research priority but rather reflects a purely Western-driven agenda or elitist frivolity. We profoundly disagree, and will demonstrate how research on sexual minorities reveals hidden power dynamics in many spheres of social, political, and intellectual life that are of great concern to Africans, however they understand and express their sexuality or gender identity and however far they may be from elites.

The empirical component of this book presents a wide tapestry of issues that testify to the complex, multifaceted nature of sexuality, sexual practices, and gender performance in Africa. The evidence is fascinating and important to know in its own right: well-established same-sex networks in Accra and Bamako; African "traditions" defined by European observers; the weird mix of faith, pharmaceuticals, and pseudo-science to "cure" homosexual men; scandalous allegations against Cameroon's first president; and so on. The evidence also demonstrates that simplistic constructions of homosexuality versus heterosexuality, modern versus traditional, Africa versus the West, or progress from the African closet towards Western models of "out" politics – all (often implicit) staples in much of the existing literature, including scientific studies of HIV/AIDS – are insupportable. We hope the empirical evidence discussed here contributes to the theorization of sexualities in Africa that, while learning from the pioneers of the queer canon coming from the West, is capable of greater sensitivity to African experiences and perspectives than has tended to be the case in so-called global queer studies.

The multidisciplinary approach adopted for this volume has been essential to that effort and is justified by the elusiveness of the main sources of data about sexual diversity, namely, the agents involved in the bodily, discursive, and legal transformation of hegemonic constructions of sexuality in Africa. These are for the most part lesbians, gays, bisexuals, trans, and intersex people (LGBTI) but also men who have sex with men (MSM) but do not identify as GBTI and women who have sex with women (WSW) but do not identify as LBTI. We do not accept the lazy stereotype that such people are "hard to reach," but acknowledge that reaching and learning from them requires more sophisticated tools and methods than one methodology or discipline could ever encompass. The broad umbrella of African feminism offers such tools, and most of the authors here generally agree with Epprecht's statement that "methods pioneered by feminist social historians and anthropologists are well-suited to the task of teasing out [data, analysis] from silent or evasive sources" (chapter 3, this volume, backed by reference to the rich tradition of African feminist scholarship). This aligns us with Ugandan legal scholar Sylvia Tamale (2011), whose underlying premises are feminism, anti-colonialism, human rights, and sex positivity. Tamale argues that none of these ideas is a Western import. On the contrary, much of the optimism in her book *African Sexualities* stems from the conviction that such ideas are embedded in African traditional cultures and can, therefore, be nurtured without inciting a patriotic backlash if approached with sensitivity to local context. We share that conviction.

There is also a strong consensus among the authors here that critical analysis and theory should be a double-edged sword aimed first at assumptions about the construction of identity and political engagement that come out of Western intellectual and activist traditions. The authors then apply this double-edged critique to African societies and regimes of thought when they analyze local discourses around African identities and essentialisms. The term *local* refers to a particular position that Africa occupies as a *project* and an *object* of a contentious sexual and human rights discourse. This simultaneous critique of outsider and insider presumptions tied to the study of sexualities in Africa is, we believe, the prerequisite for an effective approach to our understanding of sociopolitical transformation across the broadest canvas in Africa.

With respect to terminology, we the editors agreed to disagree. There is a lot of controversy on these issues. Where exactly is "the West"? Who exactly is an African? Some authors prefer the term *queer*, some *homosexualities*, some *lgbti*, and so on. Rather than explain the justifications and debates each and every time, we opted for a term that everyone can agree is the least controversial and most widely-used: LGBTI. There was also the question of referencing. Of course it is important not to reinvent the wheel or appear naïve about the powerful insights brought to bear on the study of sexuality by scholars like Michel Foucault and Judith Butler. But at what point does genuflection to the celebrity of Western queer theorists become colonial? Rather than impose a party line – or worse, try to stake out an all-encompassing original "Africanist" position – we decided to let the contributors bring their own perspectives and preferences as developed through their engagement with diverse specific local scholarship and struggles. While the prevailing ethic is to listen respectfully to the perspectives of the main subjects of the research, we also recognize that the personal subjectivity of the researchers has an important role in shaping the direction of the debates. Since this book is intended to further those debates, rather than to definitively resolve them, let the range of approaches, referencing, and terminology bloom.

No single volume could possibly capture the geographical vastness and cultural diversity of the continent, and we acknowledge with regret that we have no contributions from arabophone and lusophone Africa or from some of the biggest and most controversial countries on the continent. We have managed to cover a wide swathe, however, with case studies from very poor, mostly Muslim, and mostly rural Gambia to the highly urbanized and Christian or secular context of Cape Town. We also note some important thematic weak points that scholars deal with in more substantive fashion elsewhere. Readers interested in topics related to transgender issues and spirit possession, notably, may consult emerging scholarship on Africa such as Nkabinde (2009), Morgan et al. (2009), and Wieringa (2011).

With these gaps in mind, we greeted the recent publication of *African Sexualities: A Reader* (Tamale 2011) with enthusiasm. Its essays, poetry, and polemics from many of the countries we have missed are an important complement to this book. Conversely, this book addresses some of the geographical and thematic gaps in *African Sexualities*. We can also respectfully point out some worrisome contradictions in *African Sexualities* when seen from a queer perspective; for example, the word "queer" does not appear in the index, notwithstanding the acknowledged importance of disrupting heteronormative discourses. Nkiru Nzegwu's rather romantic ruminations on a matrifocal, sex-positive, pan-African sexual culture that allegedly existed before Christianity and Islam are another example. Nzegwu lumps homosexuality together with bestiality, sadomasochism, and paedophilia as a "counter-natural quality" eroticized in the West and then exported to the detriment of that pan-African idyll. This approach is uncomfortably close to two of the staples of homophobic rhetoric that Nyanzi, for example, dissects in this volume. In other cases, however, authors' silence on homosexuality in *African Sexualities* is simply frustrating. In her chapter on the potential of Islam to foster a culture of sex positivity, Sa'diyya Shaikh makes a strong case on topics like abortion, birth control, and male chauvinism. Her failure to consider how "moderate" forms of Islam historically dealt with same-sex desire is thus an important missed opportunity. This is not something that we resolve (although see Broqua, chapter 11), but we do feel all of our contributors understand the need to counter the invisibility of non-normative sexualities in the hegemonic discourse at each and every turn.

The chapters that follow are grouped together in three parts according to their theoretical frames, regional emphasis, and comparative debates and historiographical/pedagogical applications. The first part details the large stage on which to understand subsequent case studies: the continental human rights framework, the meaning and potential of "queer" in relation to diasporic debates, the history of how the ideology of a singular African sexuality was constructed, and the politics with regards to Africans studying same-sex sexuality in Africa. Taken together, this introductory section contextualizes the country-focused chapters that follow.

The first two chapters deal with the role of international institutions, diaspora links, and transnational mobilization in shaping discourse and contestation over LGBTI rights in Africa. In chapter 1, Akandji and Epprecht present the global and continental structures of the "human rights challenge" for LGBTI people in Africa. While at the international level, discourse over human rights is progressing from women's rights to include types of discriminations based on individual sexual orientation, conventional wisdom in Africa tends to associate the idea of rights with groups rather than individuals. However, this logic is not always easy to promote because the international instruments that protect group rights are mostly not binding. Calculated ambiguity in the language further allows states to go behind emerging conventions or to hold contradictory positions for international versus domestic audiences. At the continental level, this problem is illustrated with a review of political and legal fuzziness embedded in the Banjul Charter in light of the non-recognition of LGBTI people as a collective minority in African countries. With references to some recent controversies and the constitutional negotiations in Zimbabwe in 2011, Akanji and Epprecht suggest that any attempt to bring in international norms, conventions, and agreements on LGBTI-related issues in national politics in Africa will have to grapple with this institutional asymmetry. Despite some notable setbacks and the demonstrated risk of reaction against sexual minorities who challenge homophobia on this platform, there have been some promising developments using the instruments of the African Union.

In chapter 2, Massaquoi sheds light on the roles of transnational migration and organizing by African refugees in Canada. The chapter is built on a series of rare interviews with forty LGBTI Africans who have sought or are currently seeking asylum in Canada. African LGBTI people in the diaspora bring remarkable and fresh insights to an academic field that "has historically focused on Western examples," primarily the migration from rural closets to big city pride. From the perspective of African LGBTI migrants, the international arena offers some relief to immediate threats but remains far from perfect. Here, demands for rights go hand in hand with reflection on new forms of vulnerabilities, including not only encounters with overt racism but also more subtle demands for African LGBTI people to conform to Western expectations of being out. In particular, Massaquoi asks, "Whom am I putting at risk as I push for [a particular] articulation of rights, identity, home, and refuge?" For her, African queerness is a matter of positioning and agency that does not flow automatically or intuitively from the migration experience. While the fight for rights may not be settled with the crossing of national borders, the perspectives on migration she presents encourage further research, both empirical and theoretical, on the sexualized dimensions of diasporic displacement.

In chapter 3, Epprecht presents the historiography of "African sexuality" – from colonial representations to public health discourse to current debates about sexual rights – as an ideological construction. He shows how multiple sources often unwittingly depended on each other to promote a certain ideal or expectation of being a "real" African, notwithstanding their otherwise very diverse or even oppositional politics and temperaments (dour Christian missionaries and fiery African revolutionaries, for example). He thus not only traces the origin of African sexuality as a discrete problem for colonial rulers, but also reviews the epistemological negotiation the African intellectuals effectuate to erase the traces of unconventional sexuality from national consciousness. He makes several direct suggestions for ways to pursue the research and apply it in learning situations. He also provides an extensive bibliography of early ethnographic and other ostensibly scientific sources that will be of interest to teachers introducing the topic in African classrooms.

In chapter 4, Nyanzi deals with various techniques the state and media use to repress, ascertain, or problematize sexuality through an examination of President Yahya Jammeh's threats to kill or imprison homosexuals in the Gambia. State-sponsored homophobia, Nyanzi shows, is rooted in the local construction of nationalism and religion, in this case Islam. Nyanzi finds links between a "wider strategy to entrench an undemocratic regime," which is in imminent danger of losing whatever legitimacy it could claim as a result of criticism by Islamic leaders, and the persecution of sexual minorities. To some extent this is an old story – scapegoating an unpopular minority and exploiting cultural taboos for short-term political gain. However, this is the first time such a situation has been closely documented in a predominantly Muslim country and as such it provides an important rebuttal to Joseph Massad's (2002; 2007) critique of "the gay international" in the Arab world. What makes Nyanzi's contribution especially interesting is her direct challenge to homophobes who dismiss research on same-sex sexualities, and hence the concept of human rights for sexual minorities, as a Western or neocolonialist project. "Living and studying in the West did not teach me about homosexuality," Nyanzi writes, suggesting that until Africans start to critically engage with homophobia and heterosexism within the academic culture, research on African sexuality will remain marginalized and compromised.

The essays in the second part of this book focus on South Africa, a country generally considered to be unique on the continent on account of the relative protection it offers to sexual minorities. South Africa has also produced far and away the greatest quantity – and often the boldest expressions – of activist, artistic, and scholarly literature and documentary films on LGBTI issues in Africa. Notwithstanding the so-called South African exceptionalism, however, the three essays in this section point to important commonalities between South Africa and the rest of the continent. In chapter 5, Reddy, Wiebesiek, and Munthree provide a historical account of how the apartheid state linked the containment of homosexuality among whites to the maintenance of racial capitalism. That system was threatened in the 1970s and 80s, both by black revolutionary movements and by young white men's own uncertain loyalty to the cause of an idealized, military, heterosexual, white masculinity. The authors describe South Africa's Truth and Reconciliation Commission's relative neglect of the military forces' pre-emptive torture and abuse of suspected homosexual recruits, as documented by the LGBTI community's own Aversion Project, which also notes the impact of trauma on victims' sense of identity and political consciousness. Reddy, Wiebesiek, and Munthree strive to theorize sexual justice as central to the political theory of transitional justice. Their argument holds powerful lessons for countries elsewhere struggling to heal from other forms of national, ethnic, and sectarian conflict.

In chapter 6, Hackman sheds light on a potential cultural threat to South Africa's constitutional protection of sexual minority rights, again with lessons for (the many) other countries experiencing assertive or fundamentalist religious movements. She examines the phenomenon of the so-called ex-gay ministry, that is, a movement of Christian men who have renounced (or who are struggling to renounce) their "addiction" to homosexuality. Hackman finds connections between the ex-gay ministry in Cape Town and in the United States. Her main contribution, however, is to examine the internal dynamics that explain how South Africa, the first state on the continent to constitutionalize sexual minority rights, also hosts the most successful "ex-gay" movement. This apparent contradiction, Hackman argues, is best understood through an analysis of the confessional technologies (Nguyen 2009; 2010) that "help reproduce an ideal ethical subject" in a context of national healing from the trauma of apartheid (that is, the Truth and Reconciliation Commission). South Africa in this sense is a playground for hybrid and contradictory forces, local and transnational ideas, united primarily through the techniques they employ. Hackman alerts us to similar concerns about the rise of aggressive Christian homophobia in states such as Uganda, and the links between this phenomenon and the export of potted ideologies from the United States.

In chapter 7, Dworkin, Swarr, and Cooky return to the issue of the relationship between African nationalism on the one hand, and rival notions of appropriate gender identity, physical body, and sexuality on the other. They focus on the case of Caster Semenya, who in 2009 won the world championship running as a woman but was stripped of her medal after a committee ruled she was not physically female. The international uproar that ensued included accusations of racism, denial that "hermaphrodites" existed in Africa, and politicians' and media embracing Semenya as a victimized "real woman" who was a cherished part of the (again, victimized) African family. That Semenya became a cause célèbre, while at the same time black lesbians who suffered so-called corrective rape or murder on the basis of their sexual orientation were largely ignored, speaks to a profound difficulty at the heart of a kind of populist, anti-white supremacy politics that are on the ascendancy in southern Africa.

The essays in part 3 are in-depth analyses of debates over homosexuality in West Africa. In chapter 8, Nyeck revisits the 2006 media controversy that surrounded homosexuality in Cameroon, but treats the "homosexual category" as a residual. That is, Nyeck's contribution derives mainstream and normative inferences about African political institutions, citizenship, and the study of non-normative sexuality from the analysis of homophobic attacks on state institutions, not the other way around. This analytic trajectory rests on the premise that the study of non-normative sexuality brings a fresh breath to mainstream political science, which has traditionally focused on political institutions and shied away from the study of sexuality and social change in Africa. Nyeck's analysis also disaggregates homophobic discourse and deals with its rational and irrational features, and so disrupts the common assumption that "African homophobia" can be understood as a simple form of political demagoguery. Through a comparative reading of newspapers and editorial cartoons, Nyeck documents attacks on state institutions from the private sector and uncovers interesting puzzles for political scientists. She argues that to take homophobia as a core value for political mobilization against the state and its institutions in Cameroon is costly for the party that chooses to do so. Above all, partisanship is never reliable when the political message is too fuzzy. In Cameroon, homophobia is a complex and confused genre of resistance against real or imagined western imperialisms. Homophobia may be intelligible as a discourse that rationalizes political membership and shapes core beliefs, but it does not do so in a smooth and predictable way. Perhaps ironically, the very violence of the homophobic rhetoric in Cameroon gives grounds for cautious optimism about political space for making new claims about inclusive citizenship.

In chapters 9 and 10, Dankwa and O'Mara offer another pair of complementary comparative studies from a single country, in this case Ghana. They wrestle with the construction of social and communal citizenship from a cultural viewpoint, which leads them both to criticize Western presuppositions about identity and sexual expression. O'Mara writes: "The West's discourse of coming out of the closet privileges the act of self-naming ... whereas the Ghanaians' narratives tell about a partner, an experience, not the recognition of an authentic self." She draws on (and reproduces) in-depth discussions with Ghanaians who have same-sex sexual practices and shows that they often critique mainstream ideas about freedom associated with the trappings of new technologies of information and communication.

This juxtaposition of discreet communal understandings of sexual difference and behaviour and the confrontational strategies of global models has important lessons for organizing for sexual rights in Ghana. While foreign gay models encourage public demands for human rights, discretion allows Ghana's non-normative sexual citizens to quietly build community, in contrast with the political activists described in the Cameroon case (Awondo 2010).

In her investigation of female-female relations in Ghana in chapter 9, Dankwa examines the rhetoric and condition of masculinity performance among women. The condition of and access to masculinity, Dankwa finds, are related to the social understanding of men as breadwinners. Thus, working class women who love other women often adopt roles that mirror butch/femme relations in the West. Dankwa further contends that there is more to the Ghanaian performance of "masculinity without men" that transcends the binary between "anatomy and masculine gender identification, which so potently constitutes the term female masculinity." She exposes the relational dynamic for working class women who enter erotic relationships with other women and theorizes the perpetual renegotiation of power especially for the partner who "takes the first step to verbalize her desire." This journey into social negotiation, poverty, and erotic assertiveness illustrates the intricacies of economic entrepreneurship and gender-bending performance in Ghana. Thus, both Dankwa and O'Mara give this volume a narrative from same-sex practicing Africans, however they identify, that is not always included in mainstream political campaigns for sexual minority rights in Africa.

In chapter 11, Broqua continues this line of argument with an astute critique of the presumptions of progress towards "liberation" in Western terms that pervade recent scholarship on male-male sexuality in Africa. Drawing on his ethnographic work among same-sex practicing men in Bamako, the capital of Mali, he finds that Western ideas of homosexuality are present and influential. However, there is no obvious direct and continuous link between contemporary forms of homosexuality in Bamako and an early Western model of coming out. Rather, there are plural forms that draw on indigenous traditional concepts and discourses and respond to specific local conditions as well as external influences. Interestingly, among the latter, not all relate to contemporary global queer struggles and identities but rather are anachronistic to the pre-liberation scene in the West. Broqua argues that we need to be sensitive to the complex interplay of factors that shape emerging homosexual identities and activism if we are to avoid the traps of an evolutionary and Western-centric model. To be sure, this argument has been made before (e.g., Altman 1997), but with polemical attacks on "the gay international," "queer imperialism," "homonationalism," and "pinkwashing" gaining traction (e.g., Puar 2008; Douglas et al. 2011), evidence from less developed and predominantly Muslim countries greatly strengthens it.

All of this leaves us with more – *many* more – questions than answers. How can we address homophobia without threatening democracy (majority rule) and freedom of speech and faith? How can we address the gap between theoretical rights on paper and the ability to live with dignity and respect in day-to-day situations? How can we disentangle the various historical and cultural streams that feed into homophobia from the economic, political, and social stresses that seem to be hardening prejudices in the present? What should be the relationship between academic researchers on this topic and the popular media, the state, and Western donor agencies? How can African LGBTI people come out on their own terms without conforming to the sometimes-suffocating expectations of Western friends and allies, and bearing in mind the complex issues of class, race, shade, and other factors that impact ideas about indigeneity or authentic African identity? How can we negotiate between (somewhat) empowering silences and the (very risky) impetus to be visible? How can we build curricula that alert young people to the many pressing issues around same-sex sexualities without inciting a backlash from parents or other conservative forces? How can we "Africanize" the research, empirically and theoretically, when the environment in the field is generally so unwelcoming for African scholars?

No single answer to any of these questions will apply smoothly across the continent. By way of conclusion to this introduction, however, we can say one thing for certain. The essays that follow show very clearly that more research needs to be done – research from north of the Sahara, from the Horn of Africa, from rural areas and small towns, into love and intimacy (rather than conflict and disease), and so on and on. They also show, however, that it *can* be done, notwithstanding the often seemingly impossible obstacles. And they show that African scholars are as willing and able to take on the task as anybody. That gives us confidence that the study of sexuality in general, and non-normative sexuality in particular, is intellectually and politically sustainable in Africa.

PART ONE
Framing the Debates

1

Human Rights Challenge in Africa: Sexual Minority Rights and the African Charter on Human and Peoples' Rights

OLAJIDE AKANJI AND MARC EPPRECHT

The issue of sexual minority rights has been gaining currency in human rights discourse, with the United Nations (UN), some regional bodies, human rights agencies, and even the World Bank focusing on the subject (see Beyer et al. 2011 and Global Commission on HIV and the Law 2012 for strong interventions). Whereas in the past sexual minority rights were commonly associated with liberal societies in the West, some noteworthy initiatives in recent years have come from the global South. These include the Naz Foundation's dramatic victory in court to overturn inherited sodomy laws in India in 2009, legal recognition of same-sex marriage in Mexico and Argentina, and South Africa and Brazil's 2011 co-introduction of the UN resolution that names sexual orientation as a universal human right.[1] Yet at the same time there has been an increasing wave of state repression and public outrage against sexual minorities in parts of Asia and Africa. As several authors in this volume closely attest, homosexuality has been criminalized in many African countries with varying degrees of sanctions, while hate campaigns, discrimination, and brutal attacks by state security officials against LGBTI people are widespread. South Africa, with its equality clause that prohibits discrimination on the basis of sexual orientation, is a remarkable exception. But even here, the currently tabled Traditional Courts Bill has emboldened traditional leaders to call for the excision of sexual orientation from the constitution, while activists have criticized the "lamentable" failure of the South African government to speak out against human rights abuses in other African countries (Vilikazi and Ndashe 2010, notably).

These contradictions raise a number of questions. What is the status of sexual minority rights under the African Charter on Human and Peoples' Rights (Banjul Charter)? What are the implications of the tensions between group and individual rights in the charter for human rights protection more generally in Africa? What are the prospects for using the African Commission on Human and Peoples' Rights – the "last hope" as Isaack (2010) called it – to educate and put pressure on states towards turning around the tide of political and social homophobia in Africa? In addressing such questions, we find reasons for cautious optimism. We illustrate our argument with reference to provisions of key international human rights documents, above all the Banjul Charter, and to some of the specific issues that were raised in the constitutional negotiations in Zimbabwe, a country notorious for its long-standing rejection of extending human rights protections on the basis of sexual orientation or gender variance.

SEXUALITY IN AFRICA: THE DISCOURSE, THE REALITY

The dominant trend in the historiography of homosexualities in Africa in the last two decades has been to show that homosexual acts are indigenous to Africa and were not necessarily regarded as problematic or scandalous in traditional cultures, but that views changed over time as new types of relationships emerged and new attitudes coalesced. These changes came in response to a wide range of factors including the spread of a cash economy, carceral institutions like prisons, and homophobic ideologies introduced from outside the continent (e.g., Dynes 1982; Murray and Roscoe 1998; Greenberg 1988; Epprecht 1998; 2009; Gaudio 2009). Meticulous as much of this scholarship is, it has not noticeably persuaded African leaders, who continue to trumpet an older, persistent, populist interpretation of history. In this interpretation, homosexual behaviour is "un-African," a foreign "disease" that was introduced to Africa by Arab slave traders, white settlers, or missionaries and is now spread principally by foreign tourists and sexual predators (see

Massaquoi, Nyanzi, and Nyeck, this volume, and Ndashe 2011 for some specific examples of such rhetoric).

Notwithstanding the divergence of scholarly opinions about the historiography of homosexualities in Africa, almost everyone can agree that many forms of same-sex relationships exist in Africa today. LGBTI movements and groups have emerged openly in some countries, including Namibia, Senegal, Nigeria, and Zimbabwe, while they exist secretly in many other countries. The Nigerian gay church, the House of Rainbow Metropolitan Community Church, Lagos, and the Sierra Leonean Lesbian and Gay Association are among many examples of LGBTI groups that have come out in defiance of societal and official state discrimination. Indeed, as Reddy, Wiebesiek, and Munthree (this volume) show, official state discrimination has sometimes contributed to the emergence of self-conscious and politically engaged LGBTI identities.

Although there is no doubt that there are lesbians, gays, bisexuals, and transgendered people in contemporary Africa, they do not, legally speaking, constitute a distinct social class. This is hardly surprising. LGBTI people themselves do not recognize LGBTI as a cohesive group, particularly considering the significant number of men who have sex with men or women with women (MSM and WSW) who sometimes emphatically do not consider themselves to be LGBTI, gay, queer, *supi*, *kuchu*, or any of the other terms that lump same-sex practicing people together in popular discourse. This implies that LGBTI, MSM, WSW, and their families are only legally entitled to individual rights. This, however, raises a number of questions, particularly in relation to whether individual rights or group rights are the ultimate value of the society, that is, whether citizens' access to group rights takes precedence over claims for individual rights. Does the recognition of a particular set of human rights (group rights) presuppose the negation or subordination of the other set of human rights (individual rights)? Many in Africa would argue yes.

Individual rights and group rights are conceptually distinct. While the concept of group rights revolves around the survival of the group as an entity, the notion of individual rights focuses on the fundamental rights of the individual, often in opposition to attempts to impose conformity to a group norm. Also, the constituents of the two sets of human rights are different. On the one hand, the constituents of group rights include the rights to self-determination and to maintain or defend a distinctive group or collective identity. Others include the right of persons belonging to minority groups to enjoy their own culture, to profess and practice their own religion, and to use their own language without coercion to belong to the majority culture. On the other hand, individual rights comprise all the inalienable rights of human beings enunciated by the International Bill of Human Rights and its derivatives. This includes, as binding instruments, the Universal Declaration of Human Rights (UDHR), the International Covenant on Civil and Political Rights (ICCPR), and the International Covenant on Economic, Social, and Cultural Rights (ICESCR) and, as non-binding instruments, the Convention on the Elimination of all Forms of Discrimination against Women (CEDAW) and the Convention on the Rights of the Child. Essentially, the set of human rights covered by the notion of individual rights includes the right to life, to fair hearing, to work, and to the rights to freedom of speech, association, conscience, and religion, among others (e.g., Ndashe 2010; Ahlberg and Kulane 2011; Epprecht 2012a; 2013b).

This distinction between group and individual rights has a particular and emotive importance in much of Africa. Most African countries contain numerous ethnic and religious minorities that have historically been vulnerable to dispossession and abuse by the state or majority culture and have in many cases sought justice through secession. Group rights are thus more essential to the preservation of national unity in Africa than people in more established and linguistically or culturally homogenous states might appreciate. Conversely, the very notion of individual rights has an extremely bitter history for many Africans who recall the colonial regimes that introduced it. Under colonial rule, full rights adhered only to "citizens," who were arbitrarily defined to suit the political interests of the colonialists. A lesser slate of rights was available to "subjects," the vast majority of the African population. Rights for citizens may thus have been couched in the language of universal principles but in practice tended to entrench and materially benefit a racial elite to the grave disadvantage of the majority. One of many notorious cases was the extension of suffrage (the right to vote) to white women in South Africa in a 1930 act of parliament that required the disenfranchisement of African men (e.g., Mamdani 1996; Chanock 1986). In more recent times, the global reach of "trade related intellectual property rights" has primarily benefitted Western multinational corporations at the cost, by some estimates, of hundreds of thousands of African lives (Treatment Action Campaign 2012).

Another way to express the tension between individual and group rights is through the dichotomy of rights and "basic needs." Essentially, Africans have argued that universal human rights may be desirable in theory, but are an expensive and distracting luxury if people lack the basic needs for survival. How can a woman who struggles to find clean water and food, let alone put her children through school, pay for health care, or afford a lawyer to claim the rights she is entitled to according to documents she has not heard of and cannot read? How can states that cannot monitor their own borders, let alone ensure police and judges understand and respect existing laws, afford to pursue their right to, for example, compulsory licensing of life-saving drugs against Western pharmaceutical giants and their hypocritical but powerful state allies? Better to develop the means to deliver basic needs first, before squandering precious resources in such fraught pursuits.

The fact that homosexuals are not recognized as a collective or group, and so are entitled only to individual rights, leaves them vulnerable to the denial of their rights by the state in the name of a group need such as "national culture" or "development." The danger for LGBTI people now is that some lawmakers in Africa are seeking to amend national constitutions to ensure that appeals to individual rights cannot succeed against the group (for example, Zambian parliament has sought to enshrine male-female unions as the only form of marriage allowable in effect in perpetuity, though it has so far been unsuccessful). Fear of same-sex marriage creeping in through legalistic arguments has led to similar calls in Nigeria, Zimbabwe, Burundi, and elsewhere.

SEXUAL RIGHTS, SEXUAL MINORITIES, AND INTERNATIONAL HUMAN RIGHTS LAW

Concern for sexual rights, particularly of persons of diverse sexual orientations and gender identities (i.e., sexual minorities), at local and international levels is in fact a quite recent development even in the West. Reflective of the times (the late 1940s), the UDHR actually employs sexist language and was oblivious to the specific needs for women rooted in the long history of patriarchy. The concepts of sexual minorities and homophobia had not yet been invented, and consequently do not appear in the foundational documents. The UDHR did, however, leave the door open to the development of non-sexist language and the inclusion of new forms of discrimination or abuse as they became known. Through the declaration, the UN affirmed that all human beings are born free and equal in dignity and rights and that everyone is entitled to all rights and freedoms set forth without distinction of any kind, such as race, colour, sex, language, religion, political or other opinion, national or social origin, property, birth, *or other status*, wording which allows new insights into forms of discrimination to be added.

This wording has helped to gradually broaden human rights discourse and the contestation for human right protection, including sexual rights of women and LGBTI people. For example, the United Nations, through conferences like the UN Conference on Population and Development in Cairo (1994); the UN Conferences on Women in Nairobi (1985), Copenhagen (1990), and Beijing (1995); and the activities of the World Health Organization (WHO), among others, has provided platforms for scientists, human rights NGOs, and many other interested parties to argue for greater international awareness of the plight of women, and for actions against violence against women. The Beijing conference in particular emphasized the link between – and the indivisibility of – women's sexual, reproductive, and broader human rights. The attainment of those rights was moreover linked to and indivisible from men's rights and well-being. The Beijing conference, for instance, stated that:

> The human rights of women include their right to have control over and decide freely and responsibly on matters related to their sexuality, including sexual and reproductive health, free of coercion, discrimination and violence. Equal relationships between men and women in matters of sexual relations and reproduction, including full respect for the integrity of the person, require mutual respect, consent and shared responsibility for sexual behaviour and its consequences. (Beijing Platform for Action 1995, paragraph 96, cited in UNFPA 2004)

A number of scholars, including Correa and Petchesky (1994), Fried and Landsberg-Lewis (2000), Miller (2005), and Petchesky (2000), emphasize that claims for sexual and reproductive rights are both affirmative demands for women's right to fully exercise their citizenship and to entitlement to protection against human rights violations, and that affirmative programs are required to promote gender equality and social justice to overcome the legacy of patriarchal culture and institutions. The Millennium Development Goals (MDG) then bridged the theoretical gap between rights and basic needs by emphasizing the centrality of women's equality to economic development (five of the eight goals require it, implicitly or explicitly). They also stress the indivisibility of women's empowerment as individuals through legal rights (among other things) from the health and material well-being of society as a whole.[2]

The discourse on sexual rights, which initially focused on women's right to sexual and reproductive health, has now been extended in international law and development practice to include persons with diverse sexual orientations and gender identities. Much of this is a result of the recognition of the link between public health and human rights, long-standing in theory but hugely amplified in practice by HIV/AIDS. As early as the mid 1980s, the WHO recognized the need to fight homophobia (in law and cultural expressions) as a key element of the struggle for sexual health for the whole population (e.g., Mann 1995). The organization further stressed that a holistic approach, rather than a narrowly biomedical one, is essential to dealing with HIV and indeed any other public health issue. This requires understanding sexuality in a holistic manner as well. Sexuality, according to the organization, is "a central aspect of being human throughout life and encompasses sex, gender identities and roles, sexual orientation, eroticism, pleasure, intimacy and reproduction" (cited in UNFPA 2004). Sexuality is experienced and expressed in thoughts, fantasies, desires, beliefs, attitudes, values, behaviours, practices, roles, and relationships. It is influenced by the interaction of biological, psychological, social, economic, political, cultural, ethical, legal, historical, and religious and spiritual factors (cited in UNFPA 2004). Attempts to police conformity to a heterosexual ideal in the face of such complex factors thus not only squandered resources in a futile effort but also actually enabled the spread of HIV (see below for how this is manifest in Africa).

At the UN, progress towards incorporating these insights by interpreting "other status" to include sexual orientation and gender identity has been fitful, in many cases thwarted in the General Assembly by opposition from the majority of African countries in alliance with the Vatican, conservative Islamic states and, at times, the United States. A key moment was the 1994 decision by the UN Human Rights Council in *Toonen v. Australia*, in which, for the first time, the council held that human rights law prohibits discrimination based on sexual orientation (O'Flaherty and Fischer 2008, 216). A setback quickly followed, however, as a majority vote removed the reference to sexual orientation. In 2003, Brazil put forward a resolution to reinstate it. That vote was postponed several times on account of the controversy it stirred (and likelihood of defeat), but lobbying efforts outside the UN picked up the pace. On 17 May 2005, the launch of the International Day Against Homophobia commemorated the date fifteen years earlier when the WHO removed homosexuality from its list of diseases. The following year saw the Declaration of Montreal at the first International Conference on LGBT Human Rights, and the release of the Yogyakarta Principles on the Application of International Human Rights Law in relation to Sexual Orientation and Gender Identity. The latter was prepared by a panel of leading jurists who built on an erudite and comprehensive analysis of legal precedents around the world. The Yogyakarta Principles emphasize the "importance of the freedom to express oneself, one's identity and one's sexuality, without State interference based on sexual orientation or gender identity" (O'Flaherty and Fischer 2008, 235).

This global movement emboldened supporters of the stalled Brazilian resolution. The UN General Assembly Declaration on Sexual Orientations and Gender Identity of 18 December 2008 was the result. Signed initially by sixty-six countries, including Cape Verde, Central African Republic, Gabon, Guinea-Bissau, Mauritius, and South Africa, the declaration reads in part as follows:

(4) We are deeply concerned by violations of human rights and fundamental freedoms based on sexual orientation or gender identity;
(5) We are also disturbed that violence, harassment, discrimination, exclusion, stigmatization and prejudice are directed against persons in all countries in the world because of sexual orientation or gender identity, and that these practices undermine the integrity and dignity of those subjected to these abuses;
(6) We condemn the human rights violations based on sexual orientation or gender identity wherever they occur, in particular the use of the death penalty on this ground, extrajudicial, summary or arbitrary executions, the practice of torture and other cruel, inhuman and degrading treatment or punishment, arbitrary

arrest or detention and deprivation of economic, social and cultural rights, including the right to health ...

(10) We call upon all States and relevant international human rights mechanisms to commit to promote and protect human rights of all persons, regardless of sexual orientation and gender identity;

(11) We urge States to take all the necessary measures, in particular legislative or administrative, to ensure that sexual orientation or gender identity may under no circumstances be the basis for criminal penalties, in particular executions, arrests or detention;

(12) We urge States to ensure that human rights violations based on sexual orientation or gender identity are investigated and perpetrators held accountable and brought to justice. (ILGA 2009)

A major problem with the UN declaration is that it is non-binding. Like the MDGs, it represents aspirations, ideals, and targets to aim for rather than laws to enforce. It is not mandatory for parties to the declaration to implement its content. By signing it, states simply acknowledge a willingness to be advised by it. There are reasonable suspicions that some of the more aid-dependent African countries that signed did so with a degree of cynicism about how seriously they would heed its advice. Guinea-Bissau and Central African Republic have certainly not been at the forefront in the struggle for sexual minority rights in the past, though they are highly vulnerable to pressure from their main aid donors.

Another problem with the UN declaration is the spate of antagonism it has received from state and non-state actors in the international system that flatly reject the basic premise on which it stands. For instance, the Catholic Family and Human Rights Institute and a group called "the State of America" condemned the Yogyakarta Principles as "an affront to all human and natural rights" and "a farce to justice" that "encourage[s] (physically, psychologically and morally) unhealthy choices" (cited in O'Flaherty and Fischer 2008, 247). This perspective assumes that sexual orientation is not an innate quality and that same-sex acts consequently represent a conscious decision to commit a criminal act. That act is typically equated with rape, prostitution, and bestiality in the discourse but also, for some Muslims, with apostasy, a capital offence. Accordingly, Marks (2006, 34) points out: "For LGBT in such [most] countries, abuses perpetrated against them are not viewed as human rights violations."

On the contrary, efforts to stop or mitigate those abuses by tying general development aid to them are the real human rights violations. Africans, Muslims, and so on in this perspective are the victims of pressure from the West, a new form of colonialism that denies their presumed greater group right to self-determination.

Nonetheless, support for the declaration is growing. In June 2011, the Human Rights Council was further empowered to produce annual reports that would name the names of specific rights offenders and provide a vehicle to press countries to decriminalize homosexuality (UN 2011). The number of signatories to a revised declaration by that year had risen to eighty-five, including four additional African countries (Rwanda, Sao Tome and Principe, Seychelles, and Sierra Leone). The non-binding nature remains. However, as the number of signatories from the Global South rises, and as African civil society speaks out more forcefully (see, for example, Centre for Human Rights 2010), it will get harder for opponents to claim victimhood as a result of Western imperialism.

SEXUALITY, SEXUAL RIGHTS, AND THE AFRICAN CHARTER ON HUMAN AND PEOPLES' RIGHTS

The African (Banjul) Charter on Human and Peoples' Rights, which entered into force in 1986, is the bedrock of Africa's human rights system. If progress is to be made on LGBTI issues beyond the level of tokenism, it will need to come from the charter rather than from the UN. There are reasons for rights advocates to be worried, but also to take confidence in the document and in the institutions that promote its values. Key among the latter are (a) the African Commission on Human and Peoples' Rights, which meets twice a year in different African cities to consider submissions by African civil society groups and to interpret the charter as new information becomes available; (b) the African Court on Human and Peoples' Rights, which began to adjudicate cases from its seat in Arusha in 2009; and (c) the African peer review mechanism, in which African Union members voluntarily assess the state of human and peoples' rights in their own country and allow review teams from other members to monitor their adherence to the principles of the charter. A country that violates those principles could, after all attempts at constructive dialogue and mutual assistance have failed, be formally reprimanded by the African Peer Review Forum (Ousmane 2005; Jourdaan 2006).[3]

The charter's preamble unequivocally expresses the need to have "due regard to the Charter of the United Nations and the Universal Declaration of Human Rights" and affirms adherence to the principles "contained in the declarations, conventions and other instruments adopted by the Organization of African Unity, the Movement of Non-Aligned Countries and the United Nations." Among the most directly pertinent other instruments is the African Union's Protocol on the Rights of Women, which provides for a wide range of sexual and reproductive rights and commits states to eradicate "harmful practices" in traditional culture (such as, a good lawyer could argue, compulsory heterosexuality). Article 2 of the charter almost verbatim commits to the UDHR, including its reference to "sex" and "other status" as grounds for protection from discrimination. Then, beginning with the unequivocal statement that "every individual shall be equal before the law," individual rights are placed first in the order of presentation (articles 3–13 cover political and civil rights, while articles 14–17 focus on economic, social, and cultural rights).

On that basis, African states seem to be obliged to follow the UN's path outlined above. Indeed, as noted, ten African countries have already signed the UN declaration on sexual orientation and gender identity (nearly a fifth of the continent by membership, although much less by population size). African LGBTI people are meanwhile – and sometimes quite boldly – claiming their rights to equality before the law, privacy, non-discrimination, freedom of association, adopt children, and more through the courts and using arguments derived from their countries' own jurisprudence or constitutional obligations. At the time of writing, for example, Caine Youngman and allies are seeking to overturn Botswana's sodomy laws inherited from the British (*Botswana Gazette*, 24 August 2011), while as Massaquoi (this volume) describes, Sexual Minorities Uganda (SMUG) has had a number of legal victories and has cases pending against their tormentors. In May 2006, a loose alliance of LGBTI groups began a series of remarkable workshops through the NGO Forum of the African Commission on Human and Peoples' Rights, and began to present evidence in favour of sexual minority rights directly to the commissioners (see Ndashe 2011 for an insider account).

Public advocacy and litigation for individual rights, however, remains controversial and many African LGBTI people strongly oppose it. It is expensive, which feeds into the stereotype that LGBTI people are either rich elites out of touch with the real needs of the people or, should they accept donor funds, pawns of the West. There is also the high risk that they will attract undue attention, and that politicians will respond not with positive reforms in line with international norms, but with making existing laws even worse (as is happening in Uganda and several other countries). Hardening homophobic laws would be simple enough to do in terms that remained consistent with uncontroversial (majoritarian) interpretations of the charter. Notably, article 18 provides that "the family shall be the natural unit and basis of society. It shall be protected by the State which shall take care of its physical health and moral [*sic*]" and "the State shall have the duty to assist the family which is the custodian of morals and traditional values recognized by the community."

The bottom line for advocates of sexual minority rights is that even initiatives that use subtle or coded language to protect individuals can incite homophobic attacks. In Zimbabwe's constitutional negotiations in 2012, for example, the ruling party first rejected a draft that called for no discrimination based "on natural difference or condition or ... other status." It then similarly rejected an amended draft amended that read "circumstances of birth." According to parliamentarian Jonathan Moyo, such language indicated the commission was using "trickery and deceit" to sneak gay rights into the constitution against the imputed democratic wishes of the majority of the population (*Bulawayo24 News*, 8 May 2012).

The charter's other distinctive feature – the strong provisions it makes for group rights – also holds ambivalence for LGBTI advocates. The charter uses the term "peoples," and scholars debate the actual meaning and beneficiaries of the term. Umozurike (1992), for example, argues that "peoples" implies both minority and majority groups. Alfredsson (1998) disagrees, and argues that it does not connote minorities. To him, there is no universally accepted definition of "peoples," but in international practice it has been applied almost exclusively to national self-determination in the context of decolonization. The charter's preamble showcases the strong emotions that national decolonization still evokes, calling as it does for the "total liberation of Africa, the peoples of which are still struggling for their dignity and genuine independence, and undertaking to eliminate colonialism, neocolonialism, apartheid, Zionism and to dismantle aggressive foreign military bases."

Umozurike's argument that peoples includes minorities is also somewhat undermined by the unavailability of a universal definition of minorities and the commonplace usage of definitions that could be interpreted specifically to exclude LGBTI access to rights as a minority. For instance, Thornberry (1991, 2) defines *minority* as "the cohesive group" with enduring characteristics and that regards itself or is regarded by others as different from mainstream society. The UN Sub-Commission on Prevention of Discrimination and Protection of Minorities in 1950 also defined *minority* as potentially exclusive of LGBTI people, in that it hinges on the ability of the state to define what constitutes loyalty:

> Those non-dominant groups in a population which possess and wish to preserve stable ethnic, religious or linguistic traditions or characteristics markedly different from those of the rest of the population. Such minorities should properly include a number of persons sufficient by themselves to preserve such traditions or characteristics, and such minorities *must be loyal to the state of which they are nationals.* (cited in Atsenuwa 1999, 237, our emphasis)

Meanwhile, article 27 of the International Covenant on Civil and Political Rights (ICCPR) lists some of the minorities that possess recognized rights as groups under international law, but it pointedly fails to include the "other status" loophole. The article provides only that "those States in which ethnic, religious or linguistic minorities exist, persons belonging to such minorities shall not be denied the right, in community with the other members of their group, to enjoy their own culture, to profess and practice their own religion, or to use their own language."

Almost needless to say, the Banjul Charter does not contain any specific reference to persons of diverse sexual orientations and gender identities as a typology of groups its provisions protect. The general principles of group rights in Africa spelled out in articles 19 to 24 in fact pose potential threats to LGBTI people as a non-group. These include the equality of groups (article 19); the right to group existence, self-determination, and assistance in liberation struggles against foreign domination, including cultural domination (article 20); the right to freely dispose of their wealth and natural resources (article 21); the right to development (articles 22); the right to national and international peace and security (article 23); and the right to a general satisfactory environment favourable to their development (article 24).

Those provisions, and article 20 in particular, are open to interpretations that justify the disregard of – or even active resistance to – international norms. The right to development, for example, can be taken to prioritize the basic needs as a majority group right that supersedes supposedly elitist human rights for individuals. Meanwhile, the self-determination clause is an open invitation to exclude donors, international solidarity groups, and NGOs that promote sexual minority rights in Africa. Alternative interpretations are difficult to get through the system as it is currently structured. Indeed, decisions so far by the African Court on Human and Peoples' Rights give little cause to believe that the eleven justices – who are nominated by their national governments and then elected by a majority of the state parties – will have much appetite to criticize or embarrass those governments with radical interpretations of the charter. The African Commission appears similarly willing to break its own protocols and practices in order to keep the putative dignity of the political leadership of repressive member states intact. In May 2010, the commission arbitrarily denied the Coalition of African Lesbians (CAL) observer status (see Nana 2010; Isaack 2010; and Ndashe 2011 for concededly partisan accounts of that process).

There are nonetheless grounds for cautious optimism that the cause of sexual minority rights can be pressed forward through the African Union. First, prior to the CAL fiasco, activists engaging with the African Commission found a surprisingly welcoming environment in which to forge solidarity with other human rights NGOs from around the continent and in which at least some of the commissioners listened with empathy to critiques of human rights abusers like the Cameroon government. It was, according to Wendy Isaack (2010), a participant in the early phase of workshops, "one of the most meaningful political spaces for extra-national engagement on the protection of human rights for sexual minorities in Africa." Moreover, several groups that work explicitly with MSM and other "at-risk" populations, including female sex workers, transgender people, and lesbians, were granted observer status and have continued to raise the issue in alliance with a growing circle of "straight" NGOs. Alternatives Cameroon is a noteworthy case as it focuses on seeking justice for LGBTI people (Ndashe 2011). Its major distinction from CAL appears to be not in the nature of its work but in its omission of an "offensive" word in its name. Such inconsistency leaves the commission open to challenge.

Second, and perhaps most decisively, scientific evidence establishing that homophobia threatens the rights of the majority population has burgeoned in recent years. Such evidence is argued in a range of technical languages, including medical anthropology, economics, and social science and has grown to the point that it could be used to underpin a group rights challenge to homophobic legislation and speech. Homophobia undermines effective national and regional responses to the HIV/AIDS pandemic, still ravaging the continent at an alarming rate. Put simply, the stigmatization, discrimination, and violence that sexual minorities suffer increases their susceptibility to HIV and to death by AIDS. Although national and regional HIV prevalence rates for LGBTI people are not available, reports indicate that in some countries it is extremely high among MSM. For example, while Senegal has a low overall HIV prevalence rate of about 1 per cent of the general population, 21.5 per cent of MSM were HIV positive in 2005 (Beyrer et al. 2011). This rate is related to the homophobic laws in the country, which hinder sexual minorities' access to quality health care. Sexual minorities live in an environment of fear and insecurity that denies them the opportunity to ascertain and disclose their HIV status. Because high numbers of MSM feel they must hide their male sexual partners behind the mask of a wife or girlfriend, they act as a bridge from the most at-risk population to the general population, including to children through mother-to-child transmission. The World Bank study cited above draws on other studies that suggest MSM may be responsible for up to 20 per cent of all new infections, far higher than anyone had previously imagined (Beyrer et al. 2011).[4]

Failure to provide education on the existence, let alone the dangers, of unprotected male-male sex or of homophobic practices such as so-called corrective rape puts the health and well-being of the majority population, and of youth in particular, at risk. For these reasons, ministers of health across the continent have begun to heed advice from donors on the urgency of accounting for MSM in their national strategic plans. This has resulted in an anomalous situation in which one arm of government provides education and health services to people whose practices another arm declares illegal. It is thus conceivable that a group of heterosexual women, such as mothers infected by their husbands, could take aim at that anomaly. They could take their government to court, or raise the issue for debate at the African Commission, for the state's failure to provide a "favourable environment for development" by refusing to adhere to its own national strategic plan to reduce male-male HIV infections.

Third, the African peer review mechanism is open to the obvious criticism that African states have historically been reluctant to upset their peers by meddling too closely in internal matters like domestic law. Moreover, if all peers agree (for example, on the idea that homosexual acts between consenting adults are a crime rather than a human right), then no meaningful commentary is possible. The consensus on both these points, however, is breaking down, and South Africa has begun to play a major role in pressing it further. Since 1994, South Africa has been reluctant to criticize the human rights record of its African peers, and even more reluctant to trumpet its own constitution as a model that other African countries should emulate. In 2011, however, there was a dramatic shift. Jerry Matjila was appointed as the director general of international relations and cooperation and announced that his government would henceforth adopt a more proactive foreign policy on the promotion of human rights. One of his first initiatives was to co-sponsor the UN resolution that affirms sexual orientation as a human right. Interestingly, his justification for this came from article 20 of the Banjul Charter (that is, self-determination and liberation from colonialism). As reported, Matjila "noted that most of the criminalisation of homosexuality in Africa came about through legislation enacted by colonial powers. 'When the colonialists changed, we didn't change the penal codes. Now we say it's 'culture'" (*Mamba Online*, 11 September 2011).

South Africa is meanwhile playing a lead role in the peer review process of Zimbabwe's preparations for its next scheduled elections. One requirement of this process is the negotiation of a constitution that meets the high standards of human rights protections of the charter to which Zimbabwe is a signatory, even if it has flagrantly violated its commitments over the last three decades. It is now no longer possible for peers to ignore such violations without bringing themselves into censure. South Africa in particular could hardly offer its peer approval of a new constitution in Zimbabwe that refuses to allow even the vague language of "other status" or "circumstances of birth," as opponents of sexual minority rights in

Zimbabwe demand. Were such a constitution to be tabled, South Africa would be in violation of its own constitution as well as its commitments to its peers if it failed to report the flawed document to the Southern African Development Community (thence to the African Union) for censure.

The likelihood that South Africa will publicly rebuke a constitution that definitively blocks sexual minority rights in Zimbabwe is even greater as other countries have begun to follow in its footsteps. Several countries in the immediate region have indicated they are moving toward decriminalization of homosexual acts (Malawi, Mauritius) or have already taken steps to prohibit discrimination in the workplace on the basis of sexual orientation (Botswana, Mozambique). The leader of the main opposition party and current prime minister of Zimbabwe, Morgan Tsvangirai, has indicated he is open to these ideas as well. Zimbabwe could meanwhile not rely on sympathetic homophobes at the African Union to defend it against a humiliating censure by its peers. On the contrary, in July 2012 the African Union elected Dr Nkosazana Dlamini-Zuma of South Africa as its first female president. Dlamini-Zuma is a respected veteran of the struggle against apartheid, known for her quiet professionalism in her former portfolios as South Africa's minister of health and minister of foreign affairs. Though she has not gone on record in support of LGBTI rights, she enabled their progress (and that of other harm reduction initiatives) during her tenure in the Ministry of Health. She also trained and worked as a medical doctor prior to her career in politics. It is likely that she, more than the lawyers and politicians she now leads, is predisposed to understand the dangers that homophobia represents to the African Union's vision of a peaceful, prosperous, and healthy continent.

CONCLUSION

Sexual minority rights are highly controversial in Africa. For MSM, WSW, and LGBTI individuals and their families, the risks inherent in pursuing those rights range from financial costs to stigma to a negative political reaction and possible exile, injury, or death. In the absence of employment, education, and trust in the institutions of governance, the benefits of attaining rights in a distant continental court or commission (in theory) may not be apparent or meaningful in practice (on the local street). However, Africans *are* taking those risks and pushing the envelope of the debate. The Banjul Charter and the institutions that support it may indeed have some worrisome gaps and structural limitations at present. But they also have the potential to become tools and allies in the struggle to obtain equal rights – and good health for all citizens.

2

No Place Like Home: African Refugees and the Emergence of a New Queer Frame of Reference

NOTISHA MASSAQUOI

LGBT lives should not be so cheap, but nothing can change as long as LGBT people live in fear for their safety when they claim their basic human rights.
We want to be alive.
We want to be recognized as human beings because we are.
We want to be treated with dignity.
We want to live in our countries.
We want to fulfill our dreams, build families, work hard, thrive in our countries
We want to live without fear, in peace and not thinking every morning that we might end up in prison or graves at the end of the day.
We want to be free to love and to be loved.
We deserve all these and more. (Victor Mukasa, United Nations testimony, 12 December 2009)

On 28 June 2009, a group of African refugees took to the streets of Toronto, Canada, and headed the pride parade. They were led down the parade route with dignity and strength by Ugandan activist Victor Mukasa, a self-identified transgender lesbian who fled Uganda after police illegally raided his home in 2005 and confiscated documents related to human rights and LGBTI organizing.[1] Marching in one of the largest and longest running pride parades in North America, they faced up to one million spectators, cameras, and international media outlets as they shouted and chanted for human rights and denounced the persecution they had faced at home because of their sexual orientations and identities. Indeed, while this group of African activists engaged in an activity taken for granted by most Canadians who watched, the Ugandan government prepared to pass a bill submitted by a member of parliament, David Bahati. The bill aimed to strengthen his nation's capacity to deal with "emerging internal and external threats to the traditional heterosexual family" (Uganda Antigay Bill draft, April 2009. See also *Daily Monitor*, 11 January 2010; *Seattle Times*, 8 December 2009; and *Sydney Morning Herald*, 8 January 2010). It built on the claims that same-sex attraction is not an innate and immutable characteristic and that the people of Uganda must be protected against sexual rights activists seeking to impose their values of sexual promiscuity and exploitation of youth. The original proposed legislation would have strengthened the criminalization of homosexuality in Uganda by introducing the death penalty for people who were considered serial offenders, who were suspected of "aggravated homosexuality" and were HIV-positive, or who engaged in sexual acts with those under eighteen years of age (*Washington Post*, 8 January 2010; *New York Times*, 8 May 2010). People caught or suspected of homosexual activity would also be forced to undergo HIV tests. The bill further stated that Ugandans who engage in same-sex sexual relations outside Uganda would likewise fall under the jurisdiction of this law, and may be extradited and charged with a felony. If passed, the bill would also require anyone aware of an offense or an offender, including family members, companies, media organizations, or non-governmental organizations that support LGBTI rights, to report the offender within twenty-four hours. If an individual did not do so, he or she would also be considered an offender and would be liable on conviction to a fine (*Guardian*, 13 December 2009).[2]

This infamous bill catapulted Uganda to the front of the line of the thirty-eight African countries imposing repressive laws against their LGBTI citizens, with South Africa remaining the only country on the continent to offer unqualified human rights protection under its constitution. Even with protective laws on the books, however, LGBTI communities in South Africa still face abuses justified by culture, religion, or patriotism; often find only ambivalent support from authorities (*Channel4*, 12 March 2009; Mkhize et al. 2010); and also face more subtle pressure to conform to heterosexual norms (Hackman, this volume).

Around the time of this bill in 2009, I studied a group of forty queer African refugees who had sought or were currently seeking asylum in Canada. I use the term *queer* to mean an act of agency and in reference to same-sex desire or any alternative to compulsory heterosexuality. I use this term with particular reference to same-sex desire from an African context in which labels such as *lesbian* and *gay* are not fixed identities and where there are a multiplicity of sexualities not yet uniformly defined. I stress in my argument that the collapsing of *queer African* is not a natural or static category and, in the vein of Sylvia Tamale (2011), I understand that such homogenizing particularly in terms of African sexuality is out of touch with the lived experiences, identities, and relationships of African activism and scholarship. I however use the term in Spivak's (1996) sense, as a strategic use of positive essentialism for a situationally specific political movement. This positioning is what makes meaning possible in this context.[3]

I met with the individuals in my study on a bi-weekly basis over the course of the year. Drawing on their life histories, these men, transmen, women, and transwomen describe some common experiences. Although their circumstances vary greatly, such as in terms of family background, educational level, cultural background, access to resources, and sexual identity, their stories share many features that resonate with both each other and with my own experience as an immigrant child originally from Sierra Leone navigating my queer identity between my adopted home in Canada and my home of birth on the African continent. These stories will create the foundation for understanding queer communities in Africa and the mixed feelings that some members hold about both their countries of origin and also the experiences of adapting to life in the African diaspora.

These stories will become part of what I propose is a queer African framework, which will allow me to interrogate the concept of sexual orientation and identity from an African perspective. The academic study of sexual orientation, the emergence of queer politics of identity, and new queer formations have focused on Western examples and have emphasized white, middle-class gay life (e.g., Bérubé 2001; Kinsmen 2001). Africa and Africans are often added as a cursory and general footnote to global studies (e.g., Rupp 2001). Spaces and environments in which to freely articulate the current state and future of queer African lives are thus urgently needed for the creation of a queer African framework. I define an African queer framework as one that offers an analysis of the present situation of queer Africans, an interpretation of a queer African past, and movement to involve queer citizens in Africa's future, with *Africa* conceptualized in an expansive and inclusive way (e.g., Tamale 2011).

In the formation of such a framework it is important to pay attention to the process that constructs the collective queer African *we*. Every self is a storied self, and stories that support the queer African visibility need to amplify how they negotiate identities and politics across dynamic spaces. The emergence of queer African subjects thus requires changes to methodological, political, and cultural theoretical approaches used to study or represent them in order to more sensitively and accurately articulate who they are, how they can claim their space in history, and how they create a political platform in terms – rather than in spite – of their racial and ethnic differentiation from the mainstream queer community in Canada. Who is empowered and who is disempowered in a specific construction of the queer African *we*? How are social divisions negotiated in this construct? What is the relationship of this construct to other queer communities globally?[4] These are questions that need to be explored before the articulation of a framework that centralizes the lives of queer Africans.

The quotations I highlight in this chapter are based on the results of a qualitative participatory research study for my PhD thesis.[5] Conducting the interviews in Canada as opposed to on the continent allowed me to find participants who could freely share their life stories and openly discuss sexuality without fear of persecution. I also felt this group could not only best articulate their experiences in Africa as LGBTI individuals and community members, but also give a clear picture of how identity shifts through migration.

I recruited participants over a two-month period through newspaper ads, list serves, service providers, and refugee lawyers. Research participants were in four Canadian cities (Toronto, Ottawa, Montreal, and Windsor), ranged from twenty-three to forty-seven years old, and included individuals who self-identified racially and ethnoculturally as black and continental African. They originated from eleven African countries (Burundi, Uganda, Senegal, Kenya, Botswana, Swaziland, Ivory Coast, Ghana, Ethiopia, Nigeria, and Rwanda) and represent all regions except for North Africa. Participants identified themselves using the categories of queer, lesbian, gay, bisexual, and or transgendered. Of the forty people I interviewed, twenty identified as male, sixteen as female, two as a transmen, and two as transwomen. All were currently living in Canada and were in the process of or had completed a refugee claim in Canada due to persecution based on sexual orientation or identity in their country of origin. In addition, I conducted seven key informant interviews with Canadian immigration lawyers and community agency service providers. I conducted individual interviews face-to-face with all participants. I concealed the identities of the participants when requested, and have used pseudonyms.

QUEER AFRICANS?

Obviously it's difficult and we face a lot of discrimination and violence. There are very hard and fast rules culturally, traditionally and legally that prohibit us from being together or being seen together or just being yourself, you know ... there's certain things that are just taboo and absolutely no go areas. And being a homosexual and choosing a sexual orientation anything apart from being a heterosexual it's just a no. So it makes life difficult and uncomfortable and unfair so I think that's kind of the status right now. It's just very difficult and challenging and if anybody tries to challenge it, some do, some are brave enough to, then it backfires and the repercussions are always negative. (Lesbian refugee from Botswana in Canada for one year)

For reasons of urgency (to escape homophobic persecution or other violence), necessity (to escape economic hardship), and sometimes choice (to pursue educational or other opportunities, or to consume the mythologized Western lifestyle), lesbian, gay bisexual, and transgendered Africans cross borders and unfold their lives in diasporic spaces. Those who come to Canada are not alone. Approximately 69,000 transnational community members from African countries of origin reside in Ontario, the most popular Canadian destination for members of these communities, making up 6.9 per cent of the immigrant population for the province (Statistics Canada 2006). As the African population continues to grow, Canada is clearly becoming an intricate part of the African diaspora. My focus is on LGBTI Africans whom fear moved from their native homeland into an environment that is radically different in climate, culture, economy, and political and legal structures. With this in mind, the question now is,

"What kind of history of sexuality will be written with the collision of dislocated LGBTI Africans and Canadian space?" For LGBTI African refugees in particular, Canada is both a contested space where identities are forcibly constructed under the weight of dominant culture and also a subversive space where people are free to explore multiple identities – including sexual identity and orientation – often for the first time.

Prior to their arrival in Canada, many queer African refugees find themselves in a culture of compulsory heterosexuality. The pervasive belief in Africa is that heterosexuality is the only "normal" form of sexual expression (healthy, natural, respectful, and life producing), whilst homosexuality is sick, unnatural, disrespectful, and deadly (e.g., Case 2002; Helle-Valle 2004; and Nyanzi and Dworkin et al. in this volume). Across the African continent, the number of constitutional articles that regulate homosexuality varies, but the wording is virtually identical. For example, in Zambia "carnal knowledge of any person against the order of nature" is punishable; in Uganda "any person who has carnal knowledge of any person against the order of nature is guilty of an offence and is liable to life imprisonment." The Nigerian Penal Code states that "any person who has carnal knowledge of any person against the order of nature ... is liable to imprisonment for 14 years" (Behind the Mask 2005; see also Nyeck and Broqua, this volume, on commonalities that arise from the French colonial and neocolonial experience).

With national and cultural imperatives to be reproductive citizens, queer Africans are positioned as a threat to the nation and the heterosexual African who loyally builds it. This position creates intense pressure to appear to conform to heterosexual norms:

> Most of the clients in the clinic at home are married men, when I say married, married with women, they have children and a wife at home. They have sex with men in the sex trade. Which is, I mean, which is very bad because those men they can take HIV from the straight community and bring into the gay community. So they are a kind of bridge. (Gay refugee from Uganda in Canada for one year)

> You have to live a double life because I wasn't going to be a, a lesbian full-time because they want to see you with guys. Even if you are young, but then your parents like to see you with guys, even if they would beat you at least you were dating a guy at a

tender age it's fine for them. (Lesbian refugee from Swaziland in Canada for six months)

Such comments force us to examine the construction of the continent as a closet for queer Africans. In the West, activists tend to concentrate today on how to encourage individuals to come out of their personally constructed closets by focusing on internalized homophobia, private shame, and performative deception. In queer African theorizing, there is a need to refocus this gaze to look at how cultures, family, colonization, faith, neoliberalism, and other factors have created interwoven closets and oppressive conditions, and how the resulting culture of heteronormativity makes coming out heroic for most individuals. Only a few can do it. It forces some citizens to flee. As one informant, a lesbian refugee from Uganda in Canada for one year, described:

I was living with my mom but when people started knowing what happened to me, I moved to another village. And I had a girlfriend, and I remember it was 2007 in September. The girlfriend I had, I knew that girl from 2004. I used to see her, but we used to see each other secretly. I don't know what happened to her, somebody killed her. She was found on the way by my house lying down. She was stabbed. We don't know what happened to her up to now I don't know what happened to her. Because what they do if they know truly this is your character or this is who you are, chances of you getting killed, they are very high. If I didn't come to Canada I don't think now I would be alive.

Another participant, a gay refugee from Zimbabwe who had been in Canada for three years, remarked:

The president was making statements about there being no gay people in Zimbabwe and my friend had a talk show and invited me to come and talk about being gay on national television. I thought this would be an opportunity to make a statement ... I was arrested shortly after ... the harassment that followed was just unbearable.

Another gay refuge from Uganda, who had been in Canada for two years, put it this way:

I think the situation for most gays and lesbians in Africa is ... one of the concerns around safety and you know personal agency, freedom from violence, freedom from the fear of violence and just the ability to live out a full life, fully participating in the society without concern for being ill or mistreated and that being sanctioned by the state, by the state using laws to restrict their full personhood.

In arguing that queer Africans are positioned as a threat to the nation and its heterosexual citizens, I also want to emphasize that African queer communities are challenging our silencing, are creating visibility and presence, and are resisting the culture of silence. In October 2010, Ugandan tabloid *Rolling Stone* published the names and photographs of one hundred gay individuals and called for their execution. Three members of Sexual Minorities Uganda – David Kato, along with Kasha Jacqueline and Julian "Pepe" Onziema – listed in the article successfully petitioned for an injunction to stop the newspaper from publishing the names and pictures of alleged gays or lesbians. Kato was subsequently murdered on 26 January 2011. Yet in the face of such brutality, others remain active and vocal in their desire to remain in the country (and faith) of their families (e.g., Kaggwa 2011; Victor Mukasa as noted above).

I also want to emphasize, as Sylvia Tamale (2011) writes, that silence in many of our African cultures can be as powerful and empowering (or at least, enabling) as speech. Stella Nyanzi (chapter 4 in this volume) notes the powerful nature of this silence in her discussion of President Yahya Jammeh's homophobic pronouncements and the subsequent silence from the Gambia's LGBTI community. The very lack of a coordinated visible response from queer Gambians highlighted the fear, danger, and tyrannical oppression they lived under. It also shone a spotlight on the fact that even the president could no longer deny the existence of queer people in his country. While they may not have been vocal, their presence warranted his attention, and their silence drew the forceful reaction of the international community.

HETEROSEXUAL BORDERS, QUEER CROSSERS: WHAT IS AT STAKE?

Asylum in Canada, with all its legal protections for sexual minorities, is attractive from the perspective of such experiences. But the border comes first. For queer African refugee claimants, the border means difficulties making refugee claims, difficulties navigating Canadian society while waiting for a claim to be heard, possible detention and deportation if a claim is denied, and possible loss of life if returned to their country of origin.

In the past two decades, Canadian immigration has begun to decrease the surveillance and increase the movement of queer bodies across the border. In 1977, gays and lesbians were removed from the list of inadmissible bodies. In 1992, influenced by two queer refugee cases in progress in the United States (*Acosta v.* and *Toboso v.*), Canada became the first North American country to grant refugee status to a claimant on the basis of sexual orientation (Fairbairn 2005; Miller 2005). A year later, in landmark ruling *Canada v. Ward*, the Supreme Court of Canada explicitly defined the parameters of the refugee convention concept of a "particular social group" as including sexual orientation; that is, the court identified sexual orientation as an immutable, innate, or unchangeable personal characteristic, therefore declaring gay and lesbian refugee claimants as belonging to a particular social group and so deserving of explicit protection (La Violette 1997; Parrish 2006). This discourse also developed from public policy on the admission of same-sex partners through the expansion of the family class codification in the Immigration and Refugee Protection Act and Regulations (2001). In 2012, the redefinition of marriage through Bill C-38 and the ability of same-sex couples to sponsor spouses also became part of how the state produces sexual identities.

The current Canadian refugee law nonetheless struggles to acknowledge the fluidity and contextual nature of sexual orientation and gender identity. The refugee process has been criticized due to the arbitrary and subjective nature of Immigration and Refugee Board of Canada (IRB) rulings on queer refugee claims. Queer refugees must prove their queerness. Some researchers believe that many IRB adjudicators end up determining a queer refugee claimant's "queerness" based on their own heterosexist or even homophobic worldviews (Fairbairn 2005; Lidstone 2006).

I am appealing. My claim was denied in 2006. I was told that I was not believed to be gay since I have six children. How can an African man of forty-six years not have children? My father had ten children by the time he was my age. A man with no children

will not be taken seriously ... It has nothing to do with being gay.
(Gay refugee from Uganda, in Canada for four years)

They use stereotypes that are presented to them by the media
and, you know, general media presentations like the TV shows
and what they see in the mainstream, kind of gay culture and the
gay village kind of thing so a gay guy has to be femme-y, have to
wear colours that are femme-y or gay, you have to wear pink if
you have some make-up if you are doing the hairdos, and I also
saw and heard lawyers advising their clients to gay it up a little
bit in the hearing, you know? Don't dress, don't wear what you
usually dress, you're too butch, too masculine if you're a man.
Like wear a pink shirt, wear something like what you would
wear to go to a club, dancing, you know. Do you use make-up?
Maybe you can add a little bit mascara to your eyes ... all these
things that, you know is just ... really silly and they are very cos-
metic, they're very image oriented and don't really prove anything but unfortunately the system is very immature that way
and unreasonable in lots of ways and because it's not a judicial
system the refugee process is a bureaucratic system ... they're not
judges they are members who are appointed as a job, as a
bureaucratic job so they don't have that training of a judge they
don't have the process of presenting the evidence, witnesses,
arguing, all that doesn't exist, which takes away so much from
the fairness and neutrality of this process. (Trans refugee support
worker, key informant seven)

The limited research currently available on contemporary queer
Africans often overlooks an examination of specific modes and
effects of displacement and geographic movement between nations,
cultures, and regions that promotes the intricate realignment of sexual identity, sexual politics, and sexual desire. The queer African
refugee is currently defined by Western decision makers who are still
coming to terms with the other, which in this case is a lesbian, bisexual person, gay man, or transgendered person from a society that
historically was not a significant source of immigration to Canada.
Border officials must translate this experience of sexuality, gender
identity, and culture – not only into the international and national
frameworks of refugee law, but also into something they recognize
as "gay" or "homosexual." This process requires empathy and

imagination as to who the queer African refugee subject is now, and who they might be if granted admission to and protection within Canada. In the case of Francis Ojo Ogunride in June 2012, a federal judge overturned an IRB decision that rejected Ogunride's claim after concluding he was not credible and not gay. This decision came despite overwhelming evidence from roommates, landlords, LGBT organizations, past lovers, and a police report from Nigeria that all attested to Ogunride's orientation. The federal court felt that the IRB's decision was guided by stereotypes of how a gay man should behave. This case emphasizes the challenges and need for guidelines and clear standards in making rulings. According to a Canadian immigration lawyer (key informant three):

> You don't change people's attitudes, people's biases, people's lenses, and, you know, ways of looking at things over a one-day training ... this is training that should be mandatory and that should be ongoing. I think that the IRB still has to look at this more seriously because we are seeing cases of refugee claimants who are LGBTQ refugee claimants and who are unjustly refused.

Being marked as queer entails the realignment of identity, politics, and desire as one moves between cultures and nations. Being *kisi, kifi, buyazi, mashoga, supi, tousso bakari*, a grinder, AC/DC, *woubie*, a woman who does business, a Tommy boy, homosexual, lesbian, queer, or gay involves answering to those terms, acting on emotions, feeling desire, and engaging in sexual practices that have different meanings in different places.[6] Serena Dankwa (chapter 9, this volume) highlights the fact that that same-sex loving women within a Ghanaian context may not feel the necessity to organize around an identity but do express tacit knowledge of the possibilities of such relations. They may even have identifiers, such as *supi* for women who engage in same-sex sex, and they may verbalize and articulate their desires for other women without a discursive language for Ghanaian same-sex culture. What does it mean to be marked as queer and to answer to those terms in Africa, and what happens when that same queer-marked African body becomes a refugee in a Western nation? According to a Canadian immigration lawyer (key informant four):

> They are actually asking a lot of people making this claim, so for some people for the first time they're going to put on paper and

verbalize something that they have never been able to speak
about before openly ... just in my own experience with working
with African gays and lesbians, they didn't have the language
when they came, the LGBT language and then ... they ... I want
to say they weren't anticipated and when I say that I mean no
one is expecting this African person to say that they are gay,
'cause there's such limited experience that people have with gay
people who also claim to be continental African. So they don't fit
the Western stereotype and then they also don't fit the immigrant
stereotype. Immigrants from Africa aren't gay.

This is not, however, to put the onus entirely upon the issue of stereotyping by immigration officials. The context in which queer
Africans are forced to construct their lives does not always make
helping easy:

Gay African refugees are both the easiest cases and the hardest at
the same time. In terms of proving that their life will be in danger
if returned home and that they are in need of protection in
Canada – that's easy. The laws, public statements by presidents,
governments, and religious leaders are quite easy to obtain.
Human rights organizations have also compiled enormous
amounts of support info to help us ... Proving that they belong to
an oppressed group, i.e., that they are in fact gay is the difficult
part. They have spent their entire lives carefully hiding their identity so they come with no pictures, letters, evidence of living with
partners, no friends, family, or lovers who are willing to testify or
send statements on their behalf, they do not belong to gay groups
or associations publically ... there is no evidence. All my clients
have effectively erased this whole part of their lives from public
view. (key informant four)

Negotiating this need to shift identities can be re-traumatizing. A
Canadian immigration lawyer (key informant one) explains:

There's the issue of trauma that you may have experience around
this ... hypothetical case – lesbian woman who was forced into
marriage and has been in marriage for a number of years under-
going marital rape for a number of years, imagine what this does
to you as a person psychologically and emotionally and then you

may have been discovered having the very first same-sex relationship and that's the reason why you had to flee and then you
come here traumatized and you are expected to repeat and share
this story over and over so that you can get the services you need
and prepare for your refugee claim. And because of your sexuality, because you grew up in an environment that constantly told
you that you are unworthy, that you are ... you know despicable
you come here and file your claim in a way that minimizes your
traumatic experience and this creates an issue of credibility. Your
claim gets rejected but then finally you get the right counselling
or the right lawyer that tells you; yes I understand that you were
not able to speak up about your sexuality but that's the reason
why you fled and ... perhaps you had to appeal and then try to
say well this thing that was being played down in my first
account is that I am actually gay. The extent to which you have
just been unable throughout your life to actually give yourself a
voice about this issue is the thing that renders you non-credible
... and you're going to be rejected by the IRB.

RETHINKING AFRICAN QUEER INVISIBILITY

The circumstances of arrival in Canada (origin, arrival date, and
immigration status) clearly articulates many things about who an
individual will be perceived to be, how they will be treated in the
host nation, and what that nation will offer (Bannerji 2000; Li
2003). Once past the border, the African diaspora becomes an environment that facilitates the renaming and remaking of tradition. It is
a place where national pride can override ethnic or regional differences, and ethnic, sexual, and gendered identities become less important than shared experience of immigration, racism, and the search
for belonging in Canadian society. In this context, one's sexual orientation as an African living in the diaspora becomes secondary to
navigating Canadian society in the settlement phase of the immigration process and to rebuilding a sense of community within the new
nation (Gastaldo et al. 2005). Brah (1996) suggests that in a diasporic space, boundaries of inclusion and exclusion, of belonging
and otherness, and of "us and them" are contested. How is an LGBTI
African diaspora historicized, politicized, sexualized, and erased? I
asked myself this question as I marched with the LGBTI refugees in

a 2009 pride parade and as I conducted research over the course of
the year. A lesbian refugee from Ethiopia who has been in Canada
for two years says: "I live with my aunt and she is very religious. Am
I going to give up my family and my church to be openly gay? I think
this will be different when I finish my refugee claim and I can find a
job to support myself."

Many transnational subjects from African locations are prepared
for otherness based on race due to experiences of colonization,
imperialism, apartheid, and the many stories that filter back to Africa
about disappointments or traumas encountered in the West. Many
such subjects are not prepared to place themselves in the role of the
other within their communities in terms of sexual orientation (Abou-
Rihan 1994; Khayatt 2002). It is often physically dangerous to do so
in their countries of origin and although human rights are protected
by legislation in the West, the risk of loss, being ostracized from family and community, and banishment into a Canadian environment
that is not always supportive of difference, particularly racial devia-
tion from white heteronormativity, is too great. As transnational
subjects cross borders, they extract queerness from their identity as
Africans and their relations to gender, race, and class out of fear and
necessity. In so doing, they help to perpetuate the notion that queerness is equated with whiteness from a Canadian perspective and
same-sex desire is a foreign manifestation from an African perspective (Murray and Roscoe 1998; Arnfred 2004; Machera 2004). One
of my research participants, a gay refugee from Burundi who has
been in Canada for six years, explains:

> It's better than what I was, like the way I was living in Burundi.
> For example let me see ... here I'm gay, I came out, I live my life
> but it hasn't changed me, uh, the only thing which changed in me
> like I'm more free, I don't have to think all the time, oh I should
> hide, or oh I should do this. No I just be myself, you take me as I
> am and then it's funny because you come here and you think, uh,
> everything's gonna be fine, and you find people from your own
> community, from Burundi, are discriminating you again like at
> home. So it's another struggle, you know?

Tensions also arise from nostalgia for homes and families left behind.
Very often, diasporic subjects feel so dissatisfied and disillusioned by
the injustices in their new locales that they turn a diasporic gaze

back to their countries of origin. This gaze is sometimes romanticized, uncritical, and defensive in the face of the ignorance or unwit-
ting prejudices about Africa in the dominant Canadian culture. The
mainstream white queer communities also still often engages in discriminatory exclusionary patterns of behaviour with little regard for
the issues – or validation of the experience – of queer transnationals
(Patton 2000). Key informant five, an African immigration counsel-
lor, discusses this behaviour:

> What's your community? And I said well, it's the queer commu-
> nity. But that's a very white community. It's absolutely a white
> community. Most of the queer communities in Canada are white.
> Walk down Church Street [in Toronto] and any gay village and
> you can count how many people of color are walking there. Why
> don't we feel accepted in those spaces?

Key informant six, an AIDS service worker, explains that these patterns have consequences:

> I do outreach in the bathhouses. It is you know, people are ... it's
> pretty stripped down, it's pretty basic, it's pretty obvious what
> people want. And consistently people of color get looked through
> like they are invisible. There's a whole section in our cruising
> book about dealing with racism in the bathhouse context and
> what that looks like. In the bathhouse it's brutal because what
> you see is a bunch of guys searching the room for what they like
> and if you are not what they like you are invisible and most
> often they are not looking for someone Black. So eye contact is
> only made with specific individuals but consistently it begins to
> be only specific individuals of a certain preferable race. This is
> the white gay male culture that new refugees are trying to navi-
> gate. It leaves them wide open for abuse and HIV risk since you
> are not going to negotiate safer sex if you are constantly dealing
> with loneliness and rejection in the white gay world.

In this inhospitable context, diasporic subjects cultivate home with a
vengeance (Okpewho 2009), but the image of Africa that results
stands in stark contrast to the realities of the queer subjects living
there. This hunger for romanticized knowledge and intimacy with
the home country leaves queer Africans in an unstable position.

Their lives point to the reality that feeling disenfranchised in the diaspora can be painful, but the politics of home, which has been a core coping mechanism for diasporic subjects, can no longer be the remedy without a commitment to challenge the current state of affairs for queer citizens in the country of origin.

CONCLUSION: TRAVELLING THEORIES AND THE POLITICS OF LOCATION

The emergence of the queer African refugee has resulted in interrogating the complex system of sexual norms in both African and Western cultures, where the normal African is not queer and the normal queer is not African. The existence as queer Africans in the diaspora thus launches a critique of both the dominant culture in Canada and also the loud, homophobic African nationalism of men like Bahati. The locational politics where power as impossible Africans is articulated also amplifies that critique.

Such collective queer African identities acquire specific content from narratives both of belonging and ancestry, and of dislocation, displacement, adaptation, and resistance prior to and post movement. The histories of queer displacement show some diasporic features that are oriented to roots in a specific place and a desire to return home, as well as to an ability to recreate a culture in diverse locations (Gilroy 1993; Hall 2003). Identity becomes a necessary component of agency, resistance, and survival, and is attained through an ongoing process of self-analysis and interpretation of social position. I suggest that a queer African identity is not an essence but an ongoing positioning.

One of the biggest challenges queer Africans globally face is forced invisibility. The creation of an effective queer African presence behind (and across) borders would involve the active rejection of the notion of invisibility globally – within our nations of origin and within nations of the African diaspora in which African bodies are also present. It is equally necessary to address concepts of queerness on the continent and in the African diaspora, as these same concepts travel with queer African bodies as they cross borders. The struggle of queer Africans everywhere is vital testimony to the presence of same-sex desire on the African continent.

The struggles of queer African refugees make discussions of the heterogeneity of the African diaspora unavoidable. Diasporic experiences may not be obviously – but are always – sexualized. Theoretical accounts of diasporas and diasporic culture tend to hide this fact, to talk of displacement in unmarked ways, and thus to normalize the heterosexual experience and mask the queer one. A queer African framework that speaks to the refugee's experience is a project that not only affirms and celebrates the complex representations of African identity – which are privately accentuated by sexual political consciousness – but also challenges representations that are publicly regulated by those who define African cultural expression by prioritized heteronormativity.

A queer African framework, then, must clearly articulate the formation of a queer African identity, which that cannot be separated from the theory of resistance, revolution, and change. In a transnational world where cultural asymmetries and linkages continue to be mystified by economic and political interest at multiple levels, detailed, historicized, and geopolitical mappings of the circuits of power in relation to sexual orientation are a necessity.

3

The Making of "African Sexuality": Early Sources, Current Debates

MARC EPPRECHT

African sexuality – the idea that Africans share a common sexual culture distinct from people elsewhere in the world – has had numerous incarnations over the centuries. These include native custom, Black Peril, *The African as Suckling and as Adult* (Ritchie 1944) and *Voodoo Eros* (Bryk 1964 [1925]) – to name two of the more notorious volumes on the topic. Despite differences in emphasis and veneer of scientific neutrality, the overarching theme has been that African sexuality is a problem. In colonial times, Africans' supposed stunted or brutish sexuality was thought to oppress and degrade women, to engender laziness and stultify intellectual growth in men, to threaten public health and safety, and to impoverish culture and the arts (there being no love or higher emotions, just lust, superstition, and steely transactions). Whether Africans were immoral or merely perverse was a serious debate that profoundly shaped the development of colonial states (see Jeater 1993, for example, on the laws and institutions created in colonial Zimbabwe to control Africans' sexual behaviour). In modern times, African sexuality has been invoked to explain the high rates of HIV/AIDS in much of the continent (and, by implication, in the diaspora). Australian demographers Caldwell, Caldwell, and Quiggan (1989) survey the ethnography and conclude that Africans were less prone to feel guilt, less concerned with female virginity or fidelity, and hence more relaxed towards having multiple concurrent sex partners than Asians or Europeans. Even more controversially, Phillipe Rushton (1997) argues that there was a direct correlation between penis size, intelligence, respect for the law, and

sexual behaviour. In this analysis, "Negroids" were genetically predisposed to be sexually precocious, permissive, and criminal.[1]

African sexuality, in short, needed to be fixed by propaganda, legislation, and perhaps a global rescue mission.

It is tempting to decry these sweeping stereotypes and the policies
that have stemmed from them as straightforward racism – "five hundred years ... of white racist imperialism" and "white words" as Greg
Thomas puts it (2007, 21). Certainly, those who uncritically draw on
nineteenth-century European travelers for empirical facts about sexuality in Africa are at the very least extremely naive. But racism cannot
explain why so many African artists, intellectuals, and leaders also
often assert false claims of a unitary African sexual culture, in many
instances explicitly in the name of *anti*-racism. In colonial times,
African nationalists and sympathizers upheld an erotic but moral
Africa to stand in contrast with the neurotic and immoral West. In
recent years, this opposition has often centred around the claim that
"homosexuality is un-African," a claim staked out by political and
religious leaders from across the continent, as well as implied by the
pointed silences of important scholars (epidemiologists Kalipeni and
Oppong 2004, for example; also implicit in the Caldwell thesis). As
several of the studies in this volume show, the power of the state and
vigilantism against suspected gays and lesbians has backed the rhetoric of patriotic heterosexuality in many cases. Since 2005, notably, a
raft of draconian legislation has been tabled or enacted in countries
that otherwise have little in common.[2]

A quiet countermovement has achieved important gains for sexual
rights on the continent, including a host of initiatives under the ban-
ner of public health and at the level of international treaty obligations (Akanji and Epprecht, this volume).[3] Yet the broad loyalty to
what anthropologist Michael Herzfeld (1997) terms a "cultural intimacy" that otherwise disparate groups often unconsciously share
remains striking. This is particularly so as that stereotype of African
sexuality is clearly damaging to the well-being of Africans themselves. Essentialist constructions of heterosexually "predatory" masculinity are closely linked to gender-based violence with devastating
impacts on development (Population Council 2008; Jewkes et al.
2009; World Bank 2012). Moreover, while most of the tens of millions of Africans who have been infected with HIV/AIDS likely
became infected through heterosexual vaginal intercourse or mother-
child transmission, research in the last few years has shown that

heterosexual anal sex appears to have been dramatically underestimated as a risk factor. Homosexual transmission is also far more significant than research previously assumed. This research shows that African men who have sex with men (MSM) not only have especially high rates of infection, but also commonly report having female sexual partners. Denying their existence thus exposes the whole of society to risk, not just sexual minorities. Indeed, the history of colonial era campaigns against syphilis or "female circumcision" (female genital cutting, or FGC), plus lessons learned globally in the struggles against HIV/AIDS, show that denial, moralism, ideology, secrecy, and repression make a poor base upon which to build effective interventions against sexual ill health (e.g., Setel et al. 1999; Lockhart 2002; Niang et al. 2003; Allman et al. 2007; Smith et al. 2009; Beyrer et al. 2011).

This public health research, it should be added, follows on the heels of a wealth of memoirs, monographs, journalism, film, fiction, and activist literature that depicts the complex motivations, emotions, and shared humanity of sex workers, of women and girls who chose genital cutting, of sexual minorities, and of many others in Africa who do not conform to the predominant heteronormative expectations.[4]

How, then, to understand the durability of "African sexuality" in the face of such evidence? For that, it helps to trace the idea back in time to its earliest articulations in ostensibly scientific discourse: geographic exploration, ethnography, and psychiatry. These, I argue, have been profoundly influential because of the way they have largely disappeared into taken-for-granted "common sense." Methods pioneered by feminist social historians and anthropologists are well-suited to the task of teasing out that history of ideological construction from silent or evasive sources. They help us to ask, what can we learn about the making of African sexuality as an idea in the past that may suggest ways to challenge its enduring, harmful impacts in the present?[5]

The first written accounts of African societies south of the Sahara come from Muslim travellers or observers of African slaves in the Middle East from as long ago as the ninth century CE (255 AH). Akbar Muhammad (1985) shows that these were often thoughtful and respectful meditations upon difference. However, derogatory and sensational claims also percolated into Arabic accounts of Africans' "immense potency and unbridled sexuality" (Lewis 1990, 94). The framework story of *The 1,001 Nights*, for example, centres on the erotic fantasy/trauma of the male protagonists catching white women of the royal court having sex, singly and en masse, with their black servants (e.g., Burton 1885; Mardrus 1900). Muslim travelers, meanwhile, often found African Muslims to be somewhat relaxed in their interpretation of the Qur'anic injunction to modesty. Ibn Battuta was shocked to observe not just matter-of-fact female nudity but also that married Malian women met privately with male friends (Gibb 1983, 330).

Some of these ideas likely circulated in Iberia and may have influenced the ways that Portuguese voyagers regarded Africans when they began to explore the African coast in the fifteenth century. From the point of view of the Catholic church, the pre-eminent concern in that period were the African rulers' practices of polygyny and offering slaves, daughters, or junior wives as a gesture of hospitality to Portuguese visitors (Elbl 1992). Attempts to prohibit such intercourse did not succeed, and were also unsuccessful under subsequent French rule in places like Saint Louis and Gorée. By the late eighteenth century, relations between European men and African women had given rise to a local Christian aristocracy of *mulattas* or *signares* all along the West coast of the continent. Prior to their decline in economic fortune and the rise of racist ideologies in Europe in the mid-nineteenth century, these women were highly eroticized. To this day, the government of Senegal celebrates the memory of their beauty and love-making skills in its efforts to promote tourism.[6]

By the late eighteenth century, the Portuguese had been joined in writing about Africa by travelers and traders from many different European countries. They created a substantial body of literature that detailed many intimate aspects of life. Accounts were frequently exaggerated, sensationalized, judgmental, and imbued by error that stemmed from naiveté or linguistic misunderstanding. They nonetheless documented a basic truth: African societies tended to place an extremely high value on heterosexual marriage and reproduction. Marriage came in many forms, and with protections or flexibilities built in to preserve health and social harmony when ideals were breached in practice, whether those breaches occurred from necessity (such as the preservation of women's health against too many or too close pregnancies) or preference (human foibles, desire for ritual, and so on). Departures from the fecund heteropatriarchal ideals included long post-partum abstinence, ritual celibacy and incest, fictive relationships ("marriage to the grave," for example) and the use of herbs for aphrodisiacs and abortions. Same-sex exceptions to heterosexual norms and ideals were also documented, albeit usually couched in euphemistic and often strongly disparaging language. Sir Richard Burton's grand overview of world sexuality, for example, refers to a Portuguese document from 1558 that claimed "unnatural damnation" (meaning, male-male sex) was esteemed among the Kongo, as well as a "prostitute corps" used by the male-identified female warriors of Dahomey, the Amazons (Burton 1885, vol. X, 246–7). Andrew Battell, who lived among the Imbangala (in modern-day Angola) in the 1590s, was similarly disapproving, both of the male cross-dressers ("They are beastly in their living, for they have men in women's apparel, whom they keepe among their wives" (Purchas 1905 [1625], 376) and of "women witches ... [who] use unlawfull lusts betweene themselves in mutuall filthinesse" (Purchas 1613, 513). Images of African polymorphous perversity and flexible gender systems along these lines found their way into European middlebrow culture in the eighteenth century, including in ostensibly realistic novels by Castilhon (1993 [1769]) and Sade (1990 [1795]). Indeed, Sade's *Aline et Valcour* is notable for African and Africanized characters whose irascible bisexuality offends the sensibilities of the prim and proper European character.

In European accounts over the course of the nineteenth century, recognition of shared humanity with Africans (or inhumanity, in Sade's misanthropic view) and of cultural diversity within Africa gave way to overtly racist simplifications about natives and savages. These were sometimes linked to another set of stereotypes that emerged around the same time – the view that homosexuality was the result of over-civilization or decadence, and a cause of effeminacy and pacifism among men. As the Roman and Turkish empires supposedly showed, homosexuality ineluctably led to military defeat and humiliation by more virile societies. Such an understanding of history implied that homosexuality, as a so-called unnatural or decadent tendency, could (indeed, should) be contained or eliminated through rigorous moral instruction, strict parenting, and state intervention when necessary.[7]

Africans figured significantly in debates within Europe about the meaning of civilization, and of virility versus decadence. Since the prevailing prejudice was that Africans were uncivilized and close to nature, by definition they could not be decadent or exhibit social traits and behaviours that were assumed to come with a sophisticated level of culture. The emerging consensus on homosexuality thus required that Africans conform to the expectation of a supposedly natural heterosexuality and lack of sexual diversity (or even the "higher" emotions, like love). This was precisely the hope of Edward Gibbon, who first made the point in a footnote to his explanation of how "primitive Romans were infected" with homosexuality by the more civilized Etruscans and Greeks (1909 [1896; 1781], 535, 537), to their eventual doom.

Soon after Gibbon, someone who had actually travelled to Africa brought the first authoritative seal of personal observation to the theory. The English explorer William Browne spent several years wandering about the Middle East and North Africa in the 1790s. In his account of those travels, he noted simply that "paederasty" was rare in ostensibly primitive Sudan as compared to decadent western Asia (Browne 1806, 293). The idea that Africans did not engage in same-sex sexual practices gained currency as the frontiers of European rule expanded into the interior. Christian missionaries and colonial officials at the forefront of that expansion emphasized an African sexuality that was a formidable obstacle to their mission, yet also conceivably mutable to the ideals of bourgeois European culture. The main obstacle in this view was Africans' barbarous lack of control over their heterosexual instincts – an excess of natural virility. Indeed, the missionaries had their hands full challenging the array of what they regarded as heterosexual immoralities in African societies, including polygyny, child betrothals, marriage by cattle, female genital cutting, widow inheritance, widow cleansing, notions of female pollution, and so on. More secretive homosexual practices fell low on the list of priorities of behaviour to rail against or even enquire into. The absence of overt homosexual relationships may in fact have been missionaries' and administrators' one straw of hope for re-shaping African sexuality toward their ideal of civilized. Harry H. Johnston (1904, 685) offered a rare acknowledgement of this when he claimed that the "vicious propensities" of the king of Buganda "disgusted even his negro people." Likewise, Sir Frederick Jackson (1930, 326), a colonial official reflecting on the first decade of British rule over Kenya and Uganda, noted "the good sense of the natives and their disgust" toward the bestial vices practiced by Orientals. This, according to the emerging scientific homophobia, was one of the few unambiguously positive things to be said about African morals and character.

Sir Richard Burton's translation of *The Arabian Nights* was another influential presentation of African sexuality to English-speaking audiences. Through a double Orientalist gaze (that is, othering "the black" through the imagined Arab perspective), Burton inflamed the monstrosity of being African to his European readers while denying contradictory evidence. In Husain Haddaway's modern translation of the "Story of King Sharyar and his Brother," for example, the cuckolder is not named as black at all. In a French translation contemporary to Burton's, he is simply "un esclav noir," later "une solide nègre noir" (Haddaway 1992; Mardrus 1900, 4, 5). In Burton's creative hands, however, the slave who cavorts with Sharyar's wife becomes "a black cook of loathsome aspect and foul with kitchen grease and grime," and in another case "a big slobbering blackamoor with rolling eyes which showed the whites, a truly hideous sight" (Burton 1885, vol. 1, 4, 6).

Burton's "Terminal" essay to the same set of volumes is also noteworthy, and not just for its authoritative scientific-sounding claim "the negro and negroid races to the South ignore the erotic perversion" supposedly introduced by the Romans or other foreigners. One of the characters in a story Burton had translated actually contradicted his own claim. This was a black slave who had been castrated for having sex with both his mistress *and* her eldest son, and who told his tale to two other eunuchs with a sardonic sense of humour (Burton 1885, vol. X, 205, and vol. II, 56).[8]

Africans began to publish in European languages in the late eighteenth century, and it was not long before they began to attack such racist or patronizing tendencies in European accounts of African sexual mores (notably, Edward Wilmot Blyden's protests against Burton in the 1860s, described by Phillips 2006, 193). Phillips also draws attention to a Krio poem published in Freetown in 1907 that acknowledges and bemoans the moral corruption of African youth in town, which he attributes to European influence. The publication of Silas Modiri Molema's *The Bantu Past and Present* in 1920 was another important shot across the bow in this struggle. Molema was one of the first southern Africans to be a fully qualified medical doctor, a scion of the Protestant Tswana elite, and a self-styled progressive who later became a prominent member of the African National Congress. While he unambiguously embraced his Scottish teachers' hierarchy of barbarous, semi-civilized, and civilized in reference to Africans, he also roundly criticized bigoted judgments by Europeans about African morality.

Liberal and reform-minded Europeans who wanted to make colonialism more humane had to be careful not to alienate their strongest potential African allies. This is evident in the work of Henri Junod, the Swiss missionary who led the charge against the practice of "mine marriage" (whereby Tsonga men took boys as lovers/servants during their long stays in the male-only industrial compounds of South Africa). Junod was unusual in his determination to expose this practice in various media and languages (1911 and 1962 [1916], for example). But he was careful to apportion blame to Europeans for creating the evil context, not his African subjects for adapting to it. Similarly, pioneering anthropologists, such as Isaac Schapera and E.E. Evans-Pritchard, and their contemporary, psychologist Wulf Sachs, provided critical accounts of the impact of migrant labour and European racism on African morals, particularly through the rise of prostitution, promiscuity, and female sexual autonomy. On this point, European liberals and African conservatives could agree. As Lynn Thomas (2009) suggests, the element of self-censorship on the sensitive issue of male-male sexuality in Schapera's work was likely a gesture to the main African audience. Schapera may also have been influenced by the hostile reception his work received among white South Africans, which he attributed to his failure sufficiently to exoticize the Tswana in line with the dominant colonial paradigm (Schapera 1940; Sachs 1937; Evans-Pritchard 1970).[9]

The Africa/Europe, traditional/modern, and moral/immoral construction appealed to and perhaps flattered many audiences, including in Europe and among African elites. The first African to train as a professional anthropologist epitomizes this clearly. Jomo Kenyatta studied at the London School of Economics in the 1930s under the mentorship of Bronislaw Malinowski, one of the pre-eminent figures in the field. His monograph on his own people, the Gikuyu, featured a long discussion of puberty, courtship, and marriage in which he categorically denied the existence of same-sex sexuality in traditional society: "Any form of sexual intercourse other than the natural form, between men and women acting in a normal way, is out of the question. It is considered taboo even to have sexual intercourse with a woman in any position except the regular one, face to face" (Kenyatta 1961 [1938], xviii, 159). Kenyatta's translations of the term *ngweko* also hint at a kind of competitive, racialized sexuality. Among Gikuyu youth, a wholesome expression of non-penetrative sex play or fondling contributes to young people's education, including boys' obligation to respect girls. *Ngweko ya Gecomba*, however, is "European (i.e., vulgar or lustful) sexual intercourse" (327). Meanwhile, Kenyatta's views on the dignity of female circumcision and sexual passivity were picked up by European psychologists looking for ways to explain (through contrast) modern women's neurotic behaviours (Frederiksen 2008). Versions of this idea subsequently resonated at the highest levels of "comparative psychology." No less an authority than Carl Jung (1963, 247) waxed eloquent about the "utter naturalness," "confidence and self-assurance," and "stability" he thought he observed in African women as a result of the absence of "homosexualizing" factors in comparison to supposedly rational and modern (yet, in Jung's view, deeply neurotic) societies as in western Europe.

Over the middle decades of the twentieth century, close empirical studies of sexuality in Africa virtually disappeared, subsumed within sophisticated analysis of kinship networks and belief systems or new urban marital and livelihood strategies (this is the literature Caldwell et al. mostly drew on). For Africanist scholars, the explicit study of African sexualities seemed frivolous or prurient in an era that was hungry for "usable history" to fight any number of foes: fascism, imperialism, communism, patriarchy, apartheid, or underdevelopment, for example. The early Cold War years were particularly hostile to those who broached questions about same-sex sexualities, an interest that was associated with communism. Even the openly gay anthropologist Colin Turnbull, who lived in Kampala with his African-American lover in the early 1970s and whose private diaries reveal the existence of a lively gay nightlife in the city, showed little interest in his work to query received wisdom about African sexuality (Grinker 2000).

As I alluded to in the discussion above of Jung's travel memoir, this void of disciplined research did not go unfilled. On the contrary, it created space for romanticized, stereotyped, and polemical statements from across the political spectrum to go unchallenged. Those by Frantz Fanon (1962 [1957]) and Cheikh anta Diop (1960), who respectively blamed Europeans and "Moroccans" for introducing homosexuality as a corrupting influence to black Africa, were among the most influential of these on the left. Meanwhile, Egyptologist Boris de Rachewiltz (1964) and a whole genre of *National Geographic*-style soft pornography titillated Western audiences, not least of all Leni Riefenstahl's coffee table celebration of primitive or innocent black male nudity (Riefenstahl 1976).

The Heinemann African Writers' Series launched in 1962 opened a significant new front in this culture war. Many of its novels through to the 1980s articulated Africans' pent-up rage at the colonial experience by employing tropes of a romanticized and androcentric pre-colonial or pre-Christian past. This included using feminized language to portray Africa, the geographical place, being raped or dominated by masculine outsiders and African men reduced to metaphorical boyhood at the hands of racist whites. Writers in this body of literature often attempt to "remasculinize" African men through heavy-handed portrayals of their heterosexual virility, in some cases through the symbolic sexual domination of white women and in a rhetorical style that closely recalls the writing of anti-colonial revolutionary, Fanon (see Stratton 1994 for an example of feminist analysis of this type of writing, and Munro 2012 on homosexuality as a trope in apartheid-era prison and army memoirs, novels, and poetry). On the other side of the battle line, authors like Fran Hosken (1979) in polemical accounts of female genital mutilation and patriarchy nourished Western feminist outrage against "African sexuality." Contradictory evidence was overlooked in the process – Hanry (1970), for example, reports excised girls in Guinée who masturbated and had lesbian affairs. Signe Arnfred (2011) also astutely examines the ways that Western scholars wrote female sexual autonomies out of the narrative they constructed about matrilineal societies. Matriliny remained a "puzzle," in the words of the pioneering female anthropologist Audrey Richards (1950), and a basically insignificant footnote to the broad sweep of African patriarchy, only by rigorously ignoring "hidden" female-controlled rituals, spirituality, institutions, and discourses.

The advent of HIV/AIDS in the mid-1980s refocused scholarly attention on sexuality in Africa in an urgent way. However, this attention pointedly did not challenge key elements of the African sexuality stereotype. Indeed, in the rush to explain the epidemiology of HIV/AIDS and win the support of highly suspicious African political leaders to fight the disease, many sexual secrets and allusions to sexual diversity in scattered ethnographic footnotes were ignored or (self-)censored. A consensus about widespread heterosexual promiscuity that explicitly ruled out homosexual and anal transmission of HIV thus emerged several years *before* the first large-scale surveys of knowledge, attitudes, beliefs, and practices were carried out (e.g., Quinn et al. 1986). Caldwell et al. (1989) is most poignant in that respect. They demanded scientists pay attention to social science. They earnestly argued against derogatory or patronizing stereotypes about Africans by demonstrating a material basis and rationality for this putative continental culture of multiple, concurrent heterosexual partners. Yet they, too, passed over an abundance of evidence that presented a far more complicated and historically changeable situation.[10]

South Africa's liberation from apartheid was a turning point, not only in terms of national politics but also because it opened the path for activists, artists, and researchers to begin to ask new questions about sexuality in all its diverse (and sometimes embarrassing) expressions. As early as 1987, the leadership of the African National Congress acknowledged that it would respect sexual orientation in a post-apartheid setting, a position all the major political parties in the 1992 to 1994 negotiations for transition tacitly accepted (Hoad et al. 2005). Those years saw the emergence of a boldly out gay literature, including an anthology of poetry, fiction, and interviews (Krouse 1993) and a remarkable collection of memoirs and local histories from people across the spectrum of racial, gender, class, age, sexual orientation, and South Africa's many other inherited divides (Gevisser and Cameron 1994). Two other monographs published in 1994 blew the lid off one of the region's longest open secrets, the practice of male-male mine marriage among migrant workers in the Johannesburg area (Moodie with Ndatshe 1994; Harries 1994).

These publications came out in the context of the attainment of a liberal constitution, the emergence of a freewheeling post-apartheid sexual culture (including not only inter-racial and same-sex relationships, but also legalized abortion and a flowering of sexual imagery in the public sphere), and, critically, wrenching economic pain caused by the application of neoliberal policies after 1996. In regard to the latter, South Africa followed in the footsteps of the rest of the continent, where so-called structural adjustment programs had been tearing the guts out of social welfare and the formal employment sectors since the late 1970s. A conservative backlash that sought scapegoats for the economic pain often described structural adjustment as a new form of Western imperialism that it commonly lumped together with feminism as a threat to African society. The backlash took a new form in Zimbabwe in 1995, when President Robert Mugabe became the first of many African political and religious leaders to denounce homosexuality as yet another form of the threat from the West. This scapegoating of homosexuality itself attracted scholarly attention. Over the next decade, it also stimulated the establishment of sexual rights associations across the continent and sparked numerous works of fiction, film, and activist writing. In the realm of film, for example, *Woubi Chéri* (Brooks and Bocahut 1997) and *Dakan* (1998) were remarkable breakthroughs that explore the lives of transgender and homosexual or bisexual men in Côte d'Ivoire and Guinea respectively. Within social science, Murray and Roscoe (1998) gather together evidence from activists, anthropologists, historians, and literary studies to show the wide range of non-normative sexualities across Africa over hundreds of years, independent of Western influences. A new generation of African authors has emerged out of this ferment to test the hegemony of Western Africanist experts in this field of study (Achmat 1993; Gueboguo 2006; Essien and Aderinto 2009; Tamale 2011; Aken'ova 2011; Ekine and Abbas 2013; among others including Akanji, Nyanzi, Nyeck, Massaquoi, and Dankwa in this volume).

Greater attention to female sexuality in recent years has also profoundly challenged some of the phallocentric or matrifocal assumptions in much of the literature. Recent studies of female resistance to anti-female genital mutilation campaigns, for example, shift the focus from culture, narrowly conceived, to broad changes in the global political economy and to African women's own perceptions of the erotic (Dellenborg 2004; Bagnol and Mariano 2008). Novelists like Cameroon's Calixthe Beyala (1996; 2000) have explored themes of incest, abusive mothers, bisexuality, and masturbation (see also Azuah 2005; Arac de Nyeko 2007). To conservative critics, these texts may read like the end of morality, but from a feminist perspective they restore women and girls to full, troubled, complex humanity. The process reveals gender not as a timeless category that is convenient to conflate with "women" or can be easily "mainstreamed" into development, but as a site of multiple forms of contestation over the distribution of power (e.g., Arnfred 2004; 2011).

The idea of African sexuality contains important grains of truth. Much of Africa shared material conditions that encouraged fertile heterosexual union. Also, while capitalism and colonial rule came in diverse forms, recurrent trends emerged across the continent. Urbanization, migrant labour, new freedoms for women and youth, and class and ethnic formation gave rise to changes in sexuality along broadly common patterns. The appearance of "loose women" was perhaps the most visible of these, same-sex relations the least. New ideas that came from the colonial rulers or Hollywood combined with state regulation of gender and sexuality also gave rise to common political responses, including morally conservative African nationalism. Sensitivities that arose from the history of racism and

colonialism, with its lingering injustices often amplified in the neocolonial and structural adjustment eras, have intruded in a number of
debates that resonate throughout Africa, most notably how to deal
with HIV/AIDS and gender-based violence.

These commonalities across the continent have tended to obscure
a great deal of less-visible diversity and change over time. They also
sometimes obscure the fact that many of today's certainties are inherited from highly untrustworthy sources. Authors, some who never
even visited Africa and many who relied on self-serving accounts by
elite men, sometimes promoted images of African sexuality for their
own career, political, social, or artistic reasons. They cannot be
trusted to develop effective public health policy nor, as is sometimes
now happening, to justify increasingly repressive legislation. Many
evidently well-intentioned anti-racist or anti-HIV interventions have
not been careful enough in this respect (that is, in double-checking
the provenance of their facts and sources).

There have been significant challenges to African sexuality in
recent years. Perhaps the most importantly are the activism, art, and
scholarship of Africans themselves. Where seven archbishops from
across the continent joined with "conservative" religious leaders in
the Americas to split from the global Anglican community over the
issue of homosexuality, black theologians in South Africa have
aligned themselves on the liberal side of the debate. Where African
politicians have threatened death to homosexuals, African activists
have boldly established sexual rights associations linked though
pan-African and global networks to feminist, children's rights, and
other human rights and sexual health groups. Where Western scholars, missionaries, and some African leaders have promoted static
and simplistic models of African tradition, African novelists and
playwrights have produced an impressive array of dissident characters speaking to more complex truths.

History cannot predict where these debates will lead. The historiography, however, can flag stereotypes that are at times very deeply
and discreetly embedded in the sources involved in engaging the
debates. If queer is simply "a mode of being that centres on critique"
(including critique of racial privileges and global inequalities constructed through the dominant process of knowledge production,
Riggs 2006, 2) then queering local historiographies could be a vital
step to refining the understanding of current debates around sexuality and sexual identity in Africa.

Rhetorical Analysis of President Jammeh's Threats to Behead Homosexuals in the Gambia

STELLA NYANZI

On 15 May 2008, during his annual tour, President Yahya Jammeh publicly declared that he planned to behead homosexuals reported in the Gambia.[1] The threats were directed at nationals, residents, and visitors including tourists, expatriates, refugees, and foreign investors. Jammeh asserted that the Gambia was a Muslim country of believers and therefore "sinful and immoral practices [such] as homosexuality will not be tolerated." He further explained that homosexuality was un-African and therefore "un-Gambian." Issuing a twenty-four-hour ultimatum for homosexuals to leave the Gambia, the president promised to unleash massive surveillance to "weed out bad elements" – specifically drug-peddlers, thieves, criminals, and homosexuals. In the same speech, Jammeh ordered any hotel or motel that housed homosexuals to expel them, shut down, or face trouble. He threatened to introduce pieces of legislation "stricter than those in Iran." A string of arrests and corporal punishment of some nationals and foreign individuals followed his pronouncement.[2]

The story received wide local, regional, and international coverage across newspapers, radio, television, and the Internet. Media were sharply divided – either outraged by the homophobia espoused by yet another African national leader, or else supportive of his stance for reasons that included religious doctrine, morality, tradition or culture, the law, and "guarding against westernisation." For example, while Paula Ettelbrick, the director of the International Gay and

Lesbian Human Rights Commission (IGLHRC), issued a statement that called on Jammeh to retract his threats (*Freedom Newspaper*, 23 May 2008), a renowned Gambian Imam, Pa Ebou Jeng, was widely quoted in the local public media for his support of the ban (*Freedom Newspaper*, 22 July 2008).

Later in 2008, Jammeh retracted these statements, presumably under external pressure from donor governments and human rights organizations. However, at the end of his Dialogue with the People tour in 2009, he again denounced homosexuality and its tolerance in the country. Speaking at the Arch 22, a patriotism monument in Banjul, he said: "A man should marry a woman, but a man and man should never marry each other ... People should not entertain homo-sexuals in their compounds ... and not allow them to use money on them or bribe them to carry out their lifestyle" (Mhlongo 2009).

To begin this chapter, I discuss some of the methodological chal-lenges I faced while trying to study "the homosexual" as a junior heterosexual African researcher. Then I discuss the level of local organizing of alternative sexualities and gender in the Gambia; spe-cifically focusing on the cultural context that maintains the closet and the absence of sexual minority activism amidst a vibrant politi-cal economy of tourism. Next, I examine the president's rhetoric and highlight tropes and idioms of identity, belonging, and personhood, including notions of nationalism and local constructions of "how to be a good Muslim," that he deployed to build an argument against homosexuality. To conclude, I argue that Jammeh's manipulation and exploitation of local constructions of propriety and personhood in order to ostracise those who practice alternative sexualities in the Gambia are part of a wider strategy to entrench an undemocratic regime.

CONTEXT AND METHODOLOGICAL CHALLENGES

With an estimated population of 1.7 million, the Gambia is among the smallest countries in Africa. Formerly a British colony embedded within France's Senegal, it gained independence on 18 February 1965. There have been two presidents since that time: Dawda Jawara, from 1965 to 22 July 1994, and Yahya Jammeh, who seized power in a military coup (Edie 2000; Saine 1995; Wiseman 1998). Presidential elections occur every five years but Jammeh is widely suspected of corrupt practices to ensure his re-election (Perfect 2008, 427).

The Gambia's economic mainstay is agriculture (mainly ground-nuts), followed by tourism (Sharpley 2007; Dieke 1994; Sallah 1990). Though 82.9 per cent of the population lives on less than US$2 a day (UNAIDS 2007), many Gambians emigrate abroad and remit earnings from overseas. Over 95 per cent of the population is Muslim, while the rest is comprised of Christians and animists who practice traditional religions. Most Gambian Muslims practice Suni Islam, although there are also some Tabligh, Ahmadiya, Wahhabi, and Sufi sects that originated in Senegal, such as the Mouridhiyas and Tijaniyas. Religious syncretism, whereby belief in ancestral spir-its, witchcraft, *jinns,* and spirit mediums prevails, is common (Darboe 2004, 75). Islam is central to local life, everyday expression, dress code, material culture, fashion, and observances of time such as the working week, calendar, and national holidays (Nyanzi 2008). The main ethnic groups are Mandinka, Wolof, Fula, and Jola.

As a female African anthropologist, I grappled with the challenges of conducting research in this context and, more generally, doing ethnography in Africa about other Africans (Ezeh 2003; Achebe and Teboh 2007). Though I am an insider as an African of Ugandan nationality and Kiganda ethnicity born, bred, and mainly residing in Africa, I am also sometimes an outsider to other African contexts such as the "male world," other ethnic communities, and religious and spiritual organizations to which I do not belong. I am acutely aware of my fluid position as an insider-outsider researcher. Notably, when I started fieldwork in the Gambia in September 2002, I was of single marital status, and then transitioned through various gender roles. I am married to a Gambian Muslim man and the mother of three Gambian children. Thus, although I started my fieldwork as largely an outsider – i.e., a Ugandan, Christian student studying Gambian Muslims – I have become an insider – i.e., an anthropologist of sexualities in the Gambia, a Gambian wife, and a Gambian mother.

This transition did not altogether negate my outsider status to some local contexts, and indeed may have increased it in regard to Gambian alternative sexualities. First, I was mostly advised against studying LGBTI issues because doing so could "kill [my] academic career before it started." Mentors with years of academic experience discouraged my interest in alternative sexualities and argued, "oth-ers will not take [my] scholarship seriously," "funds will be withheld from you if you are associated with 'those people,'" and "there is only very limited outlet for publication in specialist journals with

almost no impact factor."[3] Literature echoes this potential danger to
me as a young female scholar: "Women in the academy and in
African studies are too vulnerable to risk their careers on 'controversial' topics. African women have argued that their feminism centers
not on sexuality, but on the economics and politics of mere survival
in present day Africa" (Amory 1997, 9). Tamale (2007a, 21) also
writes: "Yet the fact that *some* gender experts recognized the need to
support the rights of gays and lesbians is important, especially given
the fact that this stand could mean the loss of a job or ambitions for
public office." Clearly homosexuality was an othered research topic.
I risked ostracism by the mainstream scholarly body of researchers,
research funders, and research publishers (with high impact) that are
important to tenure and promotion.[4]

Secondly, the challenge of being a heterosexual studying LGBTI
issues was real. While writing this paper I consistently checked my findings to ensure I was not regurgitating heteronormative explanatory
frameworks. This strategy is not new to anthropology, which classi-
cally consisted of white Westerners who studied "natives" from far-off
lands, or men who studied women and children. My reflexivity was
largely informed by postcolonial and feminist critiques of traditional
anthropological methods. This yielded constant self-questioning; especially in regards to underlying assumptions I brought to my research
conceptualizations, data collection, interpretation, and writing. Murray
and Roscoe (1998, 16) propose double readings of anthropological
texts, that is, for both their literal meaning and in order to identify
tropes informed by implicit anti-homosexuality discourses. This double reading was useful to my own analysis and writing.

Third, as an outsider, I faced perceived suspicion from members of
various LGBTI groups. I was frank about being heterosexual. While
non-LGBTI scholars were quick to alert me of the potential dangers
of researching alternative sexualities, many LGBTI individuals were
hesitant to trust me. Understandably, the hostility expressed in everyday language towards homosexuality precluded spontaneous trust
and rapport of local LGBTI. They feared exposure and its consequent effects.

Fourth, because I set my ethnographic study of youth sexualities
in the Gambia within a public health[5] framework, specifically sexual
and reproductive health, it was important to distance myself from
biomedical theories of homosexuality. It was a constant challenge to

transcend biomedical theorizations of alternative sexualities as pathological, deviant, psychotic, and criminal; LGBTI individuals are not mere vectors of sexually transmitted infections, including HIV/AIDS, in need of control.

Last, translation of research findings in ways that are useful rather than harmful to local LGBTI individuals and communities is critical. According to Niang et al. (2004, 12), "In the Gambia MSM harbor a real fear that brutal state-sponsored violence that is used against commercial sex workers and women who use skin-bleaching cream could easily be turned against them. Official government statements violently decry behaviour that is considered sexually deviant." Indeed, in April 2012, fifteen people were arrested in the Gambia for gender transgression and on suspicion of homosexuality. The arrests highlight how the findings of even sensitive and empathetic research can be hijacked for heterosexist agendas or to criminalize alternative sexualities, thereby further dis-empowering local LGBTI people. Also worrisome is the fact that much academic research is written and published for audiences that make it simply irrelevant to intended beneficiaries. While I hope that my research findings are translated into social action or policies and programs that are relevant to study communities, I am conscious of the tensions between academic and activist or advocacy writing (Epprecht 2008, 21–2 discusses examples).

In concluding this description of challenges, allow me to digress to the persistent condemnation of African scholars who attended Western-based universities. There are allegations that neocolonialism and cultural imperialism tarnish our thought, theory, and scholarship. Considering the varied systemic failures of higher education in my home country, which especially escalated in the period I attended university, I make no apologies for my education in the West.[6] It availed me with invaluable resources. Rather than dim my critical edge, my Western-based education sharpened my ability to critically unpack underlying assumptions and implicit theories girding my and others' scholarship. Alongside reflexivity, it added urgency to the need for me to complement and/or counter global knowledge with well-theorized and grounded interpretations from the local African communities I study as an anthropologist. Living and studying in the West did not first teach me about homosexuality or homosexuals. Rather, I first encountered words such as lesbian, gay, dyke, butch, faggot, "swinging it to the left," and others while studying at Gayaza High School – the oldest all-girls' missionary boarding school in Uganda. I first encountered the ugliness and terror within homophobia when our teachers bullied and harassed scores of students named and shamed for either being lesbians or "having lesbian tendencies." It was then that my revulsion towards homophobia was ignited.

METHODS

In this chapter, I draw on a larger ethnographic study that explored the sexualities, sexual, and reproductive health and wellbeing of youths in the Gambia (Nyanzi 2008). I triangulated ethnographic data collected in rural and urban areas between 2002 and 2008, with literature review and media content analysis. The data for this chapter mainly comprise local perceptions of alternative sexualities because I failed to access an ample sample of self-identified homosexuals. The only two individuals who admitted having same-sex liaisons were beach boys (locally called *bumsters*) who exchanged their sexual services for money from tourists (Nyanzi et al. 2005). I electronically interviewed twenty-three Gambian nationals subsequent to the president's homophobic statements. Of these, eighteen resided in the Gambia and five resided in the United Kingdom. All were urban elites with email access. Content analysis of our electronic exchanges further informs this chapter. These data are supplemented with rhetorical analysis of the president's homophobic speech. According to Marcus (1980, 508): "The fundamental question concerning rhetoric as the basis of genre is the characteristic manner by which a text's language and organisation convinces its readers of the truth, or at least of the credibility, of its claims." In the ensuing analysis, I mainly appropriate the three classical appeals used in classical rhetoric analysis, namely *ethos*, *pathos*, and *logos*.

EFFEMINATE MEN, MASCULINE WOMEN, AND HOMOSEXUAL PEOPLE IN THE GAMBIA

Generally, there is widespread societal denial of homosexuality in the Gambia, mainly because of social stigma and religious prohibitions (Mah and Dibba 2008; Nyanzi et al. 2005, 565; Niang et al. 2004). In everyday life, it is presented as *haram* – taboo. According to Niang et al. (2003, 507–8), in neighbouring Senegal:

Religious reasons are the ones most frequently invoked to justify
the rejection of men who have sex with men. A Muslim dignitary
explained, "Since Muslim religion forbids homosexuality, we
cannot accept homosexuals either in our homes or in our
mosques." Another cleric explained that when a Muslim shakes
hands with a homosexual, a certain number of prayers are
required for his purification. Men often invoke religious reasons
to affirm that their homosexual life is only for a limited period of
time; they say that they expect to renounce it some day when
they have grown old in order to bring themselves in line with the
Muslim religion.

When Gambians acknowledge homosexuality in conversations and
formal interviews, they do so mainly in reference to men who have sex
with men (MSM), and often distance it using *toubabs* – the local word
for foreign white men or locals who are exposed to the West through
migration and tourism. Niang et al. (2004, 13) report that Gambian
young men offer commercial homosexual services on the beaches to
tourists. Ahmadu's (2007, 287) presentation of lesbian experience of
orgasm in the Gambia, also happens with "one white woman, she is
[a lesbian] from U.K." When I directly asked about Gambian homosexuals or lesbians, I tended to receive outright denials of their existence. However, attention to local language yielded evidence of locally
appropriate labels that revealed certain homosocial spaces and normative gender-transgressing identities. Such local homosociality
reveals degrees of acceptance for alternative performances of gender
and sexualities among Gambian sub-population groups.
  Gor-jigen is a Wolof expression that literally translates into English
as man-woman. It is a derogatory label for effeminate men and boys,
and is also used jokingly as an insult to a boy or man (Skramstad
1990; Ba 1985). During my fieldwork on youth sexualities, *gor-jigen*
was commonly hurled at male youths who loved to dance in public,
and who enjoyed cooking or hanging around kitchens with the
women and girls. Based on their study in Senegal, Niang et al. (2003,
505) elaborate:

In Wolof society, the most frequently used term for men who
have sex with men is the word *gor jigeen* [*sic*], which is translated literally in English as "man-woman." It implies a man who
is very close to the world of women, to the point of identifying

with them. *Gor jigeen* is currently considered demeaning and stigmatizing by MSM. As one MSM stated, "The term *gor jigeen* frightens us. When someone says it in our presence, it makes us shiver. The term is like a siren sound that we expect to be followed by insults, blows, or stones thrown at us by out-of-control mobs."

The concept *gor-jigen* is akin to Gaudio's (2001, 37; 2009) *'yan daudu* (singular *'dan daudu*) men in predominantly Muslim, Hausa-speaking region of Northern Nigeria, who are said to talk and act "like women." They perform their "feminine" social identities through bodily practices, including their work of cooking and selling food and frequent but variable use of *maganer mala*, "women's talk" (see Gaudio 1997). Some especially older *'yan daudu* earn money as intermediaries who introduce male patrons to women known as *karuwai*, ("prostitutes/courtesans"), or *ntata mazu zaman kansu* ("independent women"). Some, especially younger *'yan daudu*, work as courtesans themselves, providing social and sexual companionship to (ostensibly masculine) men in exchange for money, political protection, and other gifts.

Other common terms are *ibis*, which refers to men who often adopt feminine mannerisms and are less dominant in sexual interactions, and *yoos*, which refers to men who are generally the inserting partner during sex and do not identify as homosexuals. Beyond these categories, there are additional subcategories based on age, status, and type of relationship. Urban-based youths in secondary schools in the Gambia commonly used the term *homo* in English discussions or else *woubi* to refer to men who were sexually involved with other men mainly for commercial transaction. Perhaps the film *Woubi Chéri* (1998),[7] based on Abidjan's LGBTI community, popularized the label, or it may simply be a twist on *ibbi*. Similar to *Dakan* (1997), an earlier feature film based in Guinea, *Woubi Chéri* cast homoerotic relationships within Muslim West African societies in sharp relief. These two films are important to African popular culture because they reveal an established, networked, and codified system of diverse alternative relationships that are visible and meaningful to insiders, but are often hidden to outsiders. Public culture, fiction, film, and music are thus spaces with higher degrees of homosociality.

There is evidence in the literature that men who have sex with men are well entrenched in Wolof communities (Crowder 1959;

Teunis 1996; Niang et al. 2003). Niang et al. (2004, 12) report: "In the Gambia, MSM organise traditional dances and ceremonies known as *taneber*, which are not only tolerated, they are quite appreciated in some localities." They also often have the protection of powerful women and men in society. Thus entertainment is another homosocial space in the Gambia.

I found no equivalent labels for masculine women in popular language. Isatou Touray (2006, 82) states: "In the Gambia, lesbianism is taboo and many people do not believe that it exists. It is not recognised by society and is seen as an unacceptable social relationship. It is referred to as the practice of an alien culture by those who are psychologically and spiritually lost. Lesbian relationships do, however, exist among women in the Gambia, but are kept secret for fear of social rejection. Lesbianism in the Gambia has a historical association with families with powerful women." Although their study focused on MSM, Niang et al. (2004, 9) report that lesbians are often close to MSM for emotional support and financial assistance in case of need.

My data from youths in rural and urban parts of the Gambia contain multiple questions about the practicalities of same-sex sexual activities. Many of these questions were based on a heterosexist and phallocentric framework. For example: "How do two men have sex?" "Where does the one enter?" "Who sleeps on whom?" "How can a woman have sex with another woman? What do they use?" While some students from urban areas were aware of anal sex, "finger sex," and dildos, most youths lacked both knowledge and imagination.

NO SYMPATHY FOR HOMOSEXUALITY

In my interviews with heterosexual-identified Gambians immediately after Yahya Jammeh's homophobic declarations, I generally found no sympathy for alternative sexualities. Although no interviewee identified as LGBTI, I had expected some degree of tolerance based on the principle of equality of persons. While many interviewees were critical of the president's statements, they also agreed that homosexuality was and should remain illegal in the Gambia.

Many interviewees were repelled by the president's threats to decapitate homosexuals, which for them represented extreme abuse of his position. Others were offended because Jammeh implicated foreign nationals on whom the country depended for investments, development, and successful tourism returns. A few were anxious about invoking Iranian law, arguing it was a restrictive legal system. Many felt that raising such a controversial issue detracted from the functions of this tax-funded tour. Some were irate at the president for neglecting protocol by taking legislative and judicial matters into his own hands, rather than allowing the national assembly to debate the matter and hold a subsequent referendum involving diverse local opinion leaders.

However, when I asked directly about the rights of homosexual Gambians, most interviewees were decidedly homophobic. Many invoked the Arabic expression "*Astagafullulah*!" which is reserved for forbidden practices such as eating pork or pork products, drinking alcohol, and blasphemy against Allah. Some questioned whether there were any "genuinely gay Gambians." Others stated that homosexuality was criminal, sinful, a mental sickness, a disease, moral degeneration, a deprivation copied from the wayward Western world, and "against proper Muslim conduct." Most argued that heterosexuality is the standard of African values and the foundation of the human race. They found it ridiculous that I raised the issue of rights, and specifically the sexual rights of LGBTI people. These sentiments echoed responses I gathered from youths, youth workers, and community leaders in my ethnography (Nyanzi 2008).

THE ABSENCE OF LOCAL LGBTI ORGANIZING

The absence of local communal voices challenging President Jammeh's homophobic pronouncements was conspicuous. This silence was very loud. Regional, African, and international human rights organizations and sexual rights advocates responded with outrage, questioned Jammeh's audacity, clarified apparent misinformation about same-sex desire and lifestyles, and called for Jammeh to withdraw his threats. There was no similar public local Gambian rebuttal.

No civil organization specifically advocates for LGBTI issues in the Gambia. To my knowledge, there is no local support association for LGBTI individuals or their families. There is no same-sex club or bar, even in the tourist area on the Atlantic coast with its assortment of beaches, resorts, hotels, motels, lodges, restaurants, and bars. Although commercial sex work is an established industry and Gambian and foreign immigrant workers service male and female clients, interactions are generally heterosexual and very vanilla (Pickering et al.

1992; Ahmadu 2007).[8] *Chagga* (the Wolof term for female prostitutes) service male clients. *Bumsters*, youthful male hustlers on the beaches, sell their sexual services to female clients who are mostly white older tourists (Nyanzi et al. 2005). Although *bumsing* involves more than transactional sex, Mah and Dibba (2008, 4) explicitly refer to *bumsters* as "male sex workers." While reportedly lucrative, both *chagga* and *bumsters* have socially denigrated occupations that lack local organizations to advocate for their rights. However, these groups are often the first port of call for researchers interested in investigating homosexual activities because they provide sexual services (Mah and Dibba 2008; Niang et al. 2004).

According to Mah and Dibba (2008, 5), "In The Gambia, no initiative has been carried out to date to address HIV in the MSM community. No HIV prevalence data are available in The Gambia for this sub-population group." Niang et al. (2004, 4) assert that although multi-sector services for HIV prevention and AIDS treatment and care are available, "MSM are not included in those partnerships nor are they considered a target group for those services." They emphasize that in prevention and treatment services for HIV/AIDS, "programs for MSM are non-existent in The Gambia" (2004, 4).

Many civil society associations in the Gambia are fractionalized, uncoordinated, unsustainable, and largely dysfunctional (Edie 2000, 193). Consequently, they cannot organize joint operations of resistance. This malaise suppresses transparency and undermines effective strategizing to pressure the government for accountability (Nyanzi 2012). Rather than contest against the president's despotic abuse of power, many local civil society organizations rallied behind him with praise. Whether such displays are genuine support or further descent into strategies of soliciting favour through cronyism is uncertain (Nyanzi 2012). Other local civil society organizations are silent in the face of tyranny because of fear of reprisal, which has previously taken the shape of imprisonment without trial, corporal punishment, verbal threats, summoning and interrogating by the National Intelligence Agency (NIA), arson against residential compounds or offices, heavy fines, and state officials publishing or broadcasting incriminating information about daring individuals in the local press (Kandeh 1996; Wiseman 1997; Darboe 2004). Voices of critique, questioning, and resistance within civil society are largely stifled by the looming phobia of camouflaged spies who work for the NIA. This fear permeates everyday interactions among ordinary citizens. Friends and study participants, particularly in urban areas, often warned me to be careful. Said one: "You better leave that topic because the NIA boys may be hearing what you are saying. You don't want them to pick you, deh!"

Prior to President Jammeh's hate speech, the Gambian LGBTI community was generally invisible and ignored. Though the speech was negative and problematic for many reasons, it placed the LGBTI agenda at centre stage and meant the president publicly acknowledged that homosexuals exist in the Gambia. Formerly denied, invisible, and silent LGBTI individuals grabbed the attention of the president, public, locals, international media, and human rights organizations. Reactions of individuals and concerted responses of communities or institutions outside the country highlighted that homosexuals in the Gambia are not isolated, but rather are part of wider bodies of humanity with representation in Africa and the world.

YAHYA JAMMEH: THE ORATOR OF HOMOPHOBIC RHETORIC

Akin to the local-global linkages of the LGBTI movement, the Gambian president's hate-speech is not an isolated incident but rather part of a wider homophobic presidential public discourse. Thus President Yahya Jammeh joined the list of African presidents who variously made homophobic public statements. These include Zimbabwe's Robert Mugabe, Namibia's Sam Nujoma, Uganda's Yoweri Museveni, and Kenya's Arap Moi. These men at the apex of power in different African countries appear to be threatened by difference represented by alternative sexualities. According to Bujra (2000, 11): "The hysterical and angry rejoinders which queries about homosexuality often evoke from African men in positions of power, suggest that the notion of diverse sexualities is extremely threatening."

Why, then, is it critical to rhetorically examine this homophobic speech? Jammeh's words occasion analysis because they come not from a mere citizen, but from a national leader. They could amount to a state decree. Furthermore, according to the Constitution of the Gambia (6[4] of schedule 2): "The President may, by Order published in the *Gazette* and made with the approval of the National Assembly, at any time after coming into force of the Constitution make such provision as may appear necessary for repealing, modifying, adding to or adapting any existing law for bringing it into accord with the provisions of this Constitution." The president has the statutory rights and executive power to make decrees that can become law after debate by the national assembly. This is the basis of his authority when he addresses the nation – an authority that is effective. For example, consequent to the process of legal reform through the Amendment Act of 2005, the criminal code (1965) of the Gambia has laws specific to homosexuality, including the criminalization of lesbian practices (*Gambia Gazette*, 2 August 2005). Jammeh assented to this amendment on 21 July 2005. Thus, he alluded to his statutory rights when he threatened to implement "laws stricter than those of Iran." Because the constitution empowers the president to make and alter laws, his homophobic speech has virulent potential to violate people of alternative sexualities.

Media content analysis reveals that Jammeh's public stance against homosexuality has steadily worsened over time. Scholars, such as Perfect (2008, 435) predicted he would run for another term of office: "Still aged only 42 at the time of writing, there is no sign that Jammeh wishes to relinquish power, so it is likely that he will wish to stand for President once more in 2011." According to Wiseman (1997, 267), Jammeh gave "himself a free hand to alter at will" the revised constitution so that it "gave enormous powers to the presidency but to the surprise of many placed no limit on the number of terms an individual could serve" (see also Sanneh 2000, 81). As predicted, Jammeh was re-elected into his fourth presidential term, and as a result, a man with entrenched homophobia continues to influence public policy in this West African nation.

But who is Yahya Jammeh? What does he subscribe to? Understanding the private individual man has bearing on interpreting his public rhetoric. He was born on 25 May 1965 in Kanilai village. His highest level of formal education is high school. He worked his way through the army ranks to Lieutenant, his cadre during the military coup that made him president. After two years as the military head of state, he resigned from the army in 1996 and was elected president. Twice married and a father of two, Jammeh is also a traditional wrestler, wearer of *jujus*, healer of HIV/AIDS, witch-hunter of the elderly, and is fast amassing titles such as his excellency, doctor, professor, alhaji, sheikh, and lieutenant colonel, among others. He also flaunts functional titles such as commander-in-chief of the armed forces, secretary of state for defence, and chief custodian of the constitution of the Gambia. His regime has been accused of poor governance, corruption, and a growing number of human rights violations (Saine 2008, 168–9; 2002; 2000, 78). How can such a despot understand the human rights of minorities? How can he comprehend the power of allowing difference to thrive? Given his iron control, how can he fathom the protection of sexual minorities?

THE PLACE OF THE ANNUAL PRESIDENTIAL TOUR IN THE GAMBIA'S SOCIAL-POLITICAL LANDSCAPE

The president declared he would begin to decapitate homosexuals in the Gambia during the 2008 Dialogue with the People tour, which the state funded partly through taxes. Article 222(15) of the Gambia's constitution states: "The president shall undertake a nation-wide tour at least twice a year in order to familiarise himself or herself with current conditions and the effect of government policies." Jammeh publicly expressed this homophobia while fulfilling a presidential duty mandated by the constitution. He spoke to a massive audience of state officials, supporters, observers, media, traders, religious clerics from surrounding mosques, and neighbourhood residents. The event was held at the Buffer Zone grounds in Talinding-Kujang, an expansive, sand-filled clearing regularly used for public rallies staged by political, social, economic, and religious opinion leaders.

Furthermore, this public speech was at the culmination of the 2008 national tour, after Jammeh had visited all the other rural provinces. During his stops in different locales, he spoke about a range of development issues. The tour had implications for policy-making and policy-revision. Thus he expressed homophobic sentiments within an official policy-related tour that was widely televised and broadcast by local media.

IDIOMS OF POWER AND PERSONHOOD IN THE PRESIDENTIAL RHETORIC AGAINST HOMOSEXUALS

Decapitation

"Cutting off one's head" – a vivid image in Jammeh's homophobic speech – succeeds as *pathos*, the rhetorical appeal to passion using emotional language. It incited fear among LGBTI people, and disgust and revolt among the audience. This imagery symbolises the potential brutality, violence, and power within the person of President

Jammeh. It alludes to his professional knowledge of and skills in terminating human life (Kandeh 1996, 388). By asserting his power over human life through beheading, the president aligned himself with repressive regimes of terror, archaic models of justice, an inability to forgive, and disbelief in reform. On the other hand, the threat of decapitation undermines his credibility as a national leader by highlighting inconsistencies in his stance towards capital punishment.[9] In 1993, capital punishment was abrogated in the Gambia's constitution and replaced with life imprisonment. Political historian David Perfect (2008, 431) states: "President Jawara commuted all death sentences imposed by the courts except one and eventually abolished the death penalty in 1993" (see also Hughes and Perfect 2006, 291–2). Therefore as a rhetorical tool of persuasion, referring to decapitation punctures Jammeh's appeal to ethics and undermines his credibility.

The Gambia as a Muslim Country

Although the majority population is Muslim, the Gambia is a secular state (see article 1.1 of the constitution). Therefore Yahya Jammeh's claim that his is a Muslim country is unconstitutional.[10] The Gambia does not qualify as a Muslim country; Shari'a is not the law of the land.[11] The laws of the Gambia are comprised of English common law, Islamic law, and customary law.[12] Article 137 of the constitution only provides for Khadi courts to apply Shari'a in domestic matters concerning marriage, divorce, and inheritance among Muslims.

Jammeh appropriated Islam as the basis for his claims that homosexuality is "sinful" and "immoral." He appealed to the widespread local perception that homosexuality is incompatible with Muslim ethos, and the centrality of Islam in constructing sexualities in the Gambia. Touray (2006, 77) explains:

> Islam has been and remains influential in constructing lived experiences of sexuality in the Gambia. Muslim personal status law regulates issues of inheritance, marriage, custody, divorce, widowhood, sex and the sexual autonomy of Muslim women. Current constructions of "tradition" in Islam cast anything related to sex and sexuality within the framework of marriage in all its modalities, and anything related to sexual desire and pleasure in the framework of heterosexual relationships as the normative practice.

Niang et al. (2003, 508) report that many MSM believed in the possibility of abandoning same-sex relationships once their "Muslim
faith matured." This departs from other African Muslims who
believe that Islam accommodates homosexuality, for example,
through appropriating Ijtihad in the Inner Circle in Cape Town,
South Africa (see Hendricks 2008; Broqua this volume; and the
Inner Circle 2009). Scholarship (Ouzgane 2003; Gaudio 2009;
Epprecht 2013b) reveals that diverse sexualities were integrated into
everyday life in traditional ancient Muslim societies.

Given the ambivalence in the interactions between Muslim belief
and homosexualities, how does one interpret Jammeh's rhetorical
claim that the Gambia is a Muslim country? This is yet another
example of Islamism.[13] Scholars (Wiseman 1997; Saine 2000;
Sanneh 2000) criticize Jammeh's manipulation of Islamic symbols in
his private life to win over the approval and support of Muslim
Gambians. For example, Saine (2000) argues that Jammeh's pilgrim-
age to Mecca in 1997 and his second marriage to a Moroccan in
1999 were strategic ploys to strengthen ties with the Arab world and
win local Muslims' support. Jammeh's flamboyant switch in dress
code from military fatigues to flowing Muslim robes and parapher-
nalia raised critique from scholars.[14] In addition, Sanneh (2000, 80)
asserts: "Jammeh's ostentatious adoption of a Muslim public image
was as much to do with building up domestic and external support
as with personal belief." By claiming that the Gambia is a Muslim
country, Jammeh appealed to assumptions about the shared values
of his audience. His rhetorical strategy of inciting moralization based
on orthodox religious values aimed to win the approval of the
majority Muslim Gambian audience. Perhaps he hoped to deter
them from focusing on systemic failures of his regime. Darboe (2004,
73) surmises:

> Over the past fifteen years, the practice of Islam in The Gambia
> has undergone a perceptible change from a tolerant and accom-
> modating type of Qaddriyya-inspired Islam to a more radical
> form. This transformation has coincided with the rulership of
> President Yahya Jammeh, a master of manipulation of Islamic
> symbols ... [who] has frequently blurred the line between mosque
> and state to reinforce his political advantage. Gambia's recent
> experience illustrates the reciprocal relationship between religion
> and politics, and politicians' use of Islam for personal gain.

Iran

In an unexpected twist, in his hate speech against homosexuals, Jammeh proposed to introduce legislation stricter than that in Iran. The Islamic Republic of Iran is a Muslim country, and Shari'a is the law of the land. The penalty for homosexuality in Iran is death (Ottosan 2008). There are public floggings and executions of lesbians, gays, and bisexuals, although transsexuality is legal if individuals undergo sex reassignment surgery that is provided by the state. These associations were made when Jammeh referred to this theocratic Islamic country. Iran metaphorically reinforces constructions of "homosexuals as transgressors," "the claim that the Gambia is a Muslim country," "authoritarian national leaders," "capital punishment," and religious moralization that entrenches heteronormativity and patriarchy. Jammeh's reference to emulating Iranian laws was perhaps another ploy for further "cultivating support and good will with the oil-rich Arab and Gulf states" (Saine 2000, 80). The finality of death left the audience wondering what type of punishment the president planned to mete out to homosexuals at home, as he did not specify the nature of a punishment harsher than death or legislation tougher than that in Iran. Such questions remained in the audience's mind, perhaps as food for thought.

Hotels Must Throw out Homosexuals or Close Down

In his speech, Jammeh personified hotels and motels and gave them the human ability to act on his behalf – namely, to "throw out homosexuals" or "close down." To carry out this action, hotels would need to identify who is a homosexual, justify their rationale for such identification, and physically eject individuals from the premises. These tasks mimic the state roles of naming, policing, and reprimanding "criminal elements." They also reinforce President Jammeh's plans against homosexuals, namely introducing mass patrol in order to "weed out bad elements." The president declared that while the Gambia was welcome to foreigners, intense surveillance would ensure that bad elements were eliminated.

This directive to the hospitality industry had several problems. First, the president used the English label *homosexual*, but did not define it. It is not clear whether he meant MSM, WSW, *gor-jigen*, *yossi*, or transgender or bisexual individuals; people who practice anal sex;[15] or same-sex loving individuals who may not necessary act on such feelings. Second, he assumed that the liminality of hotels and motels provided temporary accommodation for short-term patrons there in order to indulge in homosexuality. This assumption negated the scores of Gambian residents and nationals who practice alternative sexualities in their own homes or other private space, as such individuals are permanent or long-term dwellers of the Gambia and not visitors. Third, by focusing on visitors to hotels and motels, the president failed to acknowledge the hotel developers, investors, owners, employers, employees, and affiliates who may also practice alternative sexualities. Would these proprietors and insiders remove themselves from their own spaces of belonging?

The reference to hotels and motels alludes to foreigners and tourists who visit the Gambia for short periods. It symbolises outsiders and temporality. As a rhetorical tool, it disassociates homosexuality from insiders, locals, or being Gambian, and instead highlights the foreignness of the practice. The allusion to temporality presupposes the fleeting nature of homosexuality in the Gambia and strategically aligns it with tourism. However, the evidence of locals who are LGBTI; their location in the Gambia as nationals, residents, and citizens; and the rootedness of local words and expressions for diverse forms of homosociality, homoeroticism, and homosexuality all dispel Jammeh's attempts to distance homosexuality from Gambians. There are people who are truly Gambian and truly homosexual, and so the *logos* presented does not withstand inspection. This idiom fails as a rhetorical trope because it punctures the president's *ethos* – specifically, his credibility as a speaker. Furthermore, because there are Gambians who practice same-sex desire and also work in the tourism industry (and ultimately contribute to government revenue), the president risked effacing this productivity by denouncing all homosexuals.

Un-African: Un-Gambian

President Jammeh employed the misnomer that homosexuality is "un-African." By reifying and trying to define what genuinely is African, he appealed to a shared sense of tradition, customary values, and norms. However, the plurality of ethnicities, cultures, and religions in the Gambia reveal multiple forms of African identity even within this relatively small country. Diversity in class, gender, generation, Western exposure, rural or urban location, and migratory experience speak to variations within experiences of being Gambian. Obviously, many more apply to African identity, which, as an individual, Jammeh has no right to determine.

It is also flawed to assume that African identity is static and fixed in time and space. African cultures are constantly being negotiated, contested, and affirmed, as Tamale (2007b, 64) highlights: "Currently the voices that are the loudest and that get listened to in African cultural discourse are mostly those of fundamentalists who view culture selectively. When it suits their hetero-patriarchal interests, they will fly the cultural flag to keep minority groups in a subordinate position. Moreover, culture is not static, but constantly changing and responding to shifting socio-economic and political conditions." It is important to consider the multitude of diverse African cultures in a holistic manner that is as inclusive as possible in order to include even those segments that accept, condone, or approve of same-sex relationships. Scholars of Africa show that alternative sexualities, including LGBTI, are a feature of many African societies (Murray and Roscoe 1998; Epprecht 2006; Morgan and Wieringa 2005; Tamale 2007b; Gaudio 2009). These scholars associate homophobia and the claim that "homosexuality is a foreign importation to Africa" with colonial myth-making that needed the creation of an African "other" close to nature and primitive man. Thus when African leaders argue that homosexuality is un-African, they regurgitate colonial stereotypes about Africans that were fabricated in times of exploration, colonization, missionaries, and long-distance trade. Rather than advocating for African tradition, these leaders instead fall for an early but remarkably enduring Western-centric trope (Epprecht this volume).

Therefore, by saying homosexuality is un-African, Yahya Jammeh buys into colonial discourse about a certain type of African sexuality. The effect is the direct opposite of his intention to purge the Gambia of all Western influences.[16] His virulent attack against homosexuality (which he presented as a foreign practice) might be part of this wider anti-Western campaign. However, it might also be another way to generate more bilateral cooperation and foreign investment from the Arab world (Sanneh 2000).

The Twenty-Four-Hour Ultimatum

President Jammeh gave homosexuals twenty-four hours to leave the Gambia. This ultimatum revealed his perception of the gravity of homosexuality. As a rhetorical device, this statement gave the speech tones of seriousness, urgency, and potency. It reinforced the president's power and acted as a deterrent against homosexuality.[17] It also begged the question, "What about Gambian nationals, residents, and citizens?" Unlike foreign diplomats with a home to return to, Gambians identified as homosexuals would not have anywhere to go. As citizens of the Gambia, they have a right to a safe home and life free from violation of their basic human rights. However, threats of expulsion meant they faced hiding, denying their homosexuality, or exposure to the multiple forms of violation the president incited.

DISCUSSION

In the above rhetorical analysis of President Jammeh's homophobic speech in which he threatened to behead homosexuals in the Gambia, I examine his case against alternative sexualities. My failure to access local self-identified homosexuals did not deter my field-based research, but rather presented a methodological challenge that demanded innovation if I was to obtain knowledge about homosexual individuals in this context. Although I interacted with few individuals who labeled themselves as homosexual, the president's homophobic speech was splattered all over public media. Thus, I used the available data to analyze this moment and aspect of the Gambia's sexual terrain.

That I was unable to get a large sample of homosexuals in the field does not mean that they do not exist. Instead, there are three possible ways to account for this absence: (1) individuals and communities who practice alternative sexualities are underground and thereby remain inaccessible for research; (2) the methodology was unable to transcend the positioning of the researcher as an "outsider" attempting to break boundaries of exclusion; or (3) the global label *homosexual* is a misnomer and does not accommodate the expressions, nuances, and realities of people who sexually desire members of the same sex in the Gambia.

The fact that Jammeh lashed out at a perceived community of homosexuals during his annual national tour indicates that there are people who practice alternative sexualities in the Gambia. By directing his attention and energies to homosexuals, the president highlighted their significance. While he sought to characterize homosexuals as an alien threat actively corrupting Gambians, he also unwittingly situated them within the Gambia (as those being corrupted). Misleading as this characterization may be, it marks a significant turn toward visibility. Gambian homosexuals cannot now be erased. They can no longer be ignored or dismissed. They can no longer be denied visibility. That homosexuals responded to this presidential homophobia with silence speaks very loudly – perhaps about fear of the oppressor, relative powerlessness, voicelessness, and indeed about a resistance that will not speak. While this silence may symbolize oppression, it may also demonstrate defiance. It may even be a mode of self-protection against state-instigated social and political retribution.

In his homophobic speech, Yahya Jammeh's strategy of manipulating diverse symbols was intended to increase local support for himself as president, particularly in light of the then-forthcoming elections. His attack on homosexual subjects and fundamentally incriminating them could only be successful if the language he employed to build his arguments echoed local Gambian ethos, values, and meaning-making systems. Thus the different elements of his speech reveal a precise selection, clever engineering, and assemblage of rhetorical devices intended to invoke strong reactions against homosexuals in the Gambia. The Aristotelian appeals of *pathos* and *logos* are much more successful than the appeal of *ethos* in this speech. On one hand, President Jammeh simultaneously incited hatred for alternative sexualities with his words, and made logical arguments based on his knowledge of local morals premised within contextual understandings of Islam, culture, African identity, personhood, and propriety. On the other hand, he also discredits himself as an orator by flagging apparent inconsistencies. He invariably asserts his power vis-à-vis the despicable caricature of homosexuals that he presents to his audience. His intent to divert from, subvert, and revert to the law in his quest to "weed out" homosexuals is succinctly manifest in this hate speech. He apparently is happy to bend whichever way in order to shame and oust alternative sexualities. Rather than alarm observers, this could be fuel for individuals and groups at local, regional, and international levels to strengthen their organizing for the rights of people who practice alternative sexualities and their protection as sexual citizens, as indeed seems to be happening in other African countries, such as Zimbabwe, Uganda, and Nigeria.

PART TWO
South Africa

5

Military Mutilation: The Aversion Program in the South African Defence Force in the Apartheid Era

VASU REDDY, LISA WIEBESIEK,
AND CRYSTAL MUNTHREE

Using narratives and accounts of victims, their families, and military personnel involved in the South African Defence Force's (SADF) aversion program, we will explore the experiences of homosexuals in the SADF during the apartheid era in South Africa in this chapter. Making particular use of narratives collected during interviews for *The Aversion Project: Human Rights Abuses of Gays and Lesbians in the South African Defence Force by Health Workers during the Apartheid Era* (van Zyl et al. 1999), we will analyze the aversion program as a form of violence that contributed to gay identity formation or political consciousness.

The motivation for van Zyl et al.'s (1999) investigation of the aversion program emanated from citations from the Health and Human Rights Project (HHRP) submissions to the health sector hearings of the Truth and Reconciliation Commission (TRC) in June 1997. The HHRP submission indicated that human rights violations had occurred on a wider scale than had previously been documented. Evidence suggested, for example, that gay conscripts and recruits were "treated" for homosexuality using aversion therapy. The submission also alleged that this treatment occurred without conscripts' or recruits' full consent, and as a consequence many homosexual men and women were psychologically and physically scarred. For example, some men report sterility as a result of chemical castration, while others committed suicide (*Mail and Guardian*, 28 July 2000). These empirical facts partially motivate the title of this chapter. In the context of the aversion program, the word *mutilation* (from the Latin *mutilāre*, meaning "to cut off") could be interpreted to mean that homosexuality is a pathology that requires dismemberment. By implication, military mutilation means the homosexual is to be cut off and removed from the heterosexual matrix of the armed forces. But this dismemberment, we believe, also historically situates, constructs, and valorizes the homosexual as a *public* phenomenon, and indeed as a queer political construction. In this chapter, we take the latter aspect as a cue to engage with the narratives of some of the conscripts and recruits that appear in *The Aversion Project*.

The SADF was one of the most important institutions used by the apartheid state in its opposition to what it described as the "total onslaught" by liberation forces – including the African National Congress (ANC), the Pan Africanist Congress (PAC), the Azanian People's Organization (AZAPO), and the South African Communist Party (SACP) – against apartheid. Although the total onslaught period became a distinct phenomenon of the presidency of P.W. Botha, the South African military was involved much earlier in counter-insurgency measures against the perceived *swart gevaar* ("black threat"). The role and presence of the military in South Africa increased dramatically in the mid-1970s due to a large scale "border war" fought primarily in South West Africa (now Namibia) and Angola against the anti-apartheid liberation forces. This increase depended on the conscription of young white men, not all of whom shared either the political vision of the apartheid regime or the type of masculinity imposed by the military. It is not simply the conscription of young men that is relevant here,[1] but the adjudication of their sexuality that became the subject of the aversion program. The SADF was concerned about conscript morale and thus morale in the military as a whole. It became particularly anxious about the impact of the sexual orientation of conscripts and recruits on its ability to successfully defend apartheid. The aversion program became one of the state's responses to homosexuality in the military.

As much as "race" defined the enemy for the apartheid state and its machinery, the state and the military were also interested in sexual orientation. It is interesting to note that the military did not immediately discriminate on the basis of sexual orientation, but once it became evident that some men were gay and some women were lesbians, the state took it upon itself to manage the homosexual pathology. This attitude (and methodology) reflected the pathological status the medical model in the context of the 1960s and 1970s accorded homosexuality, a status that the state merely subscribed to. However, the Christian nationalist ideology might also account for the state's determination to intervene.[2]

In this chapter, we profile how the aversion program as a secret SADF project was administered to "treat" homosexuals (*Mail and Guardian*, 28 July 2000). We argue that the program contributed to positioning "the homosexual" as a particular political subject, a subject that is deviant and consequently needs to be constrained.[3] We also argue that the emergence of the homosexual through this structure of oppression engendered a discourse in which the homosexual became a *productive* subject; one who not only accounts for the experience of violence, but also actively transforms the discourse to challenge the oppressive, militarized political order of the apartheid state. Through the public process of healing that was the TRC from 1996 to 1998, the homosexual subject has contributed in an important way to the construction of post-apartheid national identity.

THE MILITARY AND GENDER

Two definitive South African studies (Cock and Nathan 1989; Cock 1991) build on research elsewhere in the world on war and gender and demonstrate how the apartheid military systematically reinforced gender regimes. Studies on masculinity in South Africa (e.g., Morrell 2001; Cock 2001; Swart 2001; Xaba 2001; Munro 2012) address how aggressive masculinities have been constructed within war and physical conflict from the Anglo-Boer War of 1899 to 1902 to the dying days of apartheid.[4] The analytical perspectives of the various studies on war and gender are drawn from the disciplines of psychology, history, literature, sociology, and cultural studies. The distinctive aspect of these studies, in the context within which we locate the aversion program, is that they all critique the privileged status of masculinity in society, as well as the role of the military in reinforcing patriarchy. For us, the aversion program foregrounds the discursive silences that surround sexuality by demonstrating the pervasive secrecy of the apartheid era. In her study, Enloe (2000, 32) articulates: "Thinking about militarization allows us to chart silences. It enables us to see what is not challenged or, at the very least, what is not made problematic. The silence surrounding militarization is broken when military assumptions about, and military dependence on gender are pushed to the surface of public discussion." The phrase "public discussion" is especially relevant to the aversion program since it has received much coverage in the press, and to a limited extent at the TRC hearings. The aversion program was also the subject of a documentary film, *Property of the State: Gay Men in the Apartheid Military,* which premiered at the South African Gay and Lesbian Film Festival in 2004.[5] The film demonstrates that once conscripted into the army, homosexual individuals were cut off from civilian life and became the property of the state, which thereby owned their bodies. The film, via the narratives of the subjects interviewed, also suggests that its own production and content is a counter-narrative that affirms the idea of the political construction of queer identities.

The political construction of queer identities leads to another hypothesis we present in this chapter, namely that apartheid military culture reflects interrelated systems of oppression. Some scholars offer views that we will use to interpret the homophobia within the apartheid military. Dollimore (1991, 236, in Feinman 2000) observes: "Homophobia often intersects with other kinds of phobia and hatred: in this case, and rather economically, not only misogyny but also racism and xenophobia." The apartheid state viewed homosexual individuals in a particular structure of pathology, i.e., as *onsedelik* ("unnatural"): abnormal, perverse, immoral, sick, corrupting, and indeed an abject and diseased body that necessitates remedying. The aversion program strategies ensured the conscripts' sexuality was moved out of the arena of the private and into the public space of the military zone.

In apartheid South Africa, the army made decisions on behalf of its conscripts and recruits. The army exercises a degree of power by constructing a space in which it is difficult for queer subjects to discover sexuality. One of the military's features is that it institutionalises methods based on "control" to construct its gender regime by deploying gendered codes in relation to the power it wields over bodies. Enloe (2000, 291), writing about the disciplinary framework of the army elsewhere, emphasizes social control in the militarization of men: "There is nothing automatic about militarization. It is the step-by-step process by which something becomes *controlled by, dependent on,* or *derives its value from* the military as an institution or militaristic criteria. What has been militarized can be demilitarized. What has been demilitarized can be remilitarized."

The question of control and the values (such as obedience and respect for authority) that accrue in a militarized culture confirm what Cock (1991, 56), a South African sociologist, articulates in relation to the basic training for South African conscripts: "During 'basics' soldiers are taught two major requirements: to be submissive to authority [control] and to be aggressive to the enemy [values]." Such a view, underlined by the army as a technique of socialization, represents, according to Cock (1991, 56), a "totalitarian image, which sanctions seeing the enemy as the representative of a principle of evil one must destroy." Cock suggests male bonding is a marker of the gendered regime deployed against the racialized enemy in the apartheid military. This takes the form of the military's encouragement of an *esprit de corps* (spirit of fellowship, loyalty, and common purpose). The regimentation in the military is reinforced by socialization that encourages submission to authority.

THE AVERSION PROJECT

The Aversion Project frames sexual politics in the SADF in at least two ways. First, it shows that the state's practice of aversion therapy constitutes a breach of the human rights of its subjects, as reports of the aversion programs at the TRC confirm.[6] Secondly, as a subversive project bent on "rehabilitating" homosexual individuals, the state discloses a strategy to conceal and deny them. Patriarchy depends on heterosexual reproduction. Homosexuality is therefore a threat not simply to the moral fabric of society in general, but to the military as a patriarchal institution. The military thus moves into a defensive mode, maps the opposition between heterosexual and homosexual individuals, and, in a homosexual panic, reacts virulently. We argue that the aversion program is symptomatic of Sedgwick's (1994) *homosexual panic,* i.e., a defence that is offered by perpetrators of acts of violence, principally against gay men. We use the notion of homosexual panic to explain the apartheid military's conception of homosexuality as pathology, and to demonstrate that the techniques of the aversion program corroborate the panic as a type of state defence system.[7]

The Aversion Project is an excellent source of data that highlight the political intent beneath the aversion program and extrapolate some key issues in relation to the empirical. We have selected a number of subjects' narratives from *The Aversion Project* in order to explore some of their meanings in the context of the political construction of queer identities. We have attempted to contextualize the aversion program in relation to the context of war, the military, the state, truth, gender, race, and sexuality, all of which operate as modalities of power-knowledge. We turn now to the summaries of selected narratives.

Interviewed Subjects and Their Narratives

Transcripts of the interviews conducted with all the subjects are catalogued at Gay and Lesbian Memory in Action (GALA) in the historical papers section of the William Cullen Library at the University of the Witwatersrand. *The Aversion Project*'s reference team (van Zyl et al.) conducted the interviews in 1998 and 1999.[8] We have selected a sample representative of subjects of both genders, as well as the parents of one of the conscripts, using Swarr's (2000) *Summaries*. Most of the subjects interviewed in the summaries are anonymous, and their names and identifying information have been changed. The summaries focus on the period of military service, the duration and type of treatment, the doctors involved, the family context, and the locations of treatment. We have numbered the selected interviews based on *Summaries* to reflect the historical record, and include the dates on which the interviews took place. Without affecting the content of the narratives, we have shortened the interviews we present in this chapter.

INTERVIEW 1: CLIVE, 17 OCTOBER 1998

Clive was referred to Dr Villesky, from whom he thought he would receive counselling (c.f. sec. 3.4). Instead, Villesky forced Clive to come out to his parents in his office and gave him electroshock therapy in which he showed Clive pictures from "boy magazines" and told him to talk about what he thought. While Clive spoke, the doctor administered shocks that were "terribly painful, very disorientating." The treatment made him feel completely depressed and "confused." There were twenty or thirty patients in the ward, but Clive does not specify if they all received the same treatment.

INTERVIEW 2: HILARY, 13 JANUARY 1999

There were at least two other out lesbians in Hilary's basic training – the two petty officers above her – and many of the women would discuss lesbianism openly. Nolan, a woman who was the "golden girl" of the lieutenant, "named all of us," and they were called in to the lieutenant for questioning. Hilary admitted that she was a lesbian and was referred to counselling, as were a number of other women. Hilary says that the therapy was not effective. She ends the interview by remarking that her homosexuality was noted in her military file.

INTERVIEW 5, PART 1: NEIL, 28 JANUARY 1999

According to Neil, during basic training, "the humiliation of gays was very, very common" and they were called "*holnaaier, poefter, moffie*" (derogatory words that translate as "arse-fucker, poofter, moffie"). Gays were often scapegoated and beaten up to build cohesion among the rest of the group and they were treated terribly in the detention barracks (e.g., burned with cigarettes). Neil also speaks of a sexualized environment of "circle jerk-offs," genital-based rituals, and the rape and gang rape of Ovambo and Herero women.

INTERVIEW 5, PART 2: NEIL, 29 JANUARY 1999

Neil was referred to Dr Reynders and his team for evaluation as to whether he should enter the army. Reynders gave Neil "tablets that [would] dampen my sexual drive which I presume would have been hormonal tampering." He did not know what these medications were and states: "I was given tablets to drink with no name or substance whatsoever [listed]." These tablets resulted in devastating psychological, hormonal, and physiological damage. Neil feels that hormonal tampering might be "irreversible" and may have resulted in even more harm than behavioural therapy. He is very angry about his treatment and wants to have Reynders "scrapped off the role," even if only symbolically. Neil committed suicide in 1999 shortly after his interview for *The Aversion Project*, which is dedicated to him.

INTERVIEW 9: MR AND MRS ROBERTS, 17 SEPTEMBER 1998

In 1973, Dr Villesky subjected the Roberts' son, Sichma, to drug and aversion therapy. Sichma called his parents after he enrolled in the army and said that he was fainting from being in the sun during training. His parents brought him medication, but soon afterwards he was put into a psychiatric ward at 1 Military Hospital and "within a few days he had broken down to nothing." The Roberts report that while drugged at the hospital, "[Sichma's] eyes were glazed, his skin was dull, and his speech was slurred." He was discharged after two months, could no longer stand glaring light, and was diagnosed with epilepsy. Emotionally, he was never the same; he would run away from home and could not hold down a job.

INTERVIEW 12: CHARLES, 21 SEPTEMBER 1998

Charles was eager to tell his story and happy to have his name used in *The Aversion Project*. Charles is gay and found that gays were very suppressed at Oudtshoorn. There were worms in their food, it was cold and they were not given sufficient clothes, and their training was very physically demanding. He "didn't cope there" and was sent to Pretoria and offered a place in military intelligence and then foreign affairs. He was not out at this time. In 1983 he had to go back to the army at Vootrekkerhoogte, where all of the gay people were put together.

INTERVIEW 15: LINDA LEONARD, 2 APRIL 1999

Linda knew a lot of other women in the navy who were gay, but did not mix with them because she would have made it worse for herself. Linda rebelled and went AWOL and, as a result, was tied up and interrogated. She was subjected to extreme measures compared to other people who also went AWOL, and was forced to choose between resigning, being shot as a deserter (as it was wartime), or being dishonourably discharged. Linda never admitted that she was gay and the military had no proof, but she faced discrimination. She was locked up, covered with polish as a kind of "initiation," and not cleared for security. A female officer also targeted her and unsuccessfully tried to "trap" her into a relationship.

Silence and Emotion

The narratives reveal a modality of suffering and pain that is a direct consequence of the aversion program. The extent to which emotions underpin the subjects' experiences as reflected in their narratives, and the capacity of the subjects to contain those emotions, is relevant. For example, Sichma was "emotionally, never the same; he would run away from home and couldn't hold down a job" (interview 9). This alludes to the fragmentation of the subjects in respect of identity and personality.

These stories exemplify a type of constructed testimony of which Swarr (2000) is the grand narrator. A defining feature of the narratives is that the experiences of the conscripts (and one conscript's parents) call into question and challenge the silences informing it. In their testimonial project on Holocaust survivors, Auerhahn and Laub (1990) argue that silence helps to heal victims. Indeed, silence does not have only a negative meaning in the narratives. Even if the prime strategy of the military is to silence LGBTI individuals, it must identify – and thereby acknowledge – them in order to do so. The homophobia of the military also depends on language. The military attempts to erase homosexual individuals through naming them in pathological terms. Consider Neil's account of basic training, in which he was called "*holnaaier, poefter, moffie*" (interview 5.1). The use of the words promotes *esprit de corps,* and "build[s] cohesion among the rest of the group" of heterosexuals, which simultaneously marginalizes homosexuals as other. Naming homosexual individuals in pejorative terms is an attempt to shame them to give up their homosexuality and be assimilated into a heterosexual group. But there is also a productive moment in this naming: if silence indicates a lack of power on the part of the traumatized homosexual, it is also a sign of liberation and resistance. In these narratives, the homosexual subject is constructed and formed through trauma, and so silence in this instance can be a sign of resistance that questions the morality, or rather the abuse, that the apartheid military circumscribed.

As noted earlier, the abuse operates fundamentally within a system of violence that interfaces with other systems of oppression such as racism and misogyny. For example, Neil (interview 5, part 1) also speaks about the "rape and gang rape of Ovambo and Herero women" in which gay men were obliged to participate (as they would in a ritual) in order to reinforce their masculinity. Here, rape functions not only as a form of sexual and gendered violence, but also as a weapon of masculinity in the context of war. The Herero and Ovambo women represent the people on whose behalf SWAPO (South West Africa People's Organization) engaged in a war with the apartheid state in what was then known as South-West Africa (Namibia). The aversion program and the narratives show that another of the state's enemies was the homosexual, whom the military also had to silence.

Swarr (2000) writes: "Charles was eager to tell his story and happy to have his name used in this research" (interview 12). Swarr's mention of Charles's eagerness may be interpreted as an attempt to break the silence that circumscribed the aversion program and those who suffered under it. Auerhahn and Laub (1990, 454) argue that countering silences produces an effect of a reunion with others and emphasize a rehumanization when dealing with the effects of trauma, which is realized through a "shared recognition of the individual's subjectivity." Charles' narrative explicitly states this, but all the above narratives are formulated in a performative mode to recover a sense of dignity and self.

Medical and Psychological Abuse

The narratives encompass a number of themes at a denotative level. The main underlying theme is that of medical abuse alleg-edly committed by Dr Villesky, who appears in the narratives above. In reality, Villesky is Colonel (Doctor) Aubrey Levin, who emerges as the chief antagonist in this drama. During the 1970s and 1980s, Levin was the head of psychiatry at 1 Military Hospital in Pretoria. He proudly proclaimed far-right views, his support of apartheid not least among them. Many former conscripts hold Levin responsible for the abusive and inappropriate treatment they received in the SADF. Following the HHRP submission to the TRC, Levin, along with a number of other doctors, was served notice that he had been named as a possible violator of human rights. By that time, however, he had fled to Canada, ostensibly to escape South Africa's high crime rate (*Mail and Guardian*, 28 July 2000). Levin did not apply for amnesty from the commission, nor was he granted amnesty, implying he could be prosecuted for his apartheid-era activities should he return to South Africa. The TRC, however, made no effort to serve Levin with a subpoena. Levin worked in the forensic department of the University of Calgary until his suspension following allegations of (and his subsequent conviction for) sexual assault against male patients (Calgary Herald, 12 April 2013).

As the chief antagonist in *The Aversion Project*, Levin's uncon-ventional treatment regime entailed aversion therapy. Although aversion therapy uses various therapeutic treatments including chemicals (such as injections or drugs), noxious sensitization, and

electric shocks, Levin's treatment primarily consisted of shock therapy and electrotherapy combined with a drug regime (van Zyl et al.
1999, 72).[9] Some of the drugs administered had irreversible hormonal effects (see interviews 5.2; 9; 13). Shock therapy also led to
long-term problems among Levin's patients, who note extreme mental instability (interviews 1; 5; 9), photosensitivity (interview 9),
hormone-related disorders (interview 5.2), headaches (interviews
5.2; 9), depression (interviews 9; 15), and new medical conditions,
such as epilepsy (interview 9). In cases that did not involve Levin,
treatment of conscripts also included psychological and psychiatric
counselling, which in some cases patients did not take seriously
(interviews 1; 2; 5.2; 15). In the cases of Clive (interview 1), Hilary
(interview 2), and Neil (interview 5), a clear pattern of unethical
psychological manipulation pervaded the counselling. Such manipulation entailed gender stereotyping, which resulted in serious depression for the subjects, and deliberate attempts to undermine their
self-esteem. These counselling sessions did not seem to change conscripts' perceptions of their sexual orientation, but did result in psychological distress.

   The military also used a strategy of publicly outing people it suspected were homosexual. Linda (interview 15), Charles (interview
12), Hilary (interview 2), and Clive (interview 1) verify such practices. Outing questions the private, often repressed sexuality that is
an effect of social homophobia, which compels homosexuals to
retreat to the closet. This is in direct opposition to a forced public
coming out when someone who is suspected of being homosexual is
outed. Outing could be viewed here as a form of persecution that, in
conjunction with the other methods used as part of the aversion
therapy, deepened the trauma of the homosexual subjects. The above
narratives suggest that the psychological consequences of enforced
outing are depression, psychosis, and in some instances, possibly suicide (cf. interview 12).

   The use of drugs in aversion and conversion therapy in the military
was based on the belief that homosexuality was a medical disorder,
despite important changes in psychiatric theory. In 1973, the American
Psychiatric Association (APA) removed homosexuality from its
Diagnostic and Statistical Manual of Mental Disorders (but retained
the category "ego-dystonic homosexuality").[10] Despite this change,
Levin's practices epitomize the medicalized view of homosexuality as
pathology, and he continued to use aversion and conversion therapies

to rehabilitate homosexuals. Van Zyl et al. (1999, 66) explain: "Though this was not written into the policy, for many years the doctors in charge of the psychiatric units were allowed to proceed with such treatment in contempt of contemporary medical practices at the time."

Levin initiated a drug treatment program at a farm called Greefswald in the Northern Transvaal (now the Northern Province). Van Zyl et al. (1999, 67) report that inmates in the program were isolated from friends and family for approximately three months: "During the time Greefswald was operating, it was used as some form of implicit threat to give patients the choice of going there, or consenting to aversion therapy in the psychiatric unit. By 1980, Greefswald had been closed, and another centre started at Magaliesoord." Greefswald was primarily a hard labour detention camp that most conscripts feared. People were frightened into cooperation with and submission to the authority of the regime. It seems the fear that this prison instilled in the homosexual conscript or recruit minimized the possibility of resistance.

Greefswald also reinforced the heteronormative divisions within the military. One conscript explains that Ward 22 (primarily a psychiatric ward) was reserved for heterosexual shellshock cases, patients with bi-polar disorder, and drug addicts, while Ward 28 was reserved for people who dress in drag, homosexuals, and other sexual "deviants: (van Zyl et al. 1999, 74). One unnamed informant describes the ethos of Greefswald (see also interviews 1 and 9):

> I think most young boys are, or were in those days, terrified of
> authority. And growing up in that whole Christian Nationalist
> environment you just simply did what you were told. And if it
> meant paying lip-service to Caesar, you did so, because that is
> how you stayed out of trouble. Because if you didn't co-operate,
> there was always that unstated, but nonetheless very real threat
> that you would be dispatched to Greefswald. So you'd better just
> co-operate with this guy because he could make your life really
> miserable. (van Zyl et al. 1999, 74)

Such an observation emphasizes the abuse of power, not only at the macro-level of the military, but also at the micro-level of the South African Military Health Service (SAMS). The doctors who administered narco-analysis, which the broader medical community viewed as inappropriate, dangerous, and abusive, in effect broke the

Hippocratic oath. The execution of apartheid military ideology superseded the medical corps' ethical accountability and their Hippocratic responsibility to their patients. In an interview (*Mail and Guardian*, 28 August 2000), Harold, who spent time in 1 Military Hospital under the care of Levin and spoke on condition of anonymity, said: "After what has been, cumulatively, 16 years of psychoanalysis and therapy, every minute of every day is still a battle to find a way through the echoes of what happened then. More than 25 years on, I still cannot formulate a narrative of that time which I can hold on to."

Harold's observation speaks to the fragmentation of the subject as a direct result of the painful effects of the treatment, a desire to release the trauma and anguish that informed it. Harold was subject to Levin's use of narco-analysis without his parents' consent despite the fact he was a minor. According to van Zyl et al. (1999, 68–71), the medical establishment within the military disregarded the practice of obtaining informed consent when it came to treatment (an issue that if practiced today, would run counter to ethical protocols). During narco-analysis, Levin played Harold tape recordings of what he said in his clinically uninhibited state: "It was horrifying. I was shouting, screaming, sobbing, like an animal. And Levin was baiting me to get wilder still. It has taken me years to be able to conclude that Levin could have had only one motive – to drive me out of my mind. And he very nearly succeeded. Many others like me in Ward 11 at Number 1 Military Hospital were given narco-analysis by Levin. It seemed to be the rule rather than the exception" (*Mail and Guardian*, 28 August 2000, 5)

Harold's experience echoes Clive's aversion therapy using electric shock treatment (interview 1). Such treatment was intended to change a patient's behaviour patterns by associating negative sensations, such as the pain from an electric shock, with specific thoughts (van Zyl et al. 1999, 72):

> Electrodes were strapped to the arms of the subject, and wires leading from these were in turn connected to a machine operated by a dial calibrated from one to ten. The subject was then shown black and white pictures of a naked man and encouraged to fantasize. The increase in the current would cause the muscles of the forearm to contract – an intensely painful sensation. When the subject was either screaming with pain or verbally requested that the dial be turned off, the current would be stopped and a colour

Playboy centrefold substituted for the previous pictures. The
doctor would then verbally describe the woman portrayed in
glowing and positive terms. This process would be repeated
three times in a single session. Sessions were held twice daily for
three to four days. People subjected to this therapy experienced
long periods of disorientation afterwards.

The above procedure demonstrates (and confirms) that the world
of the apartheid defence force recognised two sexes, male and female,
constituted by gender as masculine and feminine in heterosexual
terms. Such procedures were intended to systematically and gradually reconstruct the homosexual's mind. The methodologies used in
the aversion program suggest that those running it believed therapy
would alter the sexual orientation of the subjects via a form of psychological surgery. The program's use of *Playboy* magazine is significant. Ironically, the apartheid government had banned *Playboy*
because of its "immoral" and "distasteful" focus on bodies (usually
images of naked or scantily dressed women that the regime perceived
as unchristian). However, in Levin's operation, *Playboy* had the
potential to stimulate heterosexual desire. The program, within the
context of electroshock therapy, used the images to condition, social-
ize, and reconstruct the homosexual into a heterosexual.

Sex-change operations, and accompanying hormonal treatments,
were also linked to the aversion program. In the preliminary stages,
often long before the actual operation, hormone adjustment is necessary, which means subjects identified male at birth who plan to
undergo such an operation must complete a regime of drugs to
restructure their androgen (male hormone) and estrogen (female
hormone) balance (see Ekins and King 1996 and Ekins 1997 for a
detailed explanation of this process). It is not difficult to interpret
the military's rationale for sex-change operations given its emphasis
on heterosexuality. The SAMS thus used surgery to remedy the deviant homosexual by changing their sex. These operations were usually preceded by limited counselling, and rarely had the consent of
the patient (*Mail and Guardian*, 28 July 2000). Approximately fifty
sex-change operations were performed each year between 1971 and
1989, and not all were successful (*Mail and Guardian*, 28 July 2000).
Those who the SAMS identified as in need of such an operation –
anyone deemed an "incurable homosexual" or who could not be
reformed with drugs or psychiatry – were sent to Vootrekkerhoogte

military hospital for screening and a rehabilitation program. Victims of this specialized program "were told to keep quiet about them and encouraged to set up a new circle of friends" (*Mail and Guardian*, 28 July 2000). Neil's testimony (interview 5.2) is evidence both of the existence of the surgical program and of its failure. Neil was chemically castrated, which resulted in severe depression and other mental ailments. *The Aversion Project* (van Zyl et al. 1999, 78) makes the following comment in relation to Neil's testimony:

> As a result of the research process, Neil has touched the core of his anger and humiliation. He decided to explore litigation. Assisted by a psychiatrist, a psychologist, an internist and a human rights lawyer, they tried to find out exactly what treatment he was given. He was given no information at the time of treatment, and it appears that all records of his treatment have been destroyed. The doctor who treated him pleaded amnesia, so without evidence the case could not proceed.

The treatment Neil received led to irreversible psychological, hormonal, and physiological damage.

Levin and other medical personnel who participated in the aversion program refused to be interviewed during the investigation that culminated in *The Aversion Project*. However, shortly before the report was released, journalists succeeded in getting a response from Levin. He emphatically denied that any sex reassignment operations were performed in the military, claiming that the political atmosphere at the time was such that reassignment surgery was not tolerated or even considered (*Mail and Guardian*, 28 July 2000). In response to questions about electric shock treatment, narco-analysis and the question of consent, Levin stated:

> Nobody was given electric shock treatment by me. We did not practice Russian communist-style torture. What we practiced was aversion therapy. We caused slight – very slight – discomfort in the arm by contracting the muscles using an electronic device. Some people used elastic bands to shock patients. Nobody was hurt and nobody was ever held against their will. At no time were patients forced to submit to treatment. Narco-analysis was used, I give you that, but it was used in very isolated cases and only to help treat post-traumatic stress. Narco-analysis was used

to help get victims to talk about the trauma they suffered. I want to reiterate, nobody was held against his or her will. We did not keep human guinea pigs like Russian communists, we only had patients who wanted to be cured and were there voluntarily. But anyway I have no doubt the *Mail and Guardian* will distort all of this. (*Mail and Guardian*, 28 July 2000)

Levin's response highlights several issues that are crucial to an interpretation of what we have labelled "military mutilation." Levin's denial that he gave anyone electric shock treatment, but admission that he practiced aversion therapy and his description of what it entailed, reveals his misunderstanding of psychiatric practices that confirm, that by whatever name, electric shock treatment or electrotherapy is a fundamental element of aversion therapy. Simultaneously, Levin's claim that "nobody was hurt" is a refusal to recognize the trauma, pain, and suffering subjects experienced. His claim that "nobody was ever held against their will" suggests the army was a democratic space – a suggestion the subjects' experience refutes. The prevailing power of the military dictated that non-compliance with authority would lead to the possibility of detention, such as that at Greefswald. Levin's assertion that his "patients" wanted to be "cured" implies that homosexuals are masochists who entered the military willingly in order to endure the trauma of the program. Levin also misrepresents his use of narco-analysis as a drug regime. Despite the negative effects of such drugs, Levin claims they facilitated the victims' capacity to talk about "trauma." The assumption here is that the victims' sexual orientation, not the effects of the narco-analysis, was the trauma. Particularly telling is Levin's use of the word "victim", which discloses his possible subconscious acknowledgement that subjects who supposedly enter the program as patients requiring ("wanting") a "cure" leave the program as "victims."

Levin's tacit aversion to anything Russian, which he labels as communist, also indicates his opposition to the liberation forces in South Africa, which were partly Soviet supported. His statement that "we did not practice Russian communist-style torture," suggests an acknowledgement that they did practice torture, but of a different kind.

Finally, Levin's language discloses a particular truth-effect. His entire response constructs a particular truth about the events in the aversion program. His response discloses the desire to suppress the truth of the events, especially as it relates to the subjects (the "victims," as Levin calls them) of his treatment. In a way, his accusation

that the *Mail and Guardian* "will distort all of this" is an acknowledgement that the truth about the victims' experiences matters less
to him than his version of events.

In response to the exposure of the aversion program, a representative of the South African National Defence Force (or SANDF, the
new name of the defence force in the post-apartheid context), Major
Louis Kirstein made the following statement:

> The South African military health service is more than willing to
> investigate or assist any investigation into the alleged actions by
> Dr Levin in the past. The SANDF is bound by the constitution
> and will not tolerate, condone or conceal any alleged infringe-
> ments of the constitution by its members. Furthermore the
> SANDF is an equal-opportunity employer and does not discrimi-
> nate against any person on grounds of race, gender, religion or
> sexual persuasion. (*Mail and Guardian*, 28 July 2000)

These sentiments confirm an interesting turn of events in history
and highlight the relationship of history to politics. The border war
project has been replaced by a new and reconciliatory post-apartheid
project in which racial, class, gender, and ethnic boundaries are
viewed not as divisive factors, but as the means to facilitate a reconciliatory politics. Whereas the apartheid military (the SADF) was a
negative space that prioritized the exclusion of particular categories
of difference, the post-apartheid military (the SANDF) represents an
inclusive order that welcomes homosexuals into its ranks. While the
SANDF has not overtly acknowledged the previous existence of the
aversion program, it has acknowledged that the existence of such a
program would have constituted an abuse of human rights. The
original submission by the HHRP to the TRC asserted that the abuse
of human rights in such a program warranted further investigation.
The Aversion Project should be seen as an important contribution to
this process. Though the SANDF planned to investigate the allegations, it has not yet done so.

CONCLUSION

The narratives of the victims problematize the psychopolitics of the
aversion program. Homosexuals were the subjects of a program that
included experiments that aimed to minimize and erase their desires
in order to "normalize" them within a heteronormative military and

social environment. The aversion program took place during a period of South Africa's military history that evinced the ideology of apartheid, and was reinforced by institutions of the state, such as the SAMS. The narratives we have presented in this chapter include a range of abuses that psychologically and physically scarred many. Of primary importance is the fact that the state sought to eradicate difference. The state accounted for the ambiguities of homosexuality from within a pathological model, especially so in its interpretation of homosexuality as perverse within the SADF in general and the SAMS in particular. The act of policing sexuality, especially in men, categorizes the homosexual as an effeminised body, a corruptive force that does not conform to the compulsory heterosexuality of the military's gendered regime. This has been demonstrated in the military rituals that disciplined conscripts to become heterosexual men, which may include encouraging conscripts to commit acts of extreme sexual violence, such as rape.

It is possible to theorize the strategy the aversion program employed in terms of the techniques of desexualization, whereby isolation, dispersal, torture, and violence structured the life of the homosexual conscript. This is not meant to essentialize the experience of all homosexuals within the military, but instead suggests that the program intensified social divisions based on gender, sex, and race, and led to a form of sexual apartheid. Not all gay men were victims of the aversion program. In fact, the narratives also show that many homosexuals bought into the system and were dedicated to the operation (interview 5, part 1). This being so, it is clear that homosexual individuals are not a homogenous group.

Despite the negative effects of the aversion program, and notwithstanding the emotional burden carried by the victims, *The Aversion Project* presents a positive opportunity for countering silence and constructing a truth that the victims feel more accurately represents their lived experiences. Following Foucault, the aversion program produced homosexual subjects as productive subjects constructed by a specific formation of power that identified them as deviant and queer in the pejorative sense. *The Aversion Project* unmasks a number of issues, the most important being the political configuration of the aversion program, its agents, its victims, and their families. However, *The Aversion Project* also re-presents the queer, and in this instance objectifies the traumatized queer subject whom it repoliticizes and reconstructs as a subject with an identity within a rights framework.

Constructing the "Ex-Gay" Subject: Cultural Convergences in Post-Apartheid South Africa

MELISSA HACKMAN

INTRODUCTION: ADRIAN'S HEALING

Adrian was a member of Healing Revelation Ministries[1] (HRM), an ex-gay and sexual addiction ministry in Cape Town, South Africa.[2] He turned thirty in 2008 but, with his unlined chubby face and quiet, earnest way of expressing himself, looked closer in age to someone still in college. He was a coloured[3] man who kept his hair short and neat, and he favoured roomy shirts and slacks that hid his body. He was easily embarrassed and avoided group gatherings when he could. I first met Adrian in 2004 when he was in his mid-twenties; he often seemed to be on the margins of conversations and was very socially awkward. I was surprised when a ministry leader told me that by the time I met him, Adrian had made significant social progress. When he first started to attend a weekly ex-gay support group for men, he could not look anyone in the eye, even in one-on-one conversations, and he stared at his hands or the table on the rare occasions he spoke. Besides attending groups for Christian men with "same-sex attraction," sexual desire for other men, Adrian also underwent weekly individual counselling sessions for over a year with Brian, the ministry's white American founder.

Adrian was in his early twenties when he first went to the ministry offices at Church of the Reborn, a Pentecostal Assemblies of God church. He had decided to undergo a sex change operation and entered the ministry without any hope that he could change his sexual preference. He went to his initial counselling appointment to prove to himself that he had exhausted all other healing options. He had already investigated the process for transitioning and planned to meet with a psychologist and begin living as a woman. Adrian spent his childhood being teased and bullied for being different. In his high school years, he thought he was a *moffie*[4] ("sissy") or that he was born in the wrong body. At their first counselling session, Brian told Adrian that if he wanted to heal from his same-sex attraction, he would have to work to drastically change his self-presentation, beginning with his voice. At various times Adrian described his voice as sounding "like a woman," "effeminate," and "thin." He was shocked when Brian explained that he himself was the one making his voice thin – he spoke like a woman because he spent so much time with women, learning to mimic their characteristics and mannerisms. Adrian thought he had a physiological problem and had never gone through puberty; he believed his voice had never broken. Brian told him that he could make his voice "thicker," but it would take time and practice.

Adrian's voice had always been a major source of shame for him and he was ecstatic at the idea that he could deepen it. When Adrian and I met for lunch in 2007, he explained how, with effort and constant attention, his voice was changing and "starting to become normal." With practice in the previous year it had become easier for him to modify his voice without always having to think before speaking. However, he said that when he "gets a fright" or is very upset he loses his self-control and his voice becomes high-pitched.

Besides controlling his pitch, Adrian also consciously changed how he walked. His high-pitched voice was accompanied by what he referred to as "effeminate walking," which involved swinging his hips. He learned through careful attention to move his body differently when he walked and to reposition his posture when he sat. During most of our lunch, Adrian had his legs crossed at the knee. Halfway through telling me about his transformation, he glanced down and stopped talking for a few seconds. He quickly uncrossed his legs, opening them up much wider and placing both feet flat on the floor. He leaned into the back of his chair and adopted a more relaxed posture. His arms rested on his upper thighs instead of his knees. His body took up more space, and he remained in this stereotypically masculine position throughout the rest of lunch.

Adrian believed his masculinity would continue to transform as he naturalized his new masculine posture and way of carrying himself.

He told me: "I think I have worked that [effeminacy] off, I don't even know how I used to walk because I've totally lost the ability to walk like that ... [*pause*] I think." Through practice, Adrian had returned to what he refers to as his "natural" voice and gait. The language that Adrian used is notable – that of work, practice, and "forcing" himself to speak and walk differently.

Adrian was working towards his ideal self – a deep voice, masculine walk, and heterosexual desires. He had an intimate relationship with God, whom he believed would guide him to express himself in a manner that is read by others as masculine. Adrian felt that with God's love he could transform himself in body and spirit. God would lead him to heterosexual desire and marriage.

In this chapter, I address how men like Adrian made the choice to be ex-gay in one of the few democracies in the world that legally protects gays and lesbians. I explain how an ex-gay ministry could thrive in post-apartheid South Africa and during a period of the institutionalization of gay rights. I argue that the Healing Revelation Ministries (HRM) flourished in South Africa in the post-apartheid period because of a conjuncture of newly open discussions of sexuality, national trauma and reconciliation processes, and the growth of cosmopolitan twelve-step recovery programs. The methods of the ex-gay ministry included the disclosure of root memories of abuse and desire with a goal of curing them through confession, counselling, and the formation and performance of a new self. Men joined the ministry to fashion a new masculinity, an identity as an ex-gay, and a new subjectivity based on commitment to the ministry's ideals.

ASSEMBLING SUBJECTIVITY

Like many other anthropologists and feminists, I theorize that subjectivity is a collage of historically and socially located cultural and personal productions. Media scholar Mary Gray explains how the young rural lesbian, gay, bisexual, transgender, and intersex (LGBTI) youth she worked with in Kentucky and the surrounding Appalachian region saw their sexual identities as the most "authentic" pieces of themselves. Gray notes, though, that what counts as authentic is itself a construction. Amy, a young queer woman from central Kentucky, was first sexually attracted to women in her teenage years. However, it was through watching the television show *Baywatch* and chatting online with other LGBTI young people that she "found" her "true identity" as bisexual. Gray (2009, 92) writes: "To suggest that queer youth must work arduously *to achieve*, not discover, LGBT identities and the sense of authenticity they confer is to approach the concept of identity as an ideal embedded in and constructed through the politics of social interactions rather than the expression of fixed traits." I follow Gray, seeing ex-gay identity as an achievement that must be constantly enacted. Subjectivities are built, not buried inside to await discovery.

Gray argues that identity work is labour that draws from a variety of available sources. American LGBTI people may view "coming out" as realizing their natural/true selves, but in actuality this process is an achievement built from accessible cultural assemblages (Gray 2009, 19). I apply Gray's ideas on how subjectivities are created from available cultural resources to South African ex-gay men, who drew from a variety of sources to become heterosexuals, including transnational Pentecostalism, American ex-gay cultures, and national ideas on trauma and healing. Ex-gay identity manifested itself similarly, as a form of work that revealed an inner essence. Ex-gays did not believe identity was an achievement. For them, "real" or "natural" masculinity was an interior essence that they uncovered through the healing process. Changing one's exterior was understood to have effects on the interior. Adrian believed that by altering his gait and posture, he would get closer to masculine heterosexuality.

Legal changes since the end of apartheid made the existence of an ex-gay ministry in the country notable. Since becoming democratic, South Africa has formed a government based on the concept of universal human rights, with equality for gay people and the rights of women enshrined in the equality clause of the constitution (Cock 2005; Stychin 1996). The South African constitution was the first in the world to include specific legal protections for gay citizens and remains the only constitution that did so on the African continent during the first decade of the twenty-first century, which is also the time period I cover in this chapter. In the past decade, South Africa has passed laws, often after tense legal battles, that allow gay men and women to adopt children, seek visas for non-native partners, and marry (Berger 2008).

However, sexual and gender inclusivity in the constitution, laws, and governance coexisted with popular disapproval of these new rights and high rates of sexual and domestic violence (Moffett 2008; Reid and Dirsuweit 2002). Between 2003 and 2007, the South African Social Sciences Research Council conducted annual national surveys on public acceptance of homosexuality. Each year it found that over 80 per cent of the population over sixteen years of age believed that sex between two men or two women was "always wrong" (Roberts and Reddy 2008).[5] Intense moral disapproval towards same gender sex contrasts sharply with the ideologies of the equality clause. HRM and those in the Church of the Reborn share with the majority of South Africans the attitude that homosexuality is wrong, including black nationalists who think that homosexuality is un-African, a Western colonial import (Epprecht 2009; Holmes 1997).

Below, I discuss the specific cultural convergences that make ex-gay subjects culturally salient in post-apartheid South Africa. I look closely at twelve-step ideas, the effects of the Truth and Reconciliation Commission (TRC), South African Christianities, and the rise of faith-based counselling. These all share a commitment to a new way to be an individual, improvement of the self through self-surveillance and care, and behavioural change to initiate new subjectivities. The technologies each offers, including confession, group accountability, and the opportunity for a new self through identity work, overlap. I examine the ways the ministry used culturally relevant ideas of healing practices and brought them together to form a new post-apartheid ex-gay subject.

HEALING HOMOSEXUALITY

HRM was not the beginning of people trying to "cure" same-sex attraction and behaviour in South Africa. Individuals experienced a variety of "cures" and went to a variety of "experts" during apartheid. For example, in the mid-1970s, black anti-apartheid activist Simon Nkoli told his parents that he was gay. They took him to three separate kinds of healers for treatment – four separate *sangomas*, traditional healers, with different opinions, two of whom said he was bewitched and two said there was no problem, a Catholic priest who told him to repent, and finally a psychologist who told him to accept himself as gay (Nkoli 1995; 1993). Beginning in 1969, the South African Defence Force (SADF) had a psychological unit to "cure" white soldiers who were categorized as homosexual. These cures included electroshock treatment, hormone prescription, and sex-reassignment surgery, which frequently occurred without patient consent (van Zyl et al. 1999; Vincent and Camminga 2009, 685; Reddy et al. in this volume). The SADF hospital example, along with

Nkoli's experiences (although his is an individual anecdotal account), illustrate not only that people identified as gay during apartheid but also that various community experts offered a variety of solutions at the same time.

Post-apartheid discourses on gayness helped produce its opposite. There are still diverse cures for homosexuality beyond HRM. I have picked up tracts in downtown Cape Town that advertise healings by *sangomas* for a variety of problems that include homosexuality, erectile dysfunction, and other forms of "misfortune." Many of the men in HRM tried a variety of other cures, including deliverance at their local churches, before learning about and joining the ministry. I situate my work within a larger historical trajectory of homosexual histories in South Africa and homophobic movements by the state and local communities.

SUBJECTIVITIES AND SPACE

The first time I went to visit HRM's white founder and leader Brian at the Church of the Reborn, where HRM has its offices, I was taken aback to see that I was in the middle of a gay neighbourhood. Standing in front of the church I saw a surprising number of publicly gay-friendly shops. These included a gay-owned travel agency with a pride flag swinging in the breeze, a café/bar where gay men gathered for meals and drinks (HRM members also had lunch there), and a "gay internet café." The twenty-four-hour cafe received the nickname not only because it had a pride flag outside but also because its smoky interiors were usually full of men at all hours of the night and day and the computer desktops held folders of gay pornographic material.

Around the corner and a few blocks down was the promenade along the ocean, a well-known pick-up site for male prostitutes. "The Wall" at the beach is a popular place for public sex at night. In one ministry newsletter, Brian wrote that the ministry purposely chose a location in the "middle of an area of prostitution, gay bars and drug sales" to bring God to the "enemy's turf." People who sought "healing from homosexuality through the power of Jesus Christ" could not enter the HRM's offices without a visual reminder of the subjectivity they were attempting to leave behind.

HRM members employed multiple levels of strategic identification, often at the same time. Anthropologist Tom Boellstorff (2005, 35) details how subjects live with multiple scales of identification: "The various subject positions through which one lives at any point in time may not have isomorphic spatial scales: one's sense of self as a youth could be global, as a man local, and as a labourer national, all at the same time. Or to be a youth could be both local and global at the same time, intersecting." Similarly, ex-gay men drew from a variety of spatial scales in their healing.

I start this discussion with the local context. The development of new subjectivities holds a special place in Cape Town. The city sees itself as unique because of its liberal views, cultural mixing, and acceptance of diversity, even if this does not always correspond to lived reality. Although the first ex-gay ministry in Africa started in Johannesburg, Cape Town's HRM had the longest running and most successful ex-gay and sexual addiction ministry on the African continent. The city of Cape Town is historically linked to the creation of new subjectivities, as well as a mixing of diverse cultures to form new hybrid selves. Ex-gay subjects are one example of this, as are coloured and gay identities.

Colonial Cape Town nurtured the creation of new subjectivities. The coloured community is descended from racial and cultural mixing of Europeans, the local Khoisan peoples, and enslaved populations from other parts of Africa and Asia (Loos 2004). Today, Afrikaans, a mix of indigenous, Dutch, and English languages, is the first language of most of the Cape coloured community and of white Afrikaners. As a separate racial category under apartheid, coloureds' status was higher than that of blacks but much lower than that of whites. The majority of the coloured community still lives in the Western Cape, comprising 49.6 per cent of the population in the province itself and 43.2 per cent in and around Cape Town (Statistics South Africa 2012). Today, coloured identity is being reconstructed, as some individuals now self-identify as black and others work to understand coloured identity outside the black-white binary (Bosch 2008).

The history of homosexuality in South Africa is intimately linked to Cape Town.[6] During apartheid, the city and surrounding areas had "proto-gay neighbourhoods," including Sea Point, where HRM is located, for white gay men and District Six for coloured gay men (Gevisser 1995, 27). Historian Dhianaraj Chetty (1995, 117) writes: "More than anywhere else in South Africa, aspects of gay life like cross-dressing and drag seem to have taken root in the coloured working class communities of the Western Cape." For example, Gayle, or *moffietaal* ("gay language") is a well-studied part of coloured culture. Gayle was a way to discuss and conceal gay life during apartheid (Cage 2003). Many believe that the language originated in the Western Cape in coloured communities and was used by a variety of speakers across racial lines. Gayle is a mix of Afrikaans and English, and was used more in Cape Town than in places like Johannesburg (Gevisser 1995).[7] There was little contact between the racial communities[8] until the 1990s due to apartheid's institutionalized racism and geographic separation (Leap 2005).

The emergence of a gay identity in South Africa in the last decades of apartheid sprang from local and international sources, such as exiled African National Congress (ANC) leaders' addition of sexuality to their non-discrimination rhetoric, a new awareness by many that there was an international and supportive gay community, and the first gay pride march in the country in 1990 in Johannesburg (Donham 1998; Gevisser 1995). The ending of strict moral censorship also allowed more international media into the country. Some men claimed that they first became aware of homosexual identity from watching American television shows like *Dallas* (Donham 1998). Part of the local effects of the international anti-apartheid movement was a change in the range of possibilities offered at home and in the larger world. Many people who participated in same-gender sexual activity began to claim a new gay self that linked them to a larger local and transnational LGBTI community.

Cape Town is now known as and markets itself as a "pink city" and the "gay capital" of Africa. This is particularly offensive to those who oppose gay rights because Cape Town is also the "Mother City" of the nation. HRM was in Cape Town because of the city's long-standing gay communities, but also because of its unique place in the Pentecostal worldview as under demonic possession. In the Pentecostal imagination, Cape Town was in spiritual bondage, possessed by the spirit of homosexuality. Pentecostals viewed the proliferation of pornography shops, bathhouses, gay bars, and the gay-identified neighbourhoods of Sea and Green Point as visual proof of Cape Town's sinfulness. Spiritually polluted places are said to lead to possessed bodies, and the spirit of a place can have dire effects on Christian bodies and sexual choices. Pentecostals believe that living in a demonic space influences sexual desires and actions. They read the landscape for seen and unseen signs of satanic influence.

Many Pentecostals claimed that there was a palpable haze of evil over the city that people could sense and feel. I heard from a number of people that Cape Town's "spiritual covering" leads to more "sexual falls" for those who struggle with same-sex attraction than other places. Stories were common about strong Christian leaders who could travel almost anywhere in the world without "falling" but who, once in Cape Town, had sex with other men almost immediately. One white ministry leader quipped that if a person wants to deal with sexual brokenness, Cape Town is the place to be. He told me, "You can stand it in Cape Town, you can anywhere, y'know?"

In sum, the imagination of new identities is linked to place, and Cape Town's history of gay public spaces makes it a place of particular importance. Over time, Cape Town has remained a place of hybridity in which people cross boundaries and create new subjectivities. HRM's location in Cape Town is part of longer histories of the creation of new subjectivities, from the colonial through apartheid to the post-apartheid period.

SOUTH AFRICAN CHRISTIANITIES

South Africa is a predominately Christian country and has been so for many years. The most recent census in 2001 found that approximately 79.8 per cent of the population self-identified as Christian.[9] There are many Christian traditions in South Africa, which include mainstream denominations like Presbyterians, the Dutch Reform Church, Anglicanism, Catholicism, a variety of African Independent Churches, evangelical church communities, and Pentecostals, the Christian group with the most growth since the end of apartheid. A comparison of census data between 1996 and 2001 shows that mainstream Christian churches had little or no growth in South Africa. In striking contrast, evangelical and Pentecostal church attendance and membership soared, increasing by 48 per cent. Schlemmer (2008, 24–5) estimated that in 2011, Pentecostals would make up almost one fifth of the population.

In the contemporary South African context, where the modern subject is legally constructed as an individual with human rights and the ability to make personal choices, particularly regarding gender and sexuality, being a Pentecostal further adds to a sense of individual agency. Changing sexual desire and behaviours is consistent with a long tradition in Christianity of radical personality changes via conversion, especially for those considered social deviants such as alcoholics, criminals, and prostitutes (Wanner 2003; Lovekin and

Maloney 1977). Early twentieth-century Pentecostal tracts made similar claims of drastic changes in subjectivities, paying special attention to how the gifts of the spirit transformed men and made them less aggressive, kinder, and more generous (Maxwell 1999). A study on contemporary Pentecostals in South Africa found that they had "much greater self discipline in regard to alcohol, drugs, pre or extra marital sex and life's other temptations" (Schlemmer 2008, 71). For men, conversion means giving up many of the activities that once formed their hegemonic masculinity. These include smoking, gambling, bonding with other men through drinking, and hetero-sexual sexual activity outside of marriage (Gill 1990; Austin-Broos 1997; Brusco 1995). For Pentecostals, transforming sexual and gen-der identities are one piece of the possibilities for becoming a new, better person through the born-again experience.

TWELVE-STEP IDEAS

Alcoholics Anonymous (AA) developed a global identity based on discourses of self-control and self-surveillance (Warhol 2002). Second-generation twelve-step recovery groups like Co-Dependents Anonymous and Sex Addicts Anonymous popularized ideas about dysfunctional families and explained the roots of addictions in child-hood trauma (Denzin and Johnson 1993). Twelve-step programs construct subjects who constantly evaluate and correct themselves. They believe that a new and better self emerges through suffering, sharing details of personal failures in a public forum, self-surveillance, and repeated confessionals to get rid of shame.

Twelve-step members discursively constitute new subjectivities through the construction, performance, and repetition of testimo-nies. Sociologist Nikolas Rose (1999 [1989], 244) writes: "In the act of speaking, through the obligation to produce words that are true to an inner reality, through the self-examination that precedes and accompanies speech, one becomes a subject for oneself." Subjectivity is not represented vis-à-vis testimonies, but is created through them. In his work on voluntary counselling and testing in faith-based orga-nizations in Burkina Faso, medical anthropologist and physician Vinh-Kim Nguyen (2009, 360) discusses how HIV positive people are taught a new vocabulary and framework to see and talk about themselves: "These confessional technologies, ostensibly used to help people 'come out' with their HIV positivity, in effect trained them to talk about their innermost selves in public." Although confession is often thought of as spontaneous outpouring of one's feelings and desires, it is also a form of learning that, like testimonies, assists in constructing the self.

Testimonies become more standardized over time, a well-noted phenomenon in twelve-step movements (e.g., Erzen 2006; Brandes 2002; Warhol 2002; Harding 2000). I also found this process in my research on ex-gay men, whose testimonies of recovery to heterosexuality became more uniform the longer they were involved in the ministry. The language ex-gay men used to describe themselves changed over time. Edwin, a twenty-four-year-old white Afrikaans man, shared his testimony with me soon after he joined the ministry. As a new ministry member, he had not yet been integrated into ministry discourse. He never employed ex-gay terms like "the lifestyle" (gay life), "same-sex attraction," or "homosexual tendencies." Instead, he discussed himself repeatedly as "gay," a term HRM frowned on because it refers to identity, not behaviour or desire.[10]

Besides the language they used to explain their desires, ex-gay men also framed their struggles differently after attending ministry classes, support groups, and counselling. HRM taught that homosexuality is an "intimacy disorder" and partly[11] results from not receiving proper emotional nurturance and gender socialization in childhood, particularly from fathers (Davies and Rentzel 1993). I noted that when men entered the ministry, they began their testimonies with an account of the first time they felt sexual desire for another man. Over time, they altered their testimonies to start with how their fathers did not emotionally connect with them in childhood, which led them to fill their "legitimate" emotional needs from childhood in "illegitimate" ways, through sexual activity with other men (HRM 2004).

Twelve-step discourses and healing methods travel globally, including to South Africa; people who follow them are unfamiliar with their lineage. Talk show hosts like Oprah Winfrey, who provided resources for healing through her choice of experts, audience participation, and the sharing of stories by guests, popularize twelve-step discourses for international audiences (Illouz 2003; Wilson 2003). HRM drew on self-help culture and shared with twelve-step groups like Alcoholic Anonymous the cultivation and care of the subject, strategies to use to become an ideal person, and a community to help with ethical formation.

HRM's founder, Brian, disavowed twelve-step ideology completely and claimed it is unchristian. However, I found that the ministry was flooded with twelve-step rhetoric and practices. Twelve-step ideas of "co-dependency," the "inner child," and "dysfunction" had the same definitions in the ministry, though terms were sometimes altered – for example, co-dependency was called relational idolatry. HRM used the popular discourses of the American recovery movement on self-esteem, self-worth, and learning how to grow. For example, at the end of one HRM leadership training session, everyone received a list of positive daily affirmations, such as "I am worthy of love." Participants were instructed to recite them in front of a mirror twice a day to increase self-esteem.

Practices like support groups and sponsors, who are called "accountability people," were common. There was also a focus on childhood as holding the key to the beginnings of dysfunction and poor self-image that later leads to poor sexual choices. HRM employed twelve-step language and methods in its program of change, and melded the twelve-step idea that the self can be improved with the Pentecostal belief that all things are possible after becoming born-again.

THE EFFECTS OF THE TRUTH
AND RECONCILIATION COMMISSION

The Truth and Reconciliation Commission (TRC) was a project of the democratically elected ANC government to heal the nation from the trauma of apartheid.[12] Full amnesty was granted to perpetrators of political violence if they publicly disclosed all the atrocities they had committed during National Party rule. The commission's stated intention was "to promote national unity and reconciliation in a spirit of understanding which transcends the conflicts and divisions of the past" (TRC 1999, 55). It tried to bring together perpetrators and victims of apartheid so that they would see themselves as new national subjects (Grunebaum 2011; Goodman 2009). Apartheid was argued to have hurt everyone – victims and perpetrators. The psychological idea that trauma is only healed through addressing the past was applied to the nation. Anthropologist Chris Colvin (2000, 160) explains: "The ground of the (new, healed) self – of the patient or of the nation – is understood to be constituted out of the mastering of a painful past."

There are three unintended effects of the TRC that are important to understand how HRM became culturally legible in the post-apartheid period. The first is how the Christian nature of the commission popularly linked trauma recovery with Christian discourse and practice. The TRC was explicitly Christian, with commissioners like Archbishop Desmond Tutu using theological language such as "redemption" (Tutu 1999). Christian rituals, especially prayers, began and ended all proceedings (Herwitz 2003). Christianity is a common language and world-view for many South Africans, so it made sense for the TRC to employ Christian discourses and practices.[13] Perpetrators' confessions of political violence and opportunities for forgiveness allowed them to be born again as members of the democratic nation. The TRC popularly linked Christianity and psychology in the healing process. Detailed confessions and pleas for forgiveness nationalized the healing process, and trauma became a recognizable psychological condition.

The second unintended effect of the TRC was that the popularization of apartheid trauma discourses led to their extension to other groups, such as survivors of rape, domestic violence, and crime. It also brought trauma discourses into popular consciousness. Although a national project, the discourses of the TRC had individual effects because of the ways they altered the boundaries of what could be discussed in public and provided new frameworks for understanding personal experiences of pain. Colvin (2008, 227) explains: "Since its early appearance in progressive mental health circles during apartheid, and its debut on the national stage with the TRC, the trauma discourse has since traveled more broadly in popular discourse and practice. It has moved out of the clinic and the TRC hearing, and into community healthcare clinics, police stations, newspaper articles and talk shows, and beyond." This process of extension is similar to what occurred in twelve-step groups, where AA's structure and language were applied to addictions other than alcohol, which led to an explosion of groups dealing with a variety of addictions.[14] HRM's use of trauma discourses and Christian recovery techniques begun by the TRC culturally normalized its work to uncover and heal trauma.

Third, the TRC changed the boundaries of what topics were acceptable to discuss in public. During apartheid, sex was a private matter and sexual violence had almost no public presence. Since the end of apartheid, discourses about sexuality and sexual violence have become more open due to the end of censorship, debates over gay rights, and high rates of HIV/AIDS (Posel 2011). The TRC was essential to a larger post-apartheid opening up of discourses about the secret and the hidden, which extended to the realms of sexuality and public discourse on sex. Sociologist Deborah Posel (2005) believes that in South Africa a "public confessional" has developed, where admissions of shame, trauma, and the exploitation of others are reconfigured as necessary to the ultimate redemption of the individual and the nation. The effects of the TRC can be seen now in the explosion of sex talk in the country by a variety of actors, including in churches and ministries such as HRM.

Detailed admissions of painful feelings and past actions as key to self-transformation added legitimacy to HRM's healing methods. For example, ministry members were expected to explore shameful experiences in depth, which frequently led to detailed descriptions of childhood abuse and sexual assault in testimonies. The ministry believed that without a detailed confession of all prior sinful activity, especially anything that involves sex, true and lasting healing would remain out of reach. To facilitate this process, it had specific worksheets to assist people in forming an exhaustive sexual history. The individual was asked to write down and explain behaviours such as masturbation and pornography use, and list the names, ages, and genders of all sexual partners.

The TRC's use of Christianity and the opening of sexual discourses post-apartheid, joined with the popularity of talk-therapy to heal trauma, situate ministry exercises like listing all sexual partners and activities in detail into larger cultural practices of confession and discussing sexual practices openly. Combined with the influence of twelve-step language and kinds of addiction, the details asked for on the intake form provide clues to how HRM was culturally legible.

EX-GAY HISTORIES

The ex-gay movement claims to "heal homosexuality through the power of Jesus Christ." It began in the 1970s in southern California, in response to larger conservative Christians' fears about the influence of feminism, gay rights, and other identity-based movements they saw as "taking over" America (Gerber 2011; Davies 1998). It is a montage of biblical inerrancy, self-help rhetoric, psychology, and science, and it links a variety of traumatic experiences from childhood and adolescence to the development of homosexual desire. These include failure to bond appropriately with the same gender parent, abuse, neglect, peer rejection, early exposure to pornography or sexual activity, and confusion about gender roles (Ankerberg and Weldon 1994; Moberly 1983). The non-profit ministry Exodus International was officially founded in 1976, and although marred by a number of scandals in the 1980s including the defection and then public love affair of two founders, it has continued to grow. There are ex-gay ministries on every continent except Antarctica. Exodus-affiliated ministries deal with a variety of named "sexual sins" and sexual dysfunction. These include homosexuality, masturbation, internet pornography use, prostitution, pedophilia, voyeurism, sado-masochism, and premarital and extramarital sex (Dallas and Heche 2009; Ankerberg and Weldon 1994). Internationally, such ministries share theologies and ideologies of "God's divine plan for heterosexuality," as well as ways of structuring and running their programs.

In 1992, a married couple in Johannesburg started Christian Uplift, the first ex-gay ministry in Africa.[15] Brian, an ex-gay white man from southern California, founded Healing Revelation Ministries in 1997 in the Western Cape as a satellite ministry of Christian Uplift. After spending his young adulthood in and out of jail for sexual assaults and pedophilia, Brian went to Switzerland, and then to Africa, as a missionary for Youth With a Mission.[16] HRM was "released" from Christian Uplift's authority in 2002 because of the male founder's "sexual fall," a sexual encounter with another man. In 2003, HRM became its own autonomous organization, which added to its credibility and reputation, though it closed in 2009.

HRM offered one-on-one counselling for men and women, as well as support groups and classes. The courses were all part of the "Life Matters Series: Ministering Into Relational and Sexual Brokenness." Classes came in a variety of forms and all offered a form of "freedom" from pre-conversion problems – freedom from addiction, from pain and anger, and from same-sex attraction. All the classes presented natal familial relations and childhood trauma as the root of later dysfunction. The development of co-dependency and shame appeared in most manuals because they are seen as an explanation for why many adults end up in bad relationships and have poor self-esteem. Biblical passages were used to reinforce psychological theories, and attendees at Life Matters courses, counselees, and ministry leaders were taught to see their pasts differently, re-reading life stages for key points of crisis and trauma.

In South Africa most ministry leaders were male, white, in their mid-twenties and early thirties, and did not have higher education. While the ministry leadership was made up of white and some coloured people, participants at HRM workshops, support groups, and lay counselling were white, coloured, and black. Like most ex-gay ministries around the world, men mostly populated HRM. The ministry believed that lesbianism is largely a problem of emotionally dependency and not sexual desire. HRM over-sexualized men and under-sexualized women as part of a larger Pentecostal view that naturalizes sexual differences. Evangelical and Pentecostal Christians believe that God made men to initiate and women to receive in all matters, including sex (e.g., Eldredge and Eldredge 2005; Eldredge 2001). They believe God designed women as "naturally" emotional and men as "naturally" sexual. The few self-identified lesbian women who entered the ministry felt like their voices and experiences were not heard and that there was no room for them to discuss female sexual desire. HRM leaders also thought that women should submit to men in all matters. Women's leadership and voices were silenced, including my own. The few women who became leaders throughout the years were such in name only and usually left HRM in frustration.

FAITH-BASED COUNSELLING

The TRC brought mental health professionals onto the national stage for the first time. During apartheid, therapy was inaccessible to almost all South Africans. Today, professional therapy still remains out of reach for most people because of its cost. Churches have stepped in to fill this void, continuing the work they did during apartheid in providing material, psychological, emotional, and spiritual resources to black and coloured South Africans (Tutu 1999; Borer 1998; Balia 1989).

The HIV/AIDS epidemic in the country and the government's unwillingness[17] and inability to meet the needs of its citizens have again brought religious-based organizations to the forefront of medical and psychological care (Burchardt 2009; Nguyen 2009). Christian counselling and support groups for people with HIV/AIDS are cultural convergences that contributed to making HRM's work culturally salient. HRM was one of many faith-based groups that offer counselling and support for sexual decision-making and its spiritual and physical effects.

Many churches provide voluntary counselling and testing. The Church of the Reborn had an AIDS Resource Centre and offered daily testing and pre- and post-testing counselling, both through drop-ins and by appointment. Its offices were next to HRM's in the church building and it frequently sent the people it categorized as "sexually broken" – anyone who was gay or it suspected had engaged in homosexual activity – to HRM's office for assistance. A white ex-gay HIV-positive leader also started an AIDS support group in 2007 at the church.

Faith-based counselling[18] is another method that South Africans use to understand disease, healing, and recovery. As with other methods, faith-based counselling is a bricolage of ideas from a variety of sources. It offers a unique mix of medical, religious, and psychological discourses and practices for transforming the self (Burchardt 2009). This is similar to what anthropologist Steve Robins found in what he calls "treatment testimonies," when people narrate changes in their subjectivities after learning of their HIV-positive status or beginning ARV treatment through the language of religious.conversion. Robins (2005, 1) writes: "Successful ARV treatment in South Africa continues to be described using quasi-religious phrases and narratives: 'the Lazarus effect,' 'God's gift of life,' *uvukile* ['he awoke' from near death] and so on." Faith-based counselling mixes a variety of spiritual and medical discourses in the same way as HRM, where it was impossible to draw a line between religion and psychology.

HRM's Christian counselling reproduced the TRC's ideas of trauma. Prayer and psychology merged in theory, discourse, and practice. However, who ultimately performed and maintained the healing differed between the two approaches. The focus in HRM was always ultimately on the real work being done by God and the Holy Spirit on each individual's heart. In this framework, healing comes from a willingness to be open to God's unconditional love. He is the one who emotionally heals the person, rather than the imagined national audience or society that bears witness through the TRC and so enables healing.

In HRM, participants learned how to review their lives and re-read situations for moments of crisis and trauma. The trauma that harmed the child can even occur while still in the mother's womb. One ex-gay coloured man in his early twenties told me that he thinks his "homosexual tendencies" began even before birth. His mother desperately wanted a girl, and he believes her desires impacted his gender identity. In his work on American Charismatic Catholics, anthropologist Thomas Csordas (2002, 5) also found that a belief in pre-birth trauma could have long-lasting spiritual effects: "In the Healing of

Memories an individual's entire life is prayed for in stages, from the moment of conception to the present."[19]

Ministry classes asked participants to look for what they called "root memories," frequently repressed abusive and humiliating experiences from childhood that they believe led to the development of homosexuality. To heal these memories and the inner child who experienced them, Christ needs to be invited into the memory itself after it is recalled in a "safe space" (Payne 1995 [1985]). The person is supposed to welcome Jesus into the traumatic memory and reimagine it with Him there, offering comfort and love.

For Christians, God can move back and forth in time. He can go into one's past and heal pain. The solution for healing trauma in Christian psychology, which HRM practiced, is the same as the healing from trauma that the TRC process popularized. The "talking cure," combined with realigning the self with knowing that the painful past is over, was the same in both. Root memories, the repressed traumatic memories discussed above, are the key to healing. Christian author Leanne Payne (1995, 20) writes: "In order that his deepest mind and heart might fully participate in this yielding, I asked him to picture with eyes closed Christ on the Cross, dying to take those very sins and sicknesses into Himself."

According to HRM theologies, Christ heals the inner child in the root memory in order for the adult to move on. In an October 2008 "Life Matters for the Family" class, white Afrikaans ex-gay leader Coenraad gave his testimony. He shared his own root memory, only remembered in his late twenties. God "revealed" to him through prayer that his same-sex desires stemmed from a "traumatic experience" with his mother. His parents decided to have him circumcised, which is not the norm in Afrikaner communities. While Coenraad was still healing from the procedure, a few family members came over and asked about his health. His mother suddenly pulled his pants and underwear down in front of the other adults and humiliated him. Coenraad said that God was healing his trauma and the resulting same-sex attraction. He encouraged others to be hopeful for their own healing. "God lives outside of time," he shared, and "can heal pains from a long time ago and seal it with a prayer."

Damon, another long-time HRM leader, recounted his own experience with Christian methods of healing during a Christian sex addicts support group he attended with other ex-gay men. A coloured man in his early thirties, he was four years old when family and neighbours began to sexually abuse him. This abuse went on throughout his childhood and Damon attempted suicide multiple times. He believed that Brian, HRM's founder, saved his sanity and life. Damon felt he made progress through Christian counselling and group process. However, he was not ready for what happened when he was repeatedly pushed by two leaders to describe his child-hood abuse in detail to the support group to reconnect with his root memory. He refused multiple times, and the leaders said he needed to remember these painful feelings in order to heal. Damon says he can tell what happened to him matter-of-factly in a detached way, but he did not feel safe remembering the experience of multiple abusive situations.

One leader instructed Damon to imagine that he was the one of the men who had abused him as a child. The process became too much for Damon and he blacked out. He does not remember trying to harm anyone, but was told afterwards that he almost hit the leader with a chair, which he smashed into pieces. The next day he called to apologize, thinking he was going to be asked to leave the support group. The leader told him that he was not angry and that it was obvious that God wanted him to release that pain and anger. Damon told me sadly after recounting the story, "Jesus still has a lot more work to do in my life." Ex-gay South Africans were one group out of many working to transform their subjectivities through meth-ods that merge psychology, science, and Christianity.

CONCLUSION

Ex-gay South African men are part of larger shifts in sexual subjec-tivity throughout sub-Saharan Africa (e.g., Tamale 2011; Morgan, Marais, and Wellbeloved 2009; and this volume). HRM employed discourses and technologies that were a unique mixture of psychol-ogy, twelve-step groups, Christian counselling, and self-help. These included getting people to work through the stages of grief, dis-course about healing one's "inner child," and technologies like group therapy, counselling, and behaviour modification. The emergence of an ex-gay identity in Cape Town was part of a cultural shift in focus on an agentive sexualized self in a national context where ideas about trauma, healing, and forming an improved subjectivity were popularized through the intersecting discourses of twelve-step ideas, the effects of the TRC, faith-based counselling, and transnational Pentecostalism. Despite opposing South Africa's constitutional protection of gay individuals, HRM flourished in democratic South Africa because it used and refashioned a variety of post-apartheid discourses on healing and sexuality.

7

The (Mis)Treatment of South African Track Star Caster Semenya

SHARI L. DWORKIN, AMANDA LOCK SWARR, AND CHERYL COOKY

On 19 August 2009, eighteen-year-old Caster Semenya from rural Limpopo, South Africa, won the gold medal in the women's 800-metre race at the World Track and Field championships in Berlin. On the day she won, the International Association of Athletics Federation (IAAF) ordered her to undergo "gender verification" testing; the IAAF and other female runners were suspicious of Caster Semenya's "rapid performance improvements." In addition, media reports described Semenya with "suspicion" given her "masculine build," "dominant performance," "deep voice," and "man-like style of running." The IAAF stated that the results of the gender verification test would determine if Semenya would be allowed to race as a woman in future competitions.

Shortly thereafter, the African National Congress (ANC) and the National Assembly Sports Committee Chairman lodged a complaint with the United Nations Human Rights Council, accusing the IAAF of racism and sexism. In November 2009, the IAAF reported that Semenya would keep her gold medal and that the results of the gender verification tests were a "private matter" between her and her doctor. In a statement released by her lawyers, she said, "I am thrilled to enter the global athletics arena once again and look forward to competing with all the disputes behind me." The IAAF cleared Semenya to compete in women's track and field competition in July 2010. She won a silver medal at the 2012 summer Olympics, and carried the South African flag in the opening ceremonies.

Since 2009, a series of events surrounding the treatment of Caster Semenya has resulted in a supportive national response to a female athlete believed to be intersexed, a category that could have disqualified her from international sport competitions. In this chapter, we examine why South Africa was the first country to stand up to international sporting bodies concerning the treatment of female athletes believed to be intersexed, placing these events in the context of southern Africa and colonial histories. We focus on groups invested in this controversy, including government officials, Semenya's family members, youth leaders, sports officials, and activists. We articulate gender, race, and class relations in sport within colonial, apartheid, and transitional South Africa and the region as integral to Semenya's treatment. Explicating the stances that groups invested in this controversy held within South Africa, we focus on the commentary of those who challenged efforts to disqualify Caster Semenya from women's sports competition. We articulate gender as a means through which claims about race and nation are made and discuss the theoretical implications of gender's obfuscation.

We are conscious of our positions as white United States-based academics writing about someone who has been extensively objectified. Keguro Macharia (*Gukira*, 20 September 2009) articulates the complexities and unease that come with addressing Semenya's treatment:

> It is difficult to write on Caster Semenya. It is difficult because it participates in an ongoing spectacularization that, at this time, could probably not have been handled better. I write this not simply to be perverse, to go against the many people who claim it could have been handled better, but because I think it exposes real fissures in the communities to which, for better and worse, I belong to and study – what the particular combination produces continues to be a source of personal anxiety and intellectual excitement. Arguably, those who can best speak to Semenya's situation are queer scholars. Yet, this group might also be the least suitable, and this is due to issues of race, nationality, and history. What does it mean when predominantly non-Africa based scholars who work on gender and history speak to an African cause?

As Macharia points out, ambivalence about Semenya's multiple allegiances and those who use her to support their own initiatives have

made her representation contentious. She occupies a complex position on the world stage as an athlete in the midst of transnational
debates about what constitutes sex. Both Macharia and Brenna
Munro argue: "The Semenya affair (and I too prefer "affair" to
"case"), and particularly Semenya's body, has been made a case of
too many things – mistaken identity, unfair advantage, impossible
being – by many combatants in the debate who display little awareness of the history of the scientific gaze on the gendered and sexualized body for, at least, the last three hundred years" (via Hoad 2010,
398). It is with careful awareness of these intricacies, and with efforts
to avoid either objectifying Semenya's liminal position or "reinforcing a narrative of South Africa as a 'tragic, hopeless scene of gender
trouble'" (Munro 2010, 384) that we begin this chapter.

GENDER INEQUALITY AND DIFFERENCE IN SPORT

Sport has played a major role in bolstering conceptions of dichotomous natural differences between women and men (Cahn 1994;
Dworkin and Wachs 2009; Messner 2002; Travers 2008), and generally reaffirms the "assumption that there are two, and only two,
obviously universal, bipolar, mutually exclusive sexes that necessarily correspond to stable gender identity and gendered behavior"
(Birrell and Cole 1990, 3). The fact that women and men are often
sport-typed into different activities that are exclusively or predominantly divided by gender helps to reaffirm assumptions of natural
male superiority and female inferiority (Kane 1995; Sullivan 2011).
Feminist scholars have long shown how female athletes who display
superior athleticism frequently face accusations that they are not "real
women," not "real females," are masculinized, are accused of lesbianism, or are even recast as men (Cooky, Dycus, and Dworkin 2012;
Kane 1995; Cahn 1994). This link between athleticism and masculinity becomes institutionalized through sex testing/gender verification policies of international and national governing bodies of sport,
given the tests are only carried out on female athletes (Davis and
Delano 1992; Dworkin and Cooky 2012).

The resulting practice of gender verification ignores the overlap-
ping continuum of muscles, genes, and hormones by gender while
gate-keeping the ideological boundaries of categorical gender difference (Cavanagh and Sykes 2006; Kane 1995; Wackwitz 2003).
Gender verification relies on the assumption that there are two, and

only two, sexes: male and female (Cooky, Dycus, and Dworkin 2012; Karkazis et al. 2012; Ritchie 2003). The link between athleticism and masculinity is based on a historically and contextually specific set of gendered proscriptions and beliefs about women's bodies (Dworkin and Wachs 2009; Messner 2002) and raced assumptions about women's labour and athleticism.

Mandatory sex testing of women athletes began at the 1968 Olympics. The International Olympic Committee (IOC) used a procedure called the buccal smear, wherein test administrators scraped the inside of an athlete's cheek for chromosomal evaluation. Prior to this, physical inspection or gynaecological examination of female athletes was conducted to verify the sex of competitors (Dickenson et al. 2002). The main claim behind sex testing is that men might "masquerade" as women in sport and prevent a level playing field for women who compete. The most frequently cited case used by sport organizations to rationalize gender "verification" of female athletes occurred during the 1936 Berlin Olympics, when Nazi Germany forced Herman (Dora) Ratjen to compete in the women's high jump event disguised as a woman. This incident, along with suspicions regarding the sex/gender of Soviet Union and East German female athletes during the 1950s and early 1960s, provided a veneer of legitimacy for the IOC's policy (Cahn 1994; Sykes 2006). Other than the case of "Dora," sex testing has not exposed any cisgender male athletes trying to pass as women, and many scholars note the lack of scientific veracity associated with gender verification testing (for a discussion see Cooky, Dycus, and Dworkin 2012). Numerous groups, including biomedical scientists, feminist scholars, women's sports advocates, and former athletes, have denounced sex testing for its lack of scientific credibility (Cavanagh and Sykes 2006; Cole 2000; Sullivan 2011; Teetzel 2006), and by 2000, most international sports federations had abandoned routine gender verification testing (Reeser 2005). Although the tests are no longer mandatory, according to the IAAF's *Policy on Gender Verification* published in 2006, the IAAF conducts gender verification tests under certain conditions, including if another athlete or team raises a "challenge" or if a suspicion is raised during anti-doping controls.

Caster Semenya is one of many female athletes required to undergo "gender verification" testing (in this case as a result of the IAAF's 2006 policy on gender verification) as questions regarding her "true womanhood" were made public. While female athletes from around the globe have been subject to such testing (Cavanagh and Sykes 2006; Cole 2000; Cooky and Dworkin in press; Fausto-Sterling 2000; Teetzel 2006), there has been a notable absence of athletes from the Global North subjected to these testing procedures, which reveals how the politics of nationalism, gender, race, and power among countries and regions are inseparable from the politics of sport (Booth, Cantelon, and McDermott 1993; Cole 2000; Cavanagh and Sykes 2006; Cooky, Dycus, and Dworkin 2012; Hargreaves 2000; Smith 2006). The tests to "confirm femaleness" or to "verify gender" (whether these are instituted on those classified as intersexed or those who identify as female or transsexuals in sport) rest on the assumption that superior athletic performances are a natural essence of cisgender males (Dworkin and Cooky 2012; Sullivan 2011).

RACING AND CLASSING GENDER AND NATIONAL RELATIONS IN SOUTH AFRICAN SPORT

The intersections of race, class, and gender relations and sport are critical when considering Semenya's treatment in this controversy. Government involvement in sport is widespread, and the role of sport in nation building cannot be underestimated in contemporary South Africa (Hargreaves 2000; Pelak 2010). In apartheid South Africa, the ruling National Party had a segregated sports policy and a diverse set of laws and regulations that limited involvement in sport to those legally designated as white, a policy that excluded South Africa from the Olympics for decades (Hargreaves 1997; 2000). During the apartheid period, references to gender and to women's involvement in sport were minimal, and very few black women enjoyed an opportunity to participate (Hargreaves 1997; Pelak 2010). This does not mean that women were not involved in sport; rather, sport was organized around highly gendered and racialized arrangements. Once South Africa was allowed back into the Olympics in 1991, black African women in sport faced significant financial and access barriers (Hargreaves 1997; 2000). During the 1992 Barcelona Olympics, the only South African woman to win a medal, Elana Meyer, was classified as white. Earlier, when South Africa had been banned from events, white athlete Zola Budd fled South Africa with a British passport and competed elsewhere, an option unavailable to black or coloured women that incited political controversy (Hargreaves 1997; 2000).

When apartheid officially ended in 1994, Nelson Mandela "brilliantly appropriated the Springbok emblem [in rugby] and transformed it from a symbol of white superiority to one of national unity," and sport was positioned as a means to bring together South Africans in the transitional period and beyond (Hargreaves 2000, 29). Since the official end of apartheid, sporting opportunities for black South Africans have improved; however, large disparities in resources, pay, media coverage, opportunities, and treatment based on gender, race, and class still exist. Most sporting opportunities are disproportionately located in urban areas, and both residential segregation and poverty in rural areas and informal settlements are deep and long lasting (Hargreaves 2000).

Within a context of apartheid politics and histories – and given the role that sport played in nation-building in South Africa's transition, along with the role that women have played in unifying nationalism with sport – track star Caster Semenya was viewed as a crucially important South African icon. She was the first black South African woman to win a gold medal at an IAAF World Championship in 2009 and, given her upbringing in a rural village in Limpopo, her success was seen as emblematic of the ascendency of the "new" South Africa. Her accomplishments – and many South Africans' overwhelmingly negative response to her gender verification testing – are contingent on this national history. The response of government officials in South Africa to Semenya's testing also cannot be understood without an examination of changing notions of race, gender, and sexuality in the country more broadly.

South Africa has undergone numerous shifts in the last several decades, including the formal end of apartheid, an emerging democratic system with a ground-breaking constitution, unsettling long-held racial divisions, and strong attempts to redress past inequities (Banda 2005). Notably, in 1996, South Africa became the first country in the world to offer constitutional protection on the basis of sexual orientation. This achievement was "largely due to the ability of a male-dominated gay rights movement to form strategic alliances with the anti-apartheid struggle, to mobilise the master narrative of equality and non-discrimination and to lobby effectively during the constitution-making process" (Cock 2005, 188–9). The collaboration during this transitional period resulted in an integration of sexuality into the ethos of human rights. Simultaneously, backlash against improving rights, combined with the failed promises of the

new South Africa, contributed to significant increases in homophobic violence, including murders and rapes intended to punish lesbians for their perceived gendered and sexual transgressions (Reid and
Dirsuweit 2002; Ratele 2011; Lahiri 2011; Swarr 2012). We will
return to these factors below.

SOUTH AFRICAN SUPPORT FOR "OUR FIRST LADY OF SPORT"

Following these histories, many of those who supported Semenya
either deployed gender modalities of "true womanhood" to defend
South Africa against a perceived racist assault or drew on regional
cultures of human rights to assert claims about race and nation. A
diverse group of South Africans challenged how Semenya was
treated and whether gender verification tests should determine
whether she could continue to compete. Underscoring the central
role that sport plays in the production of nationalism – and the role
of femininity in bolstering it – Semenya returned home and was
greeted with supportive crowds who cheered, claimed Semenya as
"our first lady of sport," and waved "our girl" posters (*Mail and
Guardian*, 24 August 2009). News reports underscored that the
numerous groups, including the ANC Youth League and Women's
League, would "be there to welcome her. There are going to be mobs
of people at the airport" (*Mail and Guardian*, 24 August 2009).
Historian Pamela Scully (*Defenders Online*, 16 July 2010) stated:
"South African responses have been almost uniformly supportive of
Caster Semenya, with little attention being given in the public to the
question of her gender. In some respects, popular culture treated the
handwringing over Semenya's gender identity as a non-issue."

Referred to as a "teenage heroine," Limpopo authorities reportedly treated Semenya as a national icon. To further indicate the
importance of links among sport, femininity, and nationalism, Sports
Minister Makhenkesi Stofile said if Semenya were stripped of her
gold and disqualified from future sporting events, "it would be the
Third World War" (ABC *News*, 12 September 2009, emphasis
added). He further suggested: "We would go to the highest levels in
contesting such a decision" (*Afrik-News*, 12 September 2009). In his
and others' views, Semenya "is a woman, she remains our heroine.
We must protect her." Indeed, South African leadership made clear
that in protecting Semenya, they were defending South Africa, and

defending South Africa(ns) from accusations of gender ambiguity (Cooky, Dycus, and Dworkin 2012).

The positions of two important political leaders provide the most striking examples of Semenya's elevation to national heroine in the face of South African histories of discrimination. President Jacob Zuma commented that Semenya's treatment "was started deliberately to cause a kind of confusion and dampen the spirits of the country unnecessarily" (*Mail and Guardian*, 25 August 2009). Zuma's support of Semenya contrasted his repeatedly stated positions against gender liminality and same-sex sexuality, which suggested that he participated in violence against gay men in his youth, not to mention the public and vitriolic trial that surrounded his alleged rape of "Khwezi" – an HIV-positive family friend who identifies as a lesbian. The former first lady of South Africa, Winnie Madikizela-Mandela, also strongly defended Semenya and had been involved in public homophobic actions (Holmes 1997). As Neville Hoad (2010, 404) writes: "The historical ironies of Winnie Madikizela-Mandela defending Semenya as a 'hermaphrodite' ('There is nothing wrong with being a hermaphrodite. It is God's creation. She is God's child. She did not make herself. God decided to make her in a way that can't be held against her.') are most extraordinary, given Madikizela-Mandela's participation in arguably the most homophobic political trial in recent South African history." While the juxtaposition of Zuma and Madikizela-Mandela's support of Semenya with their overt homophobia can be seen as duplicitous, it indicates significant differences between Semenya and other South Africans in gender liminal positions. In 2009, the newly designated first lady of sport led both the president and the former first lady of South Africa, "two such powerful political figures, who have been associated with homophobia in the past, [to align] themselves in defense of this gender-queer girl – saying firmly that she has rights, that she belongs, and that she *represents* South Africa" (Munro 2010, 393).

Some scholars interpreted this support of Semenya as a sign of increasing acceptance of gender liminality in South Africa (*Sunday Times*, 30 August 2009; Munro 2010). But as South African gender activists point out, "there was a concerted effort to normalize and feminize Ms Semenya, to turn her into a "proper symbol of national honour and pride" (Gender DynamiX, 27 October 2009), which was particularly notable in the tense climate of increased legislation against homosexuality in the region. In some ways, this tension represents South Africa's struggle with exceptionalism; the nation stands alone in its progressive constitutional policies, yet is also instantiated in the region and implicitly responsive to dismissals of homosexuality as "un-African," with a gendered twist.

Semenya could not remain in the category of heroine without being seen as an appropriate symbol of femininity, and hence efforts to recast her as more feminine were made. No efforts were more striking than a makeover featured on the front cover of South African *You* and its counterparts *Huisgenoot* and *Drum*, three magazines with the highest circulations in the country. *You* read: "Exclusive: We turn SA's power girl into a glamour girl and she loves it!" (*Mail and Guardian*, 8 September 2009). As interlocutors such as Antje Schuhmann note: "The constant reiteration that she is a woman, and support for her assumed that her treatment is unfair to a woman ... reinforces the same binary that is the cause of the problem: men have to be men and women have to be women" (*Mail and Guardian*, 21 August 2009).

Furthermore, the *You* magazine spread was not only gendered, but also a graphic assimilation of Semenya into a femininity that is distinctly based in the Global North and that erases her ethnicity. As Neville Hoad (2010, 402) points out: "There is nothing in the [*You* cover] image that could remotely signify Sepedi. The image is that of a thoroughly Westernized young woman – from power girl to glamour girl, indeed." However, it is important to avoid reading Semenya's representation in this image against expectations of Pedi identity as inherently "traditional." Transnational processes have long undermined the idea that there is one way to be Pedi and that ethnic markers are easily read. Perhaps, instead, this image did not omit Semenya's Pedi identity, but drew on complex black femininities in South Africa that are acutely classed and being refigured in the contemporary moment.

South Africans within the government, along with Semenya's fans, family, and friends, took great pains to state that she was not intersexed (or, "hermaphroditic" as media reported, a term with medical aetiology that is largely considered offensive), but rather was unquestionably a woman. Signs that welcomed Semenya at the airport read, "Our Girl" and "100 percent female woman" (*Mail and Guardian*, 24 August 2009). Her father was quoted as stating: "I raised her and I never doubted her gender. She is a woman and I can repeat that a

million times" (*Sowetan*, 20 August 2009). Others similarly reiter-
ated Semenya's incontrovertible femaleness; the head of Athletics
South Africa said: "I can assure you that Caster is a woman as far as
we are concerned" (*Sowetan*, 5 October 2009). As the ANC Youth
President reported, "these allegations about her being a hermaphrodite are unfounded. In our culture there's nothing like that. Even the
Home Affairs Department recognizes peoples as male or female"
(*Eye Witness News*, 1 October 2009). The suggestion of cultural
nonexistence, again, places the argument about Semenya's gender in
the regional context of political dismissals of homosexuality and
gender liminality.

However, the South African Home Affairs Department and other
government bodies are bound to the equality clause, which, after the
work of intersex activist Sally Gross, was amended in 2006 to
include *intersex* as "a congenital sexual differentiation which is
atypical, to whatever degree" as part of the meaning of sex (*Mail
and Guardian*, 19 September 2009). Similar to histories of African
same-sex sexuality, local governments' resistance to the idea of the
existence of intersexed individuals has often been interpreted as
regressive or uneducated. However, these histories are difficult to
unpack, given that African resistance to Northern ideals has also
been rooted in the imposition of medical definitions (such as "hermaphrodite") and the intentional pathologizing of black bodies
under colonial rule (Magubane 2004; Swarr 2009). Perhaps, as
Neville Hoad (2010, 402) cogently puts it: "The question of why the
existence of an intersexed African body must be read as racial insult
by cultural nativism can be explained by the persistence of colonial
histories."

RACISM, COLONIAL SCIENCE, EUROCENTRIC FEMININITY

One important component of Semenya's warm reception in South
Africa, according to media reports, was claims that gender verification testing was consistent with "European racism and imperialism"
and that Semenya therefore "seems assured of a special welcome from
family and friends who have never sat in judgment on her nature"
(*Mail and Guardian*, 2 September 2009). This warm welcome contrasted what many perceived as racist international media and medical communities. Indeed, individuals and groups that supported
Semenya, such as the Young Communist League, the chairperson of

Parliamentary Sports Committee, the head of the South African Track Federation, the South African Football Players Union, and the African National Congress youth leader, framed the handling of the case as reminiscent of racism during the colonial apartheid eras. News reports in South Africa made clear that Semenya's treatment paralleled a painful history of racist "pencil tests," where pencils were placed in hair during apartheid supposedly to resolve racial ambiguity (Dubow 1995).

There is strong reason for South African distrust of science and medicine. Indeed, scientific racism in South Africa defined the boundaries of race with subjective measures such as the texture of one's hair and the shape and size of one's skull (Dubow 1995). Perhaps even more disturbing were reports of medical experimentation on South Africans documented by the Truth and Reconciliation Commission (see Reddy et al. this volume). Within this context, contemporary news reports from South Africa made clear that Northern science should not be trusted and also challenged the validity of the tests by asking "whether the overwhelming evidence of Caster's life as a girl in South Africa does not count as science" (*Mail and Guardian*, 25 August 2009).

In addition, the president of the South African Track Federation, Leonard Cheune, alleged that sex verification testing was consistent with a history of "European imperialism," and "it would not be like this if it were some young girl from Europe" (*Mail and Guardian*, 22 August 2009). Several other media reports implied that Semenya was under such scrutiny because whites do not want black South Africans to excel. The chairperson of a parliamentary sports committee, Butana Komphela, said, "Just because she is black and she surpassed her European competitors, there is all this uproar" (*Telegraph*, 2 August 2009), while the South African minister of social development agreed, "These unfounded claims were perpetrated by fellow women [European] competitors who lost out in the race" (*Mail and Guardian*, 26 August 2009).

South Africans' angry responses to critical comments from European competitors were clearly justified. Carina Ray (2009, 18) explains: "The immediate effect of the news was evident in the nasty statements her competitors made about [Semenya]: Italy's Elisa Cusma Piccione called Semenya a man, while Russia's Mariya Savinova admonished journalists to 'just look at her.'" Put in this context, Leonard Cheune's declaration, "We are not going to allow Europeans to describe and

defeat our children" (*Mail and Guardian*, 26 August 2009) is arguably a reasonable defence given these circumstances.

Physical examinations required by the IAAF sparked particular
outrage and were viewed as shameful humiliations for anyone to
experience. Chuene stated that Semenya was "angry and humiliated" by the tests and that "her feet were in stirrups" and pictures of
her genitals were taken (*Mail and Guardian*, 20 August 2009). The
Mail and Guardian (20 August 2009) reported that Semenya was
"bitterly upset" when these photographs were taken. Such photographs were eerily reminiscent of colonial photography of South
African black women's genitals, study, and objectification (Butchart
1998; Davison 1993; Hayes 1996). In this vein, academics, activists,
and journalists alike paralleled the treatment of Semenya with that
of Sara/Saartjie Baartman, the well-known nineteenth-century
Khoisan woman who was sexualized, objectified, and exhibited
throughout Europe as the "Hottentot Venus," a project of scientific
racism that rendered African women's black bodies as "primitive"
(Chase-Riboud 2003; Gilman 1995; Magubane 2001). Ray (2009,
19) for instance, discusses the "shared ways in which their Black
bodies have become public spectacles and (mis)treated as anatomic
curiosities that deserve neither respect nor dignity." Further, as Swarr
(2009) points out, attention to Baartman's genitals could position
her as intersexed – between "normal" conceptions of maleness and
femaleness – given examination and discussion of her genitals by
scientists and observers.

SEXISM, FEMALE FRAILTY, AND INTERSEX CHALLENGES

In addition to drawing on ideologies of true womanhood to defend
South Africa, some political groups argued that Semenya's treatment
firmly reflected sexism in sport. The ANC Women's League stated that
questions about Semenya's gender "suggest that women can only perform to a certain level and that those who exceed this level should be
men" (Bryson 2009; *Mail and Guardian*, 22 August 2009). Julius
Malema, then ANC Youth League president, stated: "The media who
wanted to plant a seed that there was something questionable regarding her gender, including the IAAF earlier this year are undermining all
women of South Africa" (*Mail and Guardian*, 20 August 2009). These
types of statements reflect the growing acceptance of gender equality
and women's rights in the post-apartheid period in South Africa.

In addition to the claim that Semenya's treatment led to unfair gender stereotypes of women or women's athletic performances, several politicians argued that her privacy and gendered rights were violated. President Jacob Zuma weighed in on the events facing the eighteen-year-old track star in this vein, stating: "Miss Semenya had also reminded the world of the importance of the right to human dignity and privacy, which should be enjoyed by all human beings" (*Radio France Internationale*, 25 August 2009). Semenya's positioning as a woman, and even infantilization, in many articles is critical to her valorization as a national symbol, but it also points to South Africa's national reputation as a proponent for human rights. Further, the ANC and the National Assembly Sports Committee chairman lodged a complaint with the United Nations Human Rights Council, accusing the IAAF of racism and sexism. Minister Mayende-Sibiya argued to the UN Division on the Advancement of Women (DAW, headed by Carolyn Hannan) that the Semenya incident violated at least three international commitments governed by the UN on protection and promotion of rights of women.

A few groups addressed Semenya's treatment through the frameworks of both intersex rights and gender rights more broadly. Despite the advances in sexuality and women's rights within South African law and the 1996 South African Constitution, those who express gender liminality have had few advocates. However, as a result of the efforts of Intersex South Africa, the Triangle Project in Cape Town, and other invested individuals, significant legal changes now protect intersexed people. In 2005, activists pushed forward legislation to protect intersex people from discrimination. Intersex South Africa used the media attention given to Semenya's case to publicize, ground, and actualize this important legal change in intersex South Africans' lives. As Gross queried: "Caster was classified at birth as a female and has lived as a female. If she is intersexed, so what?" (*Mail and Guardian*, 31 August 2009). Indeed, others linked the Semenya controversy to the rights of intersex individuals. For instance, ANC spokesperson Jackson Mthembu stated that Caster Semenya "would not be alone to fight this matter" and that South Africa would mobilize civil society, the government, corporate South Africa, and the sport fraternity not only in support of Semenya, "but also to ascertain the prevalence of intersex people in the country and how this should be addressed" (*Mail and Guardian*, 5 October 2009). Such statements reveal an opening for a potentially productive public dialogue about the needs of intersexed people within sport and beyond.

The first organization on the African continent to centrally address transgender issues, Gender DynamiX, has similarly drawn on a rights-based approach to contextualize intersex status and Semenya's treatment in terms of broader gender rights. Gender DynamiX extends the arguments of most organizations that oppose gender violence and expands definitions of "violence" to include Semenya's treatment. In a public statement in 2009, Gender DynamiX linked the documented murders and rapes of black lesbians in South Africa's townships, often related to their perceived gender transgressions and butch identities, to fears for Semenya's safety. The group noted that as a woman gaining public unwanted attention for her sex/gender identity, the media and the sport governing bodies that facilitated her gender testing potentially expose Semenya to the violence black lesbians face in their daily lives (Gender DynamiX, 2 October 2009, 13 September 2009; Swarr 2012).

In the claims described above, including those by South African feminists, Gender DynamiX, Intersex South Africa, and others, defending Semenya raised broader issues of racial and gender equality in sport and society. One source reported: "It behoves the IAAF to introduce and recognize a third gender category in order for the talented 18-year-old athlete as well as numerous other women who will certainly be found with high testosterone levels to compete in future competitions" (*Afrik-News*, 12 September 2009). However, while moving beyond gender binaries is imperative, as Towle and Morgan (2002) and many others have pointed out, "third gender" categories continue to rely on a dichotomous gender binary and such terminology belies colonial and objectifying histories. South African activists are not simply asserting the importance of women's rights or gender rights; instead, they are arguing for the importance of recognizing a continuum, and entirely reconfiguring notions, of sex and gender. This conceptual move might yield more promising results for athletes such as Semenya. However, stances on intersex rights (or even recognition of a gendered continuum) remain at odds with the ways in which sport has been organized in both the past and present, as it asserts there are two sexes and that separating them ensures "fair competition" (Cooky, Dycus, and Dworkin 2012; Dworkin and Cooky 2012; Vannini and Fornsller 2011; Sullivan 2011).

SEMENYA'S PERSPECTIVES

Prior to her return to competition at the 2012 Olympic Games, Semenya's voice was largely absent from these conversations, not because she had nothing to say, but because she was so peripheral in both American and South African media coverage. Only a few media reports noted Semenya's anxiety regarding her mistreatment by the IAAF and her exclusion, at the time, from sport. Her sudden rise as a household name necessitated protection from a bodyguard. Semenya explained her experience: "People want to stare at me, to touch me. I don't think I like being famous so much" (*Guardian*, 14 November 2009). She has also talked publically about her gender expression. Semenya was quoted in *You* magazine saying that the gender controversy around her is a "joke" and that "it doesn't upset me. God made the way I am and I accept myself. I am who I am and I'm proud of myself." In the same article, she stated: "I'd like to dress up more often and wear dresses but I never get the chance. I'd also like to learn to do my own makeup. Now that I know what I can look like, I'd like to dress like this more often" (*Guardian*, 7 September 2009). While some have been critical of Semenya's feminization in *You*, she has clearly articulated her views. What she said and how she was treated, particularly in the media reports in the Global North, have material implications; for example, her perceived gender liminality has impacted her ability to gain and retain corporate sponsorships and economic funding for her training. Although South African politicians supported Semenya's family by building her a new home, not everyone was supportive. One article claimed that she had turned to Facebook to try to raise money for her career; as her manager explains: "Companies have said there is a lot of uncertainty about Caster. They have said, 'We can't touch her'" (*Daily Nation*, 31 October 2010).

Of the few media reports that discussed Semenya's perspective or experience, most focused more on her emotional state than on her sport performances or the social complexities associated with the controversy. At times she is presented as traumatized by her treatment and willing to give up her career: "For me, running is nothing. Honestly, it's nothing" (*Guardian*, 21 April 2010). At other times, she is presented as ready to move on, stating that she does not want to talk about the past and simply wants to push forward. These reports underscore the impact of the long-lasting processes of the IAAF on her career. The investigations, as Semenya explained, "have dragged on too long with no reasonable certainty as to their end. The result is that my athletic capabilities and earning potential are being severely compromised" (*Guardian*, 30 March 2010). In the same statement, Semenya announced her comeback to athletic competition beginning in July 2010. She went on to win the silver medal in the women's 800-metre race at the 2012 Olympics. Some suggest that Semenya may have been subject to "feminizing treatment" before the Olympics; here, media reports highlighted her voice: "Treatment? Why should I have treatment? What is the reality of this situation?" (*Universal Sports*, 28 January 2011). Similarly, why was Semenya largely excluded from conversations about her own experiences and body?

Many ostensibly spoke on behalf of Semenya, often through gender protectionist discourse or nationalist rhetoric, and these positions clearly failed to consider the broader context wherein racism and accusations of Eurocentricism obfuscate gendered forms of discrimination and oppression. Semenya's voice, albeit silenced and managed, provides a window into how the sex/gender binary is reproduced and upheld through sport organizations' policies, which created a legitimized context that enabled discrimination against Semenya. In the bigger picture, suspicions about Semenya's sex were given more attention than her view of herself or of the controversy. Gender verification policies, and the implications of such policies on Semenya, maintained gender injustice in sport (Cooky, Dycus, and Dworkin 2012; Cooper 2010; Dworkin and Cooky 2012; Sullivan 2011) and athletes themselves are lost in these discussions.

COMPARISONS AND CONCLUSIONS

While Semenya faced gender verification testing and accusations and finally returned home to a national celebration, four men accused of murdering Eudy Simelane were on trial in South Africa. Also a prominent sports figure, Simelane had been a member of the South Africa national women's soccer team, Banyana Banyana. She was the first woman in KwaThema, her hometown, to self-identify as a lesbian. On 28 April 2008, Simelane was gang-raped and murdered, part of an increase in "corrective rape" in South Africa targeting lesbians. As Mark Gevisser wrote at the time: "Two highly accomplished, young, black, female South African athletes are currently in the news. One came home to a hero's welcome and got to meet the president. The other is dead, her alleged assailants in a Delmas court this week on trial for her rape and murder" (*Sunday Times*, 30 August 2009). Why was Semenya taken up as a national (and international) hero, while Simelane was marginalized?

Much of the celebration of Semenya rested on claims of her femininity and youth; as Winnie Madikizela-Mandela put it, "she's our girl." Gevisser asks if, "given the explicitly paternalistic tone of her support – 'that girl,' 'our child' – is it predicated on her remaining shy and deferential off the field?" (*Sunday Times*, 30 August 2009). Even when Semenya's potential intersex status was acknowledged, it was positioned as something she could not prevent, a medical "defect." By contrast, Simelane's gender liminality as an out butch lesbian was much less "innocent." Public debates concerning lesbians' "choice" of sexual orientation tend to supersede the brutality of the violence they face. Indeed the idea of choice is what inspires much violence against lesbians, intended to change them into appropriately heterosexual and feminine women. In comparing the two sports stars, Gevisser (*Sunday Times*, 30 August 2009) points out: "We are perfectly happy to have our women be butch as long as they bring home the medal, but when they actually attempt to live lives independent of men, they are often subject to the most extreme violation and abuse."

Although she was objectified in particular ways, Semenya was positioned as national icon and as representative of the democratic South African nation-state (Cooky, Dycus, and Dworkin 2012). Female athletes have historically been important to the reproduction of national pride, represented as "our golden girls" worldwide (Bruce 2009). The wariness of South Africans concerning racist and sexist readings and treatment of black women also has a strong history – from the exploitation of colonialism to present impositions by the Global North (Butchart 1998; Gilman 1985; Magubane 2004). The unique salience of Semenya's position in sport as the first black woman from South Africa, and more specifically a black woman from a poor, rural locale, to win gold at an IAAF World Championship, inspired threats of a "third world war" against those perceived as undermining her historic win.

However, widely asserted claims of Semenya's femininity and womanhood by those seeking to represent her, and efforts to reinforce this femininity, ranging from her public makeover to multiple declarations of her incontrovertible femaleness, have largely ignored the elasticity of sex. While historically female athletes in international sport competition helped to facilitate changing images of femininity and womanhood (Hargreaves 2000), the mobilization of nationalist rhetoric and the defence of Semenya's womanhood suggest a reliance on the gender binary to defend against what was perceived in many ways as a racist assault. South Africans' declaration of Semenya as "our girl" was a defence not simply of Semenya and her right as a woman to participate in sport, but of South African national pride (Cooky, Dycus, and Dworkin 2012), as well as an intervention into regional debates about homosexuality and a way to bolster the social constitution of femininity that played a central role in that defence.

Support for Semenya in international sport competition had little to do with her as an individual – both the South African government and national governing bodies of sport largely dismissed her specific needs, privacy, and rights. References to the suspicions regarding her sex were construed as insulting to the nation. The possibility that Semenya was intersexed was cast as inconsistent with her "true" African femininity and she was simultaneously detached from her own national and ethnic histories by global efforts to support her gender liminality.

It is important to recognize the interplay of debates about Semenya in terms of her own self-defined gender and her re-conceptualization of African womanhood as an antidote to fights over the boundaries of femaleness that literally occur through her body. Put in the context of activist and scholarly work based South Africa concerning the importance of defining sex as mutable and multiplicitous – and the importance of redefining masculinity as a means to undercut high rates of gender and sexual violence – understanding Semenya's treatment can provide new directions in understanding gender beyond rights paradigms that rely on laws and their enforcement. Such directions can change the ways people understand and think about the messiness of gender categories and their inseparability from raced, classed, and located histories, both within and outside of sport.

Simultaneously, Caster Semenya's treatment illustrates the need for sporting organizations to reorganize and redefine sex/gender differentiations and inequalities that are built into the institution of sport. Decades ago, the IOC claimed that it was "aware of and opposed to the historical injustices that excluded women from the

Olympics or that limited the events in which women could compete. Mandatory sex testing, according to the IOC, was a means of protecting new opportunities that had opened up for women" (Cole 2000). This is paradoxical given that women are now weeded out of sport when they exhibit athletic success (Cole 2000).

Comparing Semenya and Simelane also demonstrates how categories such as race, class, gender, sexuality, and nation can actually work to obscure each other. To illustrate this point, consider a petition of support for Semenya written by South African feminists from academia, community-based organizations, NGOS, and research institutes that chastised politicians and media for distracting from the sexism in this situation in their claims of imperialism and racism in gendered tests: "While issues of racism and imperialism have and will continue to apply in various circumstances and have a sensitive history in terms of women's bodies particularly in Africa, focusing on these issues in the current context obscures the much neglected 'elephant in the room' – gender discrimination" (African Women's Development Fund 2009). The authors of the petition suggest that commonly held ideas about what it means to be a normative man or woman promote gender discrimination and violence such as rapes and murders like Simelane's. They argue that "framing the discrimination as racism or imperialism without reference to gender discrimination as the main issue risks reinforcing gender stereotypes." The comparison drawn here not only foregrounds individuals' ability and/or willingness to be gendered in ways that are deemed socially appropriate, but also points to an instance where race and nation obscure gender.

Caster Semenya's situation evoked strong responses in South Africa and beyond. Judith Butler (2009), contemplating Semenya's treatment, wonders if there is not a global effort at consensus at work: "This co-operative venture suggests that sex-determination is decided by consensus and, conversely, when there is no consensus, there is no determination of sex ... are we, in fact, witnessing in this case a massive effort to socially negotiate the sex of Semenya, with the media included as a party to this deliberation?" However, the instability of sex as demonstrated here, and the efforts at the negotiation Butler describes, are also based in colonial histories of racist objectification and policing boundaries of social categories. Tavia Nyong'o (2010, 97) fears: "In the name of protecting African femininity from a western, scientific gaze, Semenya's defenders also disguise their own patriarchal investment in naming and controlling this gender excess." But it is also important to look at the vehemence of this protection, brought about both through troublesome iterations of patriarchy and justified reactions to decades of global hierarchies in the region and beyond. In Semenya's treatment, debates about the constitution of sex and the importance of racial histories lose sight of her as a person. South Africa's complex transnational relationships and visions of its future, especially a gendered future, allow a problematic and potentially productive space to emerge in her wake.

PART THREE
Comparative Studies

8

Mobilizing against the Invisible: Erotic Nationalism, Mass Media, and the "Paranoid Style" in Cameroon

S.N. NYECK

> Social sciences as enlightenment can profitably concentrate on critical examination and reconstruction of widely employed standard stories.
>
> Tilly 2002, 42

What is the effect of affective and erotic relationships in social movements and party identification in Africa? To what extent do such relationships illustrate political core values, the success and failure of oppositional politics? In this chapter, I analyze the strategic use of homosexuality as blackmail in nationalist and political discourse in Cameroon. Political paranoid statements on "invisible homosexuals" displayed in the public sphere in Cameroon through the actions of media, government officials, and opposition leaders introduced a socio-cultural divide in the citizenry that explains the mistrust of state institutions, political compromise (Fukuyama 2004), and the stakes in the race for social capital (Fisher and Torgler 2006).[1] As a strategy for change in the context of a long rule by a dominant political party, mobilizing *against* the invisible is a recipe for failure if the party that does so cannot incorporate the invisible as its core value. The party that mobilizes new issues without identifying with them incurs credibility costs if it leaves to chance or to its rivals the task of integrating such issues into mainstream political debates.

Jeff Goodwin (1997) noted the lack of empirical and theoretical research on the effect of affective and erotic relationships in social

movements and collective action. In this chapter, I attempt to fill such
a gap by analyzing the strategic use of homosexuality as blackmail
in nationalist and political discourse in Cameroon. Political paranoid statements on homosexuality in Cameroon reveal a mistrust of
public institutions. This deficit of trust in state institutions often
expressed in forms of aversion (Brown 2006) is a serious challenge
to democracy (Tilly 2008; Sapenza, Toldra, and Zingales 2007) and
economic growth (Granovetter 1973; Mansbridge 1997; Neustadt
1997), especially in the developing world, and so the study of collective action should pay more attention to factual and symbolic realms
of affective and erotic interactions. In Cameroon, discourse[2] on
homosexuality uncovers a source of the exacerbation of intolerance
in politics: the quasi absence of political leadership committed to
moderation as a strategy to mitigate social tension and able to clearly
articulate political demands. What makes the Cameroon case particularly interesting is that, in contrast to other notorious instances
of political homophobia in Africa (e.g., Reddy et al. and Nyanzi, this
volume; Epprecht 2006), the accusations of homosexuality did not
come from the state against civil society, but from civil society against
the state. Thus, positive constitutional change in South Africa and
attempts at negative constitutional change in Uganda and Burundi to
repress homosexuality – plus the politicization of the homosexual
subject in Nigeria, Egypt, Senegal, Gambia, Ghana, Malawi, and
Cameroon today – legitimize research by political scientists on an
issue that is often marginalized in the discipline.

The baring of the deficit of trust in state institutions in Cameroon
is historically grounded in contentious political mobilization and
representation. By focusing on the use of homosexuality in public
discourse for negative mobilization of public opinion against state
institutions, one is able to capture both the *trajectory* and *strategy* of
negative mobilization over time. In this chapter, I examine the theoretical assumptions that underline the exploitation of homosexuality
through blackmail informed by contempt and by conspiracy thinking in Cameroon. I also analyze the political implications of erotic
paranoid statements on national self-representation in this country.
I demonstrate how theosophical notions of statehood and nation-
hood, invented by both nationalists and postcolonial intellectuals
obsessed with cultural determinisms, misspell political salvation
(Cioran 1968), sexual citizenship in general, and same-sex eroticism
in particular.

THE PARANOID STYLE AND MASS MEDIA

The political scientist James Glass (1985, xiv) argues that "delusional" utterances are not only expressed in the language of power, but also that their use by political fanatics can become "a vehicle for a collective identity, with the delusional world being shared publicly as national policy or revenge [creating] a specific history to link to the project of an ongoing historical event." The emphasis here is not on the seemingly "irrational" behaviour as much as it is on the "psycho-cultural narratives and dramas" (Ross 2007) stemming from contestations about power and identity that reveal not only groups' existential fears, but also the relative absence of moderate views amidst political controversy in Cameroon. I will primarily deal with the conditions that give incentives for group identification (Hardin 1995); incentives for a pre-emptive identification of the Cameroonian state with heterosexual ontology.

Before I proceed, I will clarify and contextualize my use of the term *paranoia*. Political scientist Robert Robins and psychiatrist M. Jerrold (1997) define a paranoid mind as one that believes "a vast and subtle conspiracy exists to destroy [its] entire way of life." What is noticeable about a paranoid view of history, Robin and Jerrod add, is not that the paranoid believes that conspiracies exist and are important, but that s/he sees conspiracy as "*the* motivating force in history and the essential organizing principle in all politics" (1997, 37). I attribute to "erotic paranoid nationalism" obsessive beliefs about sexual enemies and self-defence practices that compulsively hijack the public realm and saturate political discourse with retributive justice on a sequential, provisional, and/or continuing basis. Paranoid erotic nationalism aims to consolidate a homogenous national identity and pride. Paranoia in this sense is onerous because in order to make subversion and conspirators omnipresent, it must control public opinion, outlaw dissent, and obstruct critical thinking without which the sanity of the polity becomes questionable. This attempt to freeze a nation's thoughts with the fear of an overwhelming imagined danger can be confounded with contempt. So-defined, paranoia is one of many elements of the "fictional republic" (Nackenoff 1994), a style of the mind in which the "feeling of persecution is central, and it is indeed systematized in grandiose theories of conspiracy ... whereas the spokesman of the paranoid style finds it directed against a nation, a culture, a way of life whose fate affects not himself alone but millions of other" (Hofstadter 1964, 4). Paranoia may not be pervasive in everyday politics in this country. I am more interested in its breakthroughs as forms of agenda-setting through "standard stories" (Tilly 2002, 26) beyond the event that brings them to the fore and their relationship with history, the politics of opposition, and representation in Cameroon. I will start with the politicization of the homosexual subject as the "generalized other" (Herzog 1998, 218), the hidden hand of neocolonialism, and a precursor of conspiracy thinking that lead to "erotic nationalism" in Cameroon.

MISSPELLED CORRUPTION: PARANOIA STYLE AND THE POLITICS OF SALVATION

As Hofstadter (1964, 4) notes, the paranoid style is rational and disinterested in the sense that it frames political passions as unselfish and patriotic, and "goes far to intensify the feeling of righteousness and moral indignation." In Cameroon, little else inspires intense feelings of self-righteousness, moral indignation, and opportunism, as the phenomenon of corruption and the absolutist framework in which conspiracy is articulated leaves the common citizen with only one option: fight evil absolutely (Hofstadter 1964, 31).

Transparency International (TI) found that Cameroon was perceived as the most corrupt of eighty-five states surveyed in 1998,[3] a ranking that was given momentum by opposition parties and the civil society in the country. Although the Biya government first disputed TI's classification, it later conceded that work still needed to be done to ensure transparency in governance and resource management. However, Paul Biya, the president of Cameroon since 1982, and his party, the Cameroon People's Democratic Movement (RDPC/ CPDM), continue to win elections. Meanwhile, privately owned newspapers insist that governance is not transparent because the sources of power and the mechanisms of acquisition, accumulation, and distribution of wealth are not always public knowledge. The Biya government has taken some measures to fight corruption, such as sending high-ranking CEOs guilty of embezzlement and fraud to prison. However, whether jail alone is the most appropriate course of action to fight corruption in Cameroon remains to be determined. So far, proposals have been made to recover public funds illegally transferred to privately owned bank accounts abroad and the US government has offered its assistance to recover these funds (Marquardt 2006).[4] Sceptics, however, argue that real initiative to fighting corruption in this country is impossible without political change (*IRIN*, 27 January 2006).

To determine how corrupt a country is perceived to be, TI uses corruption measurements such as the Corruption Perceptions Index, the Bribe Payer Index, the Global Corruption Barometer, and the National System Countries Studies. At the national level, for instance, TI evaluates the transparency and the accountability of key institutions such as the executive branch, media, and civil society. On 31 January 2006, mimicking TI's respected style if not methodology, the privately-owned newspaper *Anecdote* published "Le Top 50 des Homosexuels Présumés du Cameroun," a list of fifty names of people it believed were the most corrupt men and women in Cameroon.[5] The crime of these government officials, economic agents, CEOs, successful journalists, church leaders, members of civil society, and cultural and sport promoters was alleged homosexuality. An expanded version of the list, "La Suite de la Liste des Homosexuels" published the following day, added twenty-seven names (*Anecdote*, 1 February 2006). The first list included three women and forty-seven men. Of the forty-seven men, three were deceased former government officials. The supplementary list of twenty-seven included two more deceased persons and former clerics of the Roman Catholic Church (*Anecdote*, 1 February 2006). This supplementary list had male high-ranking anglophone and francophone government officials, national tycoons, and a lone woman. Curiously, both lists included neither an opposition figure nor a military official.

The practice of homosexuality is illegal in Cameroon. Article 347 *bis* of the Cameroonian Penal Code classifies homosexual acts as crimes punishable by two to five years imprisonment with fines. However, regardless of this legal classification and despite the fact that homosexual suspects have often been harassed, arrested, and detained by the police, there was never a national mobilization to hunt down LGBTI individuals before January 2006. *Anecdote*'s move took everybody by surprise. While the literature on social movements and collective action often places an "event" or a cause at the centre of mobilization, *Anecdote*'s "Top 50" is a case of mobilization without such a prior event. There were no prior scandals or any particular material experience involving homosexuals that might have inspired the article.

On Christmas Eve in 2005, the Catholic Archbishop of Yaoundé, Tonye Bakot, delivered a sermon in which he denounced corruption and homosexuality. However, his predecessor had already set the tone by publicly opposing homosexuality. Consequently, while Bakot's sermon may have inspired *Anecdote*, a direct link is hard to establish for two reasons. First, *Anecdote*'s famous "Top 50" did not spare the Catholic clergy. Second, the position of the Catholic ministers framed as homosexuals did not conflict with Bakot's interests and position in the Church. Bakot might have wanted to use print media to discredit fellow Church members indirectly for whatever reason – however, most people on the list are from all major religious backgrounds in Cameroon (Catholics, Protestants, Muslims, and Animists), and so it is not likely. Finally, the idea of a conflict of interest within the Church spilling over to society is agnostic to the gender component of the list. Although only a few of them were named in the list, women in the Church of Rome in Cameroon, as elsewhere, are not yet considered for high-ranking positions. Instead, the political and militant content of the newspaper reveals its motivation. Staged contentious politics are familiar features of social and political life and the active or passive role of governments in collective contention makes a difference because it determines how discursive power may regulate social behaviour.

Making pronouncements from its editorial pages and presenting itself as the defender of the "people" against the corrupt government, *Anecdote* ignited an unprecedented public denunciation of both homosexuality and the state in Cameroon. However, unlike TI, *Anecdote* did not comment on how it had verified the accuracy of its claims. François Bikoro, the editor in chief of the newspaper, claimed to be motivated by a democratic ideal he defined as "a reasonable equation between the aspirations of the people and the means at the disposal of the governors" (*Anecdote*, January 2006), and justified *Anecdote*'s zeal to cast corruption out of Cameroon. He argued that this "open war" would not be won if the presumed "corrupted" were only publicly named in print media and removed from their offices: "They must be officially tried and condemned if found guilty. Concomitantly, their wrongly acquired wealth must be confiscated and returned to the public treasury." It follows from *Anecdote*'s logic that social privilege and wealth allegedly acquired by indulging in homosexuality could still be useful to society, but not to homosexuals. Whether the people named were indeed homosexual or not was never established, partly because that information was not necessary. *Anecdote* was able to recruit popular support across class, religion, and gender because *these* homosexuals were presented as members of the government who conspire against "the people." Such a success cannot be overstated given the personal and cultural connections that the people on the list had within society. *These* homosexuals were otherwise Cameroonians, political agents, and family members.

Anecdote's move had far-reaching consequences. As other newspapers joined *Anecdote* in this public hysteria, the only option left for the suspected homosexuals was to assert their heterosexuality through the courts, interviews, or public letters addressed to the editors of newspapers and magazines that were suddenly transformed into archives of confessions. Public masses and national prayer days were organized to purify Cameroon and protect the people against the disease of homosexuality. According to the *Post* (14 February 2006), the scandal of the publication of the names was so devastating that it left "many women and children stigmatized because their husbands and fathers have been portrayed as homosexuals. The wife of a senior government official in Yaoundé has reportedly stayed away from her office because of shame, since her husband's name was published as one of the homosexuals." *Mutations* (3 March 2006) reported that about thirty students were dismissed from their high school in Douala, the economic capital of Cameroon, because they admitted they were lesbians or were suspected of gay sexual activity. The government's embarrassment forced Biya to denounce what he called "unacceptable reporting of uncontrolled rumors" (*Post*, 14 February 2006). Meanwhile, Bakot condemned homosexuality and "criticized Western governments for expanding gay rights" (*Voice of America*, 14 February 2006). Narratives about homosexuality as allegedly introduced by white colonizers in Cameroon presented homosexuals as witches in the cultural sense and as modern bloodsuckers under the spell of the white man's Freemasonry and Rosicrucian orders and neoliberal/neocolonial networks. Numerous articles published from January to February 2006 had already argued that the economic success of these alleged homosexuals was attributed to their membership in foreign secret societies that promote "abominable western pleasures" (see *Libéral*, January 2006; *Harmattan*, January 2006; *Nouvelle Afrique*, February 2006).

Any analyst familiar with the content of these newspapers and
radio trottoir's ("informal debates and rumours") accounts on the
origin and significance of economic and moral corruptions in this
country must take into consideration the sincerity, however distorted,
of Cameroonians' desire to be part of an exemplary nation-state. This
desire to exist and perform well is in itself commendable. However,
like any other political aspiration based on ontological claims, the
temptation to exist by posing one's problem as a unique problem is
easily decipherable in the discourse over moral and economic decadence. Though corruption may touch Cameroonian society intimately, it remains "insoluble" within the destiny of a "non-tragic
nation" (Cioran 1968, 67) and inspires standard stories about the
purity of the nation's founders.[6]

Having presented the nature and the frame of the controversy
revolving around political institutions and leaders' expected behaviours, I will now analyze the political influence of background beliefs
on sexual enemies and their effects on political representation and
discourse. My examination of the politics of derision through the
popular genre of cartoons seeks to unearth what Cameroonian
economist and political analyst Celestin Monga calls the "aesthetic
of positioning" in the absence of democracy.

POLITICAL BEHAVIOUR AND GENDER TROUBLE

In his essay "Cartoons in Cameroon: Anger and Political Derision
under Monocracy," Monga (1997) notes that independent journalists introduced political cartoons in Cameroon in the early 1990s
primarily because they found caricature a safer way to disseminate
their critical views than prose articles. Walgrave and Manssens
(2000) show that in the absence of any prior mobilization machinery and when circumstances are favourable, mass media can produce mobilization and recruit for collective action. In this situation,
Walgrave and Manssens add, the use of visual materials is important
because it fills the gaps in the discourse and does things that words
cannot. The potential of cartoons to mobilize people toward democratic ideals would seem to be even higher in a place like Cameroon,
with so many languages and very few spaces for thoughtful and
uncensored political debate.

In the absence of professional training, cartoonists in Cameroon
claim to have "intuitive knowledge of national politics and national

issues." Yet rather than serving freedom and democracy, the juxtaposition of conventional journalism and cartoons in Cameroon unfortunately often promotes "a specific and demobilizing conception of politics and the surreptitious elaboration of a new dialectical and socio-cultural order" (Monga 1997, 167). As Ansolabehere and Iyengar (1995, 1) demonstrate in their study of electorate polarization in the United States, media propaganda often turn citizens from independence to apathy, and even antipathy, toward political institutions. I now evaluate the strength and weakness of the use of cartoons that convey paranoid statements on homosexuality and neocolonialism to mobilize public opinion against state institutions in Cameroon.

If the controversy is sexual in nature, it is the strategy of contention that makes it both salient and dangerous: the ability to confound legitimate issues with a paranoid style that renders the discernment of the merit of the argument almost impossible. If *Anecdote*'s editorials focused on the corruption of Cameroonian officials, other newspapers presented an elaborate explanation of the origin of homosexuality by pointing to the early days of the nation-state. *Perspectives Hebdo* (August 2005) had previously claimed that although in Europe homosexuality is associated with a natural sexual desire, Cameroon is different for several reasons:

First, homosexuality is European and un-African. This assumption is challenged by recent scholarship in the social sciences (Morgan and Wieringa 2005; Gueboguo 2006; Wieringa and Blackwood 2007; Massaquoi and Njoki 2007; Epprecht 2006; 2008).

Second, Dr Louis-Paul Aujoulat, a former governor of Equatorial French Africa, was a Freemason and consequently a homosexual who sodomized Amadou Ahidjo, the first president of Cameroon, and then established a homocractic[7] republic in the country. The idea of the transmission of political power through sodomy is captured in the cartoon below (image 8.1). Without naming him, the cartoon shows a figure too familiar to Cameroonians: the first president of the Republic of Cameroon crawling in diapers as a sodomized and infantilized man. Although political cartoons often ridiculed Paul Biya, this particular image was shockingly disrespectful and its visual effect unprecedented.

In this cartoon, homosexuality is associated with the image of excrement and political immaturity. According to philosopher and theorist Julia Kristeva (1982, 69–71), the image of excrement coveys

Image 8.1 This cartoon, published in *Le Popoli*
(1 February 2006), reads: "Fags: the media stirs up
diapers." The speech bubble reads: "MmmF!...
It stinks!"

disgust, abjection, and the idea of "defilement as an objective evil
undergone by the subject ... relate[d] to corporeal orifices as to so
many landmarks parceling-constituting the body's territory ...
Excrement and its equivalent stand for the danger to identity that
comes without ... society threatened by its outside." The "outside" in
this case is the West and homosexuality, seen as a Western conspiracy
to maintain the former colonial power in Cameroon by infantilizing
the government. This outside pressure allegedly makes the government illegitimate and incapable because it is weak and perverted.

Image 8.2 This cartoon, published in *Le Popoli* (January 2006), reads: "The country burning with... the issue of faggots of the Republic." The speech bubble reads: "The secret is revealed! Oh yes!"

Note the dual goal of mobilization and demobilization against two objective evils: homosexuality in its figurative representation as the imperial West and state institutions themselves. The ideas of demobilization anchored in distrust and contempt for state institutions is better visualized in image 8.2.

This cartoon shows Paul Biya, the current president of the Republic of Cameroon, holding a "secret" list; his secret. He is pointing a flashlight and is walking toward a blackened door, which is the office of his collaborators. The president is panicked because media has revealed the alleged homosexual secret hidden in the gloomy room of his collaborators. The antechamber of the collaborators is the site of sexual coercion where Western neocolonial capitalists and those who do not boycott the regime meet. It follows from this cartoon that homosexual identity is acquired by associating with the political regime of sodomized men.

Third, aware of France's attempts to keep Cameroon under control during the period of decolonization (1940–60), nationalist leaders who embodied the "real" faith and "indigenous" moral values of Cameroon not only resisted sexual exploitation, but also boycotted meaningless French territorial assemblies where greedy Africans were recruited in Freemason lodges, sodomized, and de-politicized (*Nouvelle Afrique*, February 2006; *Aurore Plus*, February 2006). In these territorial assemblies, the newspapers argued, "local gurus," namely French colonials and later African elites dominated by other gurus in Europe, ruled over their vassals. The practice of sodomy allegedly reinforced this unequal colonial relationship between colonizers and colonized. *Perspectives Hebdo* (August 2005) contended: "To sodomize an individual is, in African culture, a way to humiliate, dominate, and make him a vassal." The cartoon (image 8.3) below visualizes the trauma of the children of a sodomized man, namely, the father of the republic, the man-state.

This image conveys the trauma of the colonized: the Cameroonian people suffering at the hands of their fathers, namely, postcolonial elites who steal from them. Note the shift in focus from the previous cartoon. In order to exaggerate their moral debasement and economic corruption, the emphasis is no longer on political leaders' immaturity, but on their irresponsible behaviours as fathers of the nation. The absence of women in the cartoon is striking but not novel. This exclusive relationship of the fathers and their sons in national representations (Lorde 1982; Pateman 1988; Saxonhouse 1992; Nussbaum 1999; Agathangelou 2004) and hyperbolic citation of gender corruption (Butler 1993) reflects patriarchal political arrangements that already received wider attention from many scholars. The alleged sexual commerce between French colonizers and the "apatriotic" colonized homosexuals is now presumably a state practice, as the latter uses its networks and power to convert the masses to this "abominable" Western behaviour.[8]

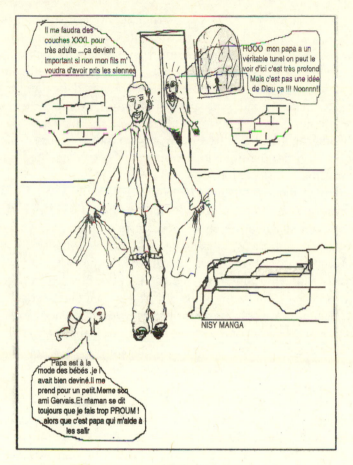

Image 8.3 This cartoon, published in *Anecdote* (31 January 2006), depicts the trauma of the children of a sodomized man.

The man-state represented here is stealing his children's diapers. In the background stands the man's older son who, looking from the rear, says: "Oh, my father has an impressive tunnel that is seen from here. It is very deep but it cannot be the work of God!!! Nooooo." The man's younger son is in the foreground, and mumbles: "My father models himself after the babies. I knew it. He thinks I am young. Even his friend Gervais ... and mum think I make excessive PROUM! [*mimics the sound of diarrhea*] But my father is responsible for the mess." In light of existing theories of postcolonial self-representation of the power struggle between new elites and society, these cartoons visualize quotidian narratives of affective interactions as the tapestries from which political meanings are made and remade. Not only do the images associated with the cartoons and historicity of homosexuality presented in these articles leave no space for consent and ambiguities in the relationships between colonizers and national elites, they also have a "talent for organizing the intentionality of others" (Glass 1985, xiv). This process of appropriation of the intentionality of sexual enemies is inherently polemical and contentious.

Arguably, the irreconcilability of postcolonial national political identities and those of alleged sexual strangers is a foundational point of reference in anti-neocolonial erotic nationalism. Nationalist warnings against the sinuous routes of homosexuality as a self-perpetuating and self-fulfilling practice of the neocolonial state are intended to inform Cameroonian citizens about how political leadership was stolen from them. Thus, self-proclaimed "voices of the people" continue to warn that if they are not repressed, same-sex relations may cause irreversible ontological damages to Cameroonians.

To move from sexual to political orientation, I argue that the contention between the imagined "apatriotic homosexuals" and the patriotic nationalists dates back to the late 1940s and early 1950s, when public opinion was divided between "immediate independence" and "gradual independence" from France.[9] It is not accidental that the Cameroonians and French citizens who supported "gradual independence," or even the prospect of Cameroon becoming a French department, are the same people who are labeled *femmes des colons*, or "colonizers' wives" (Abwa 2005, 47). From the radical nationalist viewpoint, dissent within its groups during decolonization was evidence that French colonials, and now Western capitalist sodomizers, are determined to defeat "true" freedom fighters and destroy the hope of the people of this country. Thus, the label *homosexual* is a political sentencing of dissenting ideas.

Abwa's interview of Ngouo Woungly-Massaga, an ex-guerrilla commander against French presence in Cameroon, is illuminating about the origin and the association of the French governor Aujoulat with homosexuality. Woungly-Massaga (Abwa 2005, 47) explains: "Within the circles of nationalists in 1960, we *recognized* the Aujoulatist (and they were many) fellow citizens ready to anything including homosexuality for money, or for a promise of a career."

Massaga's statement confirms that in the early 1950s, homosexuals were not self-identified gay politicians; they were only recognized as such by nationalist militants. Homosexuality was a label imposed on dissenting ideologues, both Cameroonians and foreigners, who did not fully embrace the ideas and strategies of the nationalist radical movement. Having assumed that all Africans are heterosexual by default, homosexuality becomes *something that is done to* Cameroonian nationals for political and occult reasons. One easily traces the continuity of radical nationalism in the overwhelming praises that *Anecdote* received from opposition leaders after the publication of the "Top 50" homosexuals. However, similar to the 1950s (assuming Massaga is accurate) when a nationalist homosexual label sufficed to turn other politicians into gays, *Anecdote* had failed to produce evidence of its claims and remains unapologetic to concerned families.

Nouvelle Afrique (February 2006) finally established the link between esoteric knowledge and political conspiracy when it published a new list of "confirmed homosexuals of the republic." This time, the French Dr Louis-Paul Aujoulat appeared first, followed by Amadou Ahidjo and members of the Biya government with no discernible pattern of religion or ethnicity. In less than two days, the shift from *Anecdote*'s "presumed homosexuals" to *Nouvelle Afrique*'s "confirmed homosexuals of the republic" reveals the speediness with which forty-six celebrated years of independence were contested and the concept of neocolonialism given momentum in Cameroonian politics. This "homosexual" represented in mass media is the useless and yet insidiously Westernized/apoliticized/apatriotic body, who creates a deficit of membership in collective action against neocolonialism. Such figures become an additional burden because their presence signifies defeat at a moment when victory against invisible neocolonial and neoliberal manoeuvres is most wanted.

Reacting to the publication of the lists, Jean Arthur Awoumou, member of the executive committee of the nationalist party the Union of the Population of Cameroon (UPC), argued "the reversal of values illustrates the economic exploitation by Western and local bourgeoisie, the moral and corporal destruction of the African and Kamerunian youths" (*Anecdote*, 9 February 2006).[10] Dakole Daïssala, the president of the Movement for the Defense of the Republic (MDR) party, and Ndam Njoya, the president of the Democratic Union of Cameroon (DUC), were more nuanced in their reactions than other opposition party leaders (*Cameroon Online*, 16 March 2006; *Nouvelle Expression*, 1 February 2006). Ndam Njoya called for debate on issues of sexual orientation; a debate he deemed himself not worthy to start. As the denunciation of homosexuality intensi- fied, calls were made for a change of government. Amidst this cacoph- ony, only a few voices attempted to criticize media and the political use of sexuality by arguing for the need to respect the privacy of political leaders (*Cameroun Link*, 12 May 2006; also see *Cameroon Tribune*, 2 February 2006). For example, journalist Suzanne Kala- Lobe publicly distanced herself from this homophobic chorus by arguing that the question of homosexuality should be regarded as a matter of individual liberty and freedom (*Cameroun Link*, 12 May 2006). In choosing to campaign on a platform based on unsubstanti- ated fears (none of the allegations were proven, and there is no seri- ous gay rights movement in Cameroon) and because of the esoteric nature of the alleged threats, oppositional politics in Cameroon chose to gamble with its reputation. Postcolonial nationalists wrongly or rightly concerned with multifaceted forms of "neocolonialism" in Cameroon manipulate the emotional capital invested in the *idea* of national unity to legitimate a "conspiracy theory" that could explain all the ills of their country today.

This process co-opts contemporary expressions of economic dis- content and transforms them into psychological weapons against state institutions and individuals. The second wave of multiparty liberalization in 1990s did not bring greater solidarity among oppo- sition leaders, and fatalistic feelings of being perpetually exploited continue to cripple the public sphere with anger, resentment, and venomous alienation often captured in metaphoric public articula- tions of power and ascendancy. For instance, when Frederic Kodock, then the secretary general of the nationalist party UPC, was asked to join the government as a minister in 1990s, he accepted, but declared, *"lorsqu'on se noie, on s'accroche à tout, même à un serpent,"*[11] meaning, when someone is drowning, s/he will hang onto anything, even a serpent that represents the evil incarnated in the state and the government of Cameroon.

The publication of the lists of "corrupt" men and women in Cameroonian society was not intended to initiate a debate on sexual- ity. Beyond targeting government officials and economically success- ful individuals, the outcry against homosexuality has galvanized government repressive agencies such as the police to continue to crack down on suspected homosexuals. Prior to the publication of the list, eleven young, working-class, and mostly unemployed men arrested in May 2005 had just spent about eight months in jail without trial after the police branded them as homosexuals and detained them (IGLHRC 2006). They were finally released, but not before the government ordered forensic examination of their anuses to determine whether or not they were homosexuals; a request the medical practitioner appointed by the court turned down (Human Rights Watch 2005).[12] Curiously, after *Anecdote* launched its anti-corruption campaign, homosexuality became the disease of the bourgeoisie and nobody remembered the case of the eleven that captured the attention of newspapers and national television only two years previously.

In Cameroon, once ordinary citizens are suspected of and denounced as being homosexual, their detention is increasingly accepted without question. In 2007, Alternatives Cameroon reported that five of six other young men detained in Douala since July 2007 were released after spending 1,095 days in prison while their case was pending. They owe their freedom to Me Alice Nkom, the only lawyer willing to take up cases of this nature in Cameroon today. Three days after Alternatives Cameroon's (7 February 2008) press release, the government newspaper announced that two other women were arrested for fighting after a third party called the police. The police later justified their detention not because of the fight, but because the women claimed to have been having a love quarrel (*Cameroon Tribune*, cited by Alternatives Cameroon, 7 February 2008). It seems Aristotle was right in reminding us of the importance of love quarrels and sexuality in understanding politics. Today, political theorists do not blame constitutional breakdowns on love quarrels, but explore the effects of institutional breakdowns when we fail to value all families, whether straight, gay (Polikoff 2008), or any other form.

The heavy hand of anti-corruption campaigns initiated in newspapers and legitimized by opposition to President Biya has apparently missed its target. Though it made the lives of ordinary citizens and their families more stressful, paranoid erotic nationalism has not advanced the strategic position of the opposition in Cameroon and has not changed the government or article 347 *bis* of the penal code that criminalizes homosexuality. The return to the status quo indicates that the attempt to mobilize contentious issues to unseat Biya's long rule worked against his opposition partly because the strategy involved negative mobilization only. However, *Anecdote*'s move appears to have inspired other newspapers on the continent and sparked debates about the constitutional repression of homosexuality.

CONCLUSION

In analyzing the use of homosexuality for political blackmail in Cameroonian politics after *Anecdote* published fifty names of suspected homosexuals of the republic, homophobia alone only offers a limited explanation for recent talks about sexual orientation and gender identity in the country. Instead, I propose to think of the use of homosexuality in political discourse in Cameroon as an attempt to revive a nationalist zeal among the masses. Contemporary populist nationalisms distort the political history of Cameroon *strategically* to control public opinion on the issue of economic and moral corruption. This desperate attempt to win the support of the masses is even more acute today because opposition leaders' efforts to challenge the current regime have failed since the re-enactment of multiparty electoral competition in the 1990s.

The political and religious configurations of the lists indicate that political discourse on gender and sexuality in Cameroon reveals deep-seated mistrust of state institutions. This mistrust is based on the assumption that the Cameroonian state has always been a pawn of neocolonial networks that use homosexuality to recruit allies among elites. The publication of the lists presented an elaborate conspiracy theory presented as a historical fact. Although never proven, the allegation that the French doctor Louis-Paul Aujoulat, a lay Catholic worker who became governor of the French Equatorial Africa in early 1940s, sodomized Amadou Ahidjo, the first president of Cameroon, became the rallying motto for anti-homosexual rhetoric. From Ahidjo to President Paul Biya today, homosexuality has allegedly become a mainstream practice in the circles of power. The corrupt republic is therefore a republic where men in power continue to prey on young Cameroonians and force them to participate in abominable Western pleasures. Self-appointed nationalists, the so-called defenders of the people against the state and its alleged neocolonial, capitalist, freemasons, and international exploitative networks, make this assumption.

At stake in this debate is not just the question of violence due to the alleged sexual coercion, but an ontological search for marks of purity in a country where human dignity is constantly threatened by poverty and social inequalities. From the nationalist perspective, Africans are heterosexuals by default, and resistance against homosexuality involves the denunciation of political leaders as corrupt. However, the nature of corruption is specifically threatening because African leaders are presumably under the influence of the invisible and neocolonial West. Resistance also involves calls for a change of the current regime, the suppression of any objective debate on gender and sexual politics, and, more importantly, the delegitimization of state institutions and misconceptions about the source of political power and agency.

Despite the publication of the lists of "suspected homosexuals" in early 2006, there is no evidence yet that the practice of homosexuality is compulsory to secure career advancement in Cameroon, nor did I find evidence suggesting that homosexuality sealed the relationship between Dr Aujoulat and the first president of Cameroon, and between Aujoulat and Biya, the current president. What I find is an attempt to use socially constructed phobias related to witchcraft to explain social and economic challenges that Cameroon faces today. The "homosexual" in the political discourse in Cameroon is a constructed subject arbitrarily chosen to embody the ambivalence of African discourse on self-identity. The creation of the homosexual deviant subject, and subsequent attempts to fixate state institutions within the perspective of deviance, empowers radical nationalists in all political circles with the mandate to exorcize state power. However, the ridicule of state institutions will not stop with a change of government in Cameroon unless the sting of perceived neocolonialism is broken and Cameroonians/Africans renew a dialogue with their own internal shadows, rather than running after the first ready-made Westernized scapegoat.

Regardless of what one may feel about the subject of homosexuality, the events of January 2006 in Cameroon indisputably incorporated sexuality in general, and same-sex relations in particular, as important puzzles in the study of African politics. Beyond the question of sexual orientation and sexual rights, civic morality cannot be studied in isolation from society and political institutions. Few political leaders of the opposition have called for debates on (homo)sexuality and politics in Cameroon; a call that is also addressed to the academic community as producer of knowledge. In terms of political representation and party identification, the use of homosexuality in political discourse tests the strategic strength of oppositional politics, which remains immature and polemical in nature.

9

"The One Who First Says I Love You": Love, Seniority, and Relational Gender in Postcolonial Ghana[1]

SERENA OWUSUA DANKWA

When I first met Janet Aidoo[2] in 2001, she stood bent over the open bonnet of a car, her white overalls stained with oil. We were in the centre of Accra, Ghana's capital city, in the improvised car repair shop of a friend, who – like many other young Ghanaian men – specialized in disassembling car wrecks and building "new" cars out of the functioning parts. Janet, the stocky young woman who was responsible for re-spraying the cars, was flattered when I congratulated her on doing such a difficult "man's job." When we shook hands, she scratched my palm with her right index finger – a quick but firm gesture of erotic interest that up to that point, I had only experienced from Ghanaian men.

A few years later, in search of women who love women, I remembered Janet. It took several attempts to track her down. In the meantime, she had spent two years in her rural hometown to recover from a respiratory disease from inhaling toxic paint fumes. Back in Accra, she stays in the densely populated immigrant neighbourhood in which she grew up. She shares a two-room home with her mother and younger brother, and they share the cooking and washing facilities in the compound with a dozen similar households. Periodically, Janet's infant nieces and her mother's boyfriend join them. But Janet does not go home much, and eventually her brother brought me to Vida's place, where she spends most of her time. Vida, who rents a hall-and-chamber in an airier compound around the corner, turned out be more than "just a friend."

As a native Twi-speaker and a Presbyterian Christian, Janet belongs to a majority in terms of both language and religion. In her pulsating Muslim neighbourhood, she is part of a proud minority. More significantly, she is known as a sprayer and is notorious for joking and roughhousing with her male mates, being quick-tempered and effusive, and having one too many and boasting about it – all behaviours that indicate youthful masculinity.[3] Some people recalled the police once detained her and friends and family pleaded for her release. Apparently, she was in a street fight over a girl whose father happened to be an army officer. When the angry father turned up the next day, Janet responded to his interference by telling him, "It's not you who I love, it's your daughter."[4]

FEMALE MASCULINITY

Inevitably, the way Janet carries herself, her gait, her style, her demeanour, and her trade remind me of what Judith Halberstam (1998) captured as "female masculinity." This term challenges the widespread notion that masculinity in women is "a pathological sign of misidentification and maladjustment" (2002, 360). It suggests that female-born persons who understand themselves in masculine ways cannot be dismissed as bad copies of "real" men, but instead generate distinct modes of masculinity on their own terms and in their own right.

Halberstam (2008, 1) holds that in the English language, "the very notion of a female masculinity has been contained and managed by its inevitable relationship to lesbianism." This inevitability is premised on what Judith Butler (1990) critiqued as the "heterosexual matrix" – the conflation of sex, gender, and desire that implies that the sexed body assumes not only a person's gender identity but also her sexual object choice. According to this logic, gender-bending, masculine women are sexually deviant. But what if female masculinity has not been subjected to the "heterosexual matrix" and the stereotyped image of the man-hating lesbian? What if its relationship to lesbianism is not inevitable? Does female masculinity translate into an African context where "'masculinity without men' (Halberstam 1998) has been ordinary and part of accepted gender experiences" (Miescher and Lindsay 2003, 5)? In this chapter, I argue that the binary between female anatomy and masculine gender identification, which so potently constitutes the term female masculinity, loses some of its power in the West African context.

Sexual discourse in southern Ghana has been structured by norms of discretion and indirection that relegate non-marital sexual relations, including same-sex passions, to the realm of the unnamed and the unspoken (see Dankwa 2009). In recent years, explicit anti-gay debates have probed the performativity of this silence (Broqua this volume) and the "tacit understandings" and tolerance (O'Mara chapter 10 in this volume) of same-sex lovers. In Ghana, the silence began to crumble with the media liberalization in 1992, when a sexualized public sphere emerged that allowed for the construction and condemnation of homosexuality. In the 2000s, aggressive anti-gay rhetoric gained popularity on an unprecedented level (cf. Nyeck chapter 8 in this volume). Today, political homophobia interlocks with problematic neocolonial threats to penalize the country by way of cutting aid (*BBC News*, 2011).

The term *supi* has been employed to sexualize and demonize female same-sex intimacies. Popularly associated with the affectionate ties pubescent girls forge at boarding schools, *supi* connotes close girl-friendships that are emotionally and materially significant. It started to make headlines in popular weeklies, in which Charismatic Christians worried about the erotic dimension of women's "*supi-supi* practices," supposedly carried over from boarding school. Under the headline "No 'Supi-Supi' Lesbianism," an op-ed bemoaned how a wealthy woman had been "able to snatch away a poor man's dear wife, and [to live] with her comfortably as 'husband' and 'wife'" (*Mirror*, 7 January 1998). In a more voyeuristic vein, Ghana's and Nigeria's thriving video-film industry is portraying "*supi* lesbians" as greedy bourgeois women who seduce and usher innocent young women into their secret sexual cults and are marked as a threat to biological and social reproduction (Green-Simms 2012, 40).

Such derogatory representations contrast the vibrant ways in which women like Janet flirt, gesture, and act on same-sex desires. The term *supi* is used to refer to a special female friend or lover, but not to nominalize or organize around same-sex practice. Throughout West Africa, same-sex intimacies have been concealed and celebrated through a "language of allusion" (Dankwa 2009) and "tactics of non-verbalization" (Broqua chapter 11 in this volume). Women in Ghana who suspect each other of being involved with same-sex lovers are said to "know" or "do it." Notions of being "in the know" thrive on the insight that women friends can fully satisfy each other's erotic, emotional, and economic needs and desires. Knowledge resides in the sheer awareness that a woman can pleasure and awaken the desire for such love in her fellow woman. I thus tentatively refer to experienced women who are articulate about the erotic potential and intensity of same-sex intimacies as "knowing women."

Drawing on fifteen months of ethnographic fieldwork,[5] I zoom in on the gendered dynamics of female intimacies in Ghana's urban South. I will address this by first focusing on the historical gender configurations in West Africa. Through an analysis of Janet's life story, I will explore the relation between her gendered and her erotic subjectivity. Second, I will examine how working-class women invoke gender to describe and reflect on their intimacies. The fact that self-positioning as "the man" is not necessarily enacted through a masculine gender presentation but, invoked relationally, speaks to a gender dimension I refer to as relational masculinity. Keeping in mind the growing literature on butch/femme dynamics in South East Asia (Sinnott 2004, Wilson 2004, Blackwood 2010), gender binaries must be examined through the lens of West African categories of difference.

SITUATIONAL GENDER

African gender research has provided ample evidence on the capacity of gender to outweigh and transcend biological sex. Pointing at different forms of institutionalized woman marriages throughout the continent, West African feminists argue that the primacy given to bodies and the Euro-American fixity of sex does not hold cross-culturally (Amadiume 1987; Nzegwu 2005). Ifi Amadiume's (1987) study, *Male Daughters, Female Husbands*, highlights the situationality of gender in Igbo culture. Historically, for purposes of succession and inheritance, daughters could be designated "male" and women could climb the male ladder by acquiring wives. Unwilling to imagine that the erotic might play a role in woman marriages, Amadiume attacked Audre Lorde for bringing these same-sex marriages into the realm of lesbian love.[6] The factual constraints to becoming a female husband, however, have received less attention. Conditional to attaining male status was in fact self-aggrandizement and the taking of titles, which made this position a viable option only to a minority of well-to-do female-bodied persons.[7]

In her provocative study *The Invention of Woman*, Oyèrónké Oyéwùmí (1997), one of the most ardent Afro-centric critics of feminism, insists that anatomical sex is not a foundational category to

West Africa all together. She blames "Western" feminists for buying into the "biological determinism" that underpins Euro-American epistemologies. Feminist fixations on anatomical sex and their repro-duction of the mind-body split, she argues, do not apply to Nigeria's Yorùbá culture. Unlike the "Western" nuclear family model, in which sexual difference functions as the primary source of hierarchy and oppression, the extended Yorùbá family is "non-gendered because kinship roles and categories are not gender-differentiated ... The fundamental organising principle within this family is seniority based on relative age" (Oyéwùmí 2004, 4). Concluding that Yorùbá power is tied up with seniority rather than with maleness, Oyéwùmí's work represents the far end within a spectrum of historical interven-tions that challenge the primacy of sex and gender.[8]

Like the Yorùbá language, Ghana's lingua franca Akan[9] (Twi) lacks a pronominal distinction between female and male and cher-ishes appellations that indicate a person's social age instead. Age is not measured chronologically, but compounds criteria for stratifica-tion such as marital and reproductive status, lineage ties, economic autonomy, vocational skills, or religious authority. According to Bourdieu (1985), age amounts to symbolic capital that implies eco-nomic, cultural, and social status. Miescher et al. (2007, 10) suggest, "seniority is a category as central to identity in Ghana and indeed throughout Africa as gender is." The resulting senior-junior dynam-ics work beyond chronological age: seniority marks a person's adeptness and enduring presence within a circumscribed setting. Thus, erotic resources and same-sex experience can make a younger female lover senior to an older woman.

In southern Ghana, the acclaimed power of post-menopausal women derives from Akan matriliny, which traces descent through the female line. Regardless of conjugal bonds, one remains part of and prioritizes the extended maternal family, the *abusua*. This implies that a man gives an inheritance to his sisters', rather than his own, children. In this setting, a wife's main conjugal obligation, cooking and being sexually available to her husband, does not require the establishment of a joint household. Wives are less at the mercy of their husbands, but are firmly linked to brothers and uncles and the decision-making "head" of their *abusua*, usually a "big man" whose power is contained by female elders. Companionate marriage and the nuclear family model, an ideal sought after not least by urban Christian middle-class couples, has complicated but not resolved this matrilineal logic (Clark 1999, 718). As I argue here, a matrilineal orientation remains an attractive option for women who have little or no romantic interest in men.

In most formerly colonized countries of the South, multiple precolonial, colonial, and contemporary institutions and ideologies, including different regimes of gender and sexuality, operate simultaneously. In postcolonial Ghana, globally pervasive images of youthful, bourgeois femininity and hetero-normative modernity cross-cut and coexist with older concepts of sex and gender that are based on the centrality of the male and female mode of procreation (Amoah 1990, 132). Thus, the position of post-menopausal and of pre-nubile Akan women does not, at least conceptually, differ much from that of males past or prior to reproductive adulthood. By the same token, male adulthood connotes strength and authority and female adulthood nurturing generosity and emotionality (Woodford-Berger 1997) without, however, assuming romantic notions of motherliness.

Manhood and womanhood[10] are socially achieved positions, and so it is possible for female-bodied persons to take on public leadership roles. Just like the "big man," a figure who has an enduring appeal in Ghana's history, successful female traders can become "big women" and assert authority if they can accumulate and display wealth and dependants (Akyeampong 2000). Yet, although both men and women can attain elder status, if their moral and social achievements are recognized by their *abusua*, the power of female lineage heads tends to be more hidden and indirect (Miescher 2005, 195).[11] I agree with Amadiume and Oyéwùmí that elderhood is not gender specific and that a person's gender status is situational and shifts throughout a lifetime. While they uphold the fluidity of African gender roles, I would more cautiously highlight that transient reproductive capacities, rather than sexed bodies, have shaped gender relations in Ghana.

FOOTBALL, CARS, AND MOTHERHOOD

The time I was kid, I started with football. So anytime you would see me, I hold a football ... I was twelve years of age and I decided to play the football and my mother told me if I play the football I will not give birth, so I should stop the football and go and find something better to do. So I said, I decided that I would stop the football and go and learn spraying. That's why I've

become an auto sprayer. (Janet Aidoo, personal interview with
the author, 20 February 2006)[12]

Janet and I are sitting in the dimmed hall of Janet's lover, whom she
refers to as Sister Vida. It is a hot afternoon. Sister Vida is at work, and
Janet has just returned from the military campus where she hopes to
find employment in the vehicle repair services. Janet follows my invitation to tell her life history by presenting herself as a coherent, autonomous, decision-making subject. A direct line from her favourite
childhood game to her choice of vocational training lies at the heart of
her narrative. Football and cars are inextricably and consistently
linked through her attraction to masculine spaces and activities.

Across the globe, and certainly in West Africa, the female football
arena amounts to a homosocial space in which young women's masculine styles and same-sex desires are tacitly tolerated.[13] Janet's
mother's concern that football could endanger her capacity to give
birth echoes football's image as a "modern" leisure activity, tied up
with male bodies. Nevertheless, I wondered if Janet's mother, a savvy
trader in her late forties, really believed that football causes barren-
ness. "She said my, this thing, my womb will turn and I can't have
birth," Janet insists. Was her mother concerned Janet's youthful masculinity would further thrive in the homosocial football arena and
eventually prevent her from desiring motherhood? Even if the turning uterus is Janet's own image, the fact that this explanation is conceivable speaks to a flexible understanding of bodies including the
mutability of reproductive organs through repeated exposure to
non-normative physical activity.[14]

The fear of losing her reproductive abilities may have compelled
Janet to give up football, but it did not prevent her from pursuing
equally male-connoted work against her family's will: "Because
spraying is not a job of women, it's only men who spray so I should
go and learn sewing, and I told them I can't learn sewing because I
don't know how to do woman's job, only job that I can do is job that
men do, that one I can do it." Janet does not argue that she did not
want to learn a woman's job, but that she *could* not. Her desire to
become a sprayer seamlessly emerges as the sequel and alternative to
playing football and seems not motivated by her actual skill but by
the fact that it is associated with men.[15] Janet's statement echoes the
words of one of Evelyn Blackwood's (2011, 96) respondents in
Indonesia: Robi, who identifies as *tomboi*, and states, "I feel like a

man because the things I do are more like what a man does."
Likewise, Janet's work interests amount to a key indicator of her
identification with men. Her self-portrayal draws on the certainty
that she is destined and appointed to do work "that men do."

This strong sense of self brings Janet into conflict with normative
gender expectations and impelled her to challenge her family: "I sat
down about six months, and they thought about it and they said,
okay ... they will take me to learn it." Janet resisted her family's
expectations passively and refused to leave the house until her uncles
reconsidered and found her an apprenticeship. She reckons that their
eventual consent and investment was inspired by their realization
that she would be an impressive novelty. People would say: "Hey, I
haven't seen a woman learning this job before." Indeed, remembering the graduation party that was held for her, men and women
praised her and shared their astonishment about her capacity to do
the "spraying work." Her accomplishment and perseverance in following her calling made up for her resistance and earned her the
respect of friends and family. As Blackwood highlights, it is the
"doing" of masculinity, against all odds, that makes *tombois* authentic in their own eyes, as well as in the eyes of their girlfriends and
male mates. The successful "enactment of masculinity is proof of
their status as men" (2010, 94).

Besides legitimizing the tough gait and masculine (work) clothes
that appear to be an inevitable part of her professional identity,
Janet's work ambitions must also be read as an attempt to escape the
informal sector in which most women in Ghana struggle to make a
living. As elsewhere, "jobs that men do" are more likely to be formal
and better paid (Adomako Ampofo 1997). Rather than braiding hair
or selling home-cooked food, Janet hopes for a salaried position with
the state, preferably in the armed services, and has taken a first step
by taking an unpaid internship on the military campus. Strolling
around in her work overalls and flaunting the campus identity tag in
her neighbourhood after work, she not only enacts masculinity, but
also presents herself as an upwardly mobile citizen with a formal job.
While her ideal of being self-sufficient and climbing the social ladder
complies with the modern myth of the male breadwinner, it also references the image of the maternal provider that still holds "immense
reverence and authority in Akan culture" (Clark 2001, 303).

While she defies gender norms in her vocational and erotic choices,
Janet is ready to marry, at least temporarily, "because of the birth.

Everybody wants to have a baby." In everyday usage the term *marrying* is very broadly interpreted and used synonymously with engaging in a sexual relationship (Clark 1994, 343). This fluidity is consistent with Akan models of marriage as a process that is gradually formalized (Allman and Tashjian 2000). Janet could marry without ever signing a contract or establishing a joint household,[16] and would so elude the companionate ideal of marriage that has gained currency among West African urbanites who see romantic love as the epitome of progressive individualism (Masquelier 2009, 227).

As Gracia Clark (2001, 303) explores, the ability to provide for one's offspring is more integral to motherhood than breastfeeding and physical childcare. Thus, the devoted Akan mother pursues income-generating activities and is committed to the working world. In a historical context in which urban "women have always sought wealth and autonomy" (Akyeampong 2000, 223), becoming a "big woman" is a viable option. Though motherhood alone would not render Janet big, it is the route to exceed her junior status and attain adulthood without having to compromise her desire to spray cars, make money, and court women. The imperative of motherhood and of flexibility regarding material survival allows women with little interest in male-female intimacy to hold on to older forms of marriage and remain tied to their mothers and matrilineages.

EROTIC SUBJECTIVITY

Janet is not part of a butch/femme subculture or a network of *tombois* and *girlfriends*. Nevertheless, her erotic sense of self thrives on male strength and bravery. "Because I am good at doing men's work, I am also strong at doing my work in bed. I know how to play my role very well," she chips in over a beer one evening. Elderly Akan wives often draw analogy between occupational work and sex, which they consider physically "tiresome work" after a day of farming (van der Geest 2006, 227). Janet, however, intimates her sexual competence as a working subject by comparing herself to a young man who ought to perform and take on an ostensibly active role. This charged role implies the ability to wake up in the middle of the night, initiate sex, and go back to sleep. This is vital in an environment where bedrooms are shared and one needs to be sure that one's fellow sleepers are fast asleep or can at least pretend to be sleeping. Janet prides herself on being good at setting her inner clock and waking up for the work of love.

Janet recounts her first erotic experience, which took place when she visited her older sister at boarding school: "One of her friends saw me and the girl said she wants to be *supi*, and that time I don't know what is *supi*. I went to the girl, the girl do me fine. She would serve me, she would give me everything; she would say that I should sleep with her in the school. We would sleep there, after that then I enjoyed and I started to make some [myself]." Janet aligns her early teenage experience with the "work in bed" she is strong at today. Without being asked, she further substantiates why she continued: "Because I like the *supi* very well, because I enjoy in it. From the time, I'm small then, I started to do this thing. I take a boyfriend but I did not get enjoyment in it than how I enjoy the [*pause*] so I think I choose the [*pause*]." Janet portrays her same-sex activity as a conscious and ongoing choice, but stops when it comes to naming what exactly she chose. The blank space she leaves reflects how unusual it is to nominalize same-sex intimacy.

The chronology of discovering same-sex pleasure before sleeping with men is common in the narratives of assertive "knowing women." Janet was nineteen years old when the man she referred to as her boyfriend asked to take her as his second wife – a marriage proposal her mother flatly rejected. Tellingly, Janet does not compare him to a specific girlfriend, but generalizes on doing and liking *supi* on its own terms. Though she does not invoke *supi* as a social identity, her oscillating between *supi* as an acquired practice and as an inherent mode of being complicates the "act-to-identity trajectory" (Kunzel 2002, 266), hence the assumption that same-sex activity can be understood as either practice *or* identity. Rather than separating the two, Janet's emphasis on "enjoyment" suggests a belonging to herself that echoes Audre Lorde's (1984, 57) vision of the "joy which we know ourselves to be capable of." To Lorde, "the power of the erotic" is not only about one's sexual energy. She reads the erotic through sensuality, as a powerful transcendent and transforming "lens through which we scrutinize all aspects of our existence" (1984, 57). Inspired by Lorde, Jafari Allen (2012, 231) uses the term *erotic subjectivity* to grasp a more holistic understanding of subjective agency, in which the erotic is at the heart of "an embodied human resource composed of our personal histories and (sexual, social) desires" beyond alleged dichotomies between sexual identity and practice.

Janet presents her ways of doing things, including her "tactics" for seducing non-knowledgeable women, as part of a uniquely personal style. My attempts to convey to her that female same-sex love is a global phenomenon were met by her conviction that her skills were beyond generalization. She rather imparted how unique and resourceful she is in pleasing and caring for her lovers. Certainly, allusions to her skill are constitutive of her courting repertoire, in this case directed towards me. Nevertheless, although Janet has heard of the liberties and lifestyles of "lesbians" overseas, she does not seem to connect lesbianism to her own lived reality. The ostensible lesbian representations that circulate in Ghana consist of sleazy girl-on-girl fiction geared towards men and sensational reports on the supposed homosexuality of feminine white celebrities who do not match Janet's image of adorable womanhood. Like many Ghanaians, she deems lighter skinned African women more attractive than darker skinned ones, but finds white women at best exotic.

Clothing, hair, physical stance, and adornment are key markers of identification within butch/femme cultures. In her sociological study on Black lesbians in New York, Mignon Moore (2011, 89) argues that butch/femme roles may have lost their centrality in structuring sexual interactions, but they continue to organize lesbian social worlds and amount to "a visible expression of a distinctive lesbian eroticism." To follow Moore's (2010, 73) schematic categorization of "transgressive," "gender-blender," and femme presentations of self, on a scale from masculine to feminine, Janet and many knowing women qualify as gender blending. Janet combines form-fitting jeans with sturdy shoes and a man's wristwatch, wears women's suits tailored from colourful Ghanaian fabric, and, drawn to the power and prosperity associated with motherhood, makes no attempt to disguise her ample bosom. Like most West African women, she straightens her medium-length hair. I have never seen her with elaborate extensions. Rather, she wears her hair down or in cornrows, just like elderly poor women or schoolgirls who keep their hair short or who cannot afford chemical treatment. Worn by Black American rappers, cornrows also underwent a transatlantic shift in meaning and are now fashionable among young Ghanaian men, especially musicians who see themselves as part of the Black Atlantic world. The plainness and simplicity of this hairstyle, paired with its gendered polyvalence, makes it popular among women who mould womanly and manly, "modern" and "traditional," and Ghanaian and "Western" features into a unique presentation of self.

The cultivation of a (personal) *life* or *style* is a must for young urbanites and goes beyond self-fashioning through dress. Hampered by a lack of expendable income, notions of style chiefly encompass the dimension of bodily manners that do not require the purchase of commercial goods. *Style* pertains to ways of walking, dancing, gesturing, being verbally artistic – in short, of staging a public persona. As Paulla Ebron (2007, 117) elaborates, in West African cultures, complex meanings are assigned to bodily and verbal expressions in which the enactment of an innovative aesthetic self is highly significant. In densely populated neighbourhoods configured by restrictive living quarters, everyday physical and linguistic practices are interpreted as performances that testify to an individual's resourcefulness. The invented nature of one's style is not disguised but emphasized; it speaks to one's capacity to create an intentional life (style) in spite of social control. Janet's at times peculiarly old-fashioned way of presenting herself follows a cultural ideal for self-invention that she reconfigures in a gender-specific way.

Janet's self-fashioning and erotic subjectivity confirms that masculine embodiments need to be understood as social and cultural expressions of maleness that are not tied to the male body. Yet, the normative gaze she encounters differs from the gaze she would face in North Atlantic cities. Other people in her neighbourhood do not interpret her style and "strong structure," which male passers-by compliment in ways that suggest admiration, as signs of alternative sexuality, at least not explicitly. Janet is not confronted with stereotyped images of the childless butch or "mannish lesbian," nor is her masculine stance viewed as a sign of misogyny, as it may be within heteronormative as well as lesbian-feminist spaces (Cvetkovich 1998). Rather, her physicality and her presentation of self, which avoids a potentially objectionable urban youth look, makes people believe she is older than her actual age, which in turn enhances her status and agency as an erotic citizen.

RELATIONAL MASCULINITY

In Twi, the term *obaa barima* reflects the transferability of gender.[17] In Gracia Clark's translation, an *obaa barima* is a "manly or brave woman," in which *barima* connotes young male bravery, but is also "the most polite positive way of referring to sexual virility." The market women Clark (1999, 722) heard called *obaa barima* in the 1990s were "those who had achieved the level of financial independence, considered essential for men, not those showing unusual physical strength, bravery, or sexual prowess." Consonant with historic responsibilities for farming, physically strong women did not attract particular comment. As a compliment for a savvy market woman, *obaa barima* conveys the masculine ideal most often transferred from men to women: the positive capacity for economic self-aggrandizement.

Clark (1999, 722) observes that an *obaa barima*'s subservience to her husband might be reduced, but "the sexual conduct of an *obaa barima* was not suspect." Female footballers who appropriate a cosmopolitan masculine youth look are noticeable and attract aggressive comments that mark them as deviant and lesbians. Among mature women vested with networks of friends, relatives, and dependents, however, it is economic capacity rather than physical appearance that determines if they are considered manly in the most positive sense. It is this version of female masculinity that Clark (1999, 727) grasps when she says that a woman's "economic performance of gender appears more central and more notable" than her sexual behaviour or bodily gender presentation. The significance of a person's socio-economic scope and potency informs my analysis of both the self-fashioning and the gendered roles of female lovers.

Many of my respondents were striving to become what could be considered an *obaa barima*. Ameley Nortey, for instance, is a thirty-eight-year-old mother known for her warm-hearted generosity. After attending primary school for a few years, Ameley started to sell petty items. Today she works in a field chiefly occupied by women: she walks her neighbourhood in Accra with a basket full of nail polish and gives manicures and pedicures. Her living quarters consist of a stuffy room shared with her husband and their two sons. As the room is getting too small, Ameley prefers to sleep in the airy but noisy compound her family shares with neighbouring tenants and domestic animals. Despite her impaired sight, caused by an eye disease she suffered as a child, Ameley is energetic and assertive. When she hears people gossiping about what she terms her "women friendships," she either ignores or vigorously denies them. Tellingly, she holds the term *supi* and its growing media popularity responsible for the increased level of such hostile "gossiping," which suggests that previously there was no readily available language with which to demonize knowing women.

Although Ameley wears dresses and does not visibly distinguish herself from other working-class women her age, she clearly positions herself as "the man" when it comes to same-sex love. At the time of our first interview, pregnant with her third and last child, she conveyed that she did not have a lover. Based on what she experienced during her previous pregnancy, when her long-term female friend was jealous and bewitched and prolonged the pregnancy by three months, Ameley holds that having a female lover while pregnant can harm the unborn. In the course of our interview, however, she claims that she stopped seeing women altogether for yet another reason: "You see, when you're on the *man side* ... and you have a *girlfriend*, you have to *spend* for the woman. If the woman also has some money, then you'll be helping each other. But all the people I was meeting were poor, so the *burden* always falls on you the man. Once you don't get money to cater for them, you need to stop. Because I don't want anybody to say that 'I'm going out with you and you don't give me money'" (personal interview, 4 April 2007).[18]

Initiating an intimate sexual friendship requires the capacity to offer something. The ability to invite a prospective lover out helps to arouse her interest, especially if she is not yet in the know. But Ameley is not alluding to the early stage of romance, since she knows how to seduce inexperienced women through her care and charisma rather than through monetary spending. Rather, she is concerned with the later stages of a relationship. Being on the "man side" requires a certain level of socio-economic power that allows Ameley to provide for her lovers and lay claim to an ostensibly dominant role. Her provider role should prevent her woman from having other, more gainful "men." In the worse case scenario, as Ameley further explicates, this could result in a lover presenting her with money she had received from an "outside" suitor.

Ameley's statements need to be read against a background of chronic material poverty in which the question of survival is crucial in all relationships, whether or not they are erotically charged. Framed by the obligation and desire to cater to one's close relations, serious bonds – be they between relatives, friends, or lovers – involve the exchange of monetary and material gifts. Friends are expected to house each other if the need occurs, and to share food, clothes, shoes, phones, and beds. Between spouses and lovers, such "transactions" assume additional meanings. For the South African context, Mark Hunter (2010) coins the term *provider love* to bridge the alleged gap between material transactions and romantic feelings within heterosexual relationships. Time and again my interview subjects reminded

me that at least one woman in a relationship must be able to provide
and ensure the couple's material survival. The vital necessity and the
casualness of gift exchanges do not deflect from the dependencies
that emerge from them. The resulting power dynamics are read as
signs of passion and mutual commitment.

There is yet another factor that plays out between same-sex lovers,
which enhances Ameley's seniority despite her financial insufficiency.
As discussed above, seniority is relative to one's maturity in a certain
field and can connote erotic power. Knowing of the depth and intricacies of same-sex passion, and the capacity to conceal this knowledge from outsiders, while "transmitting" it to a non-knowing lover
constitute Ameley's seniority. While she dates her first adult same-
sex experience to her age of physical maturation around sixteen, she
remembers kissing and playing with girls from the age of seven. But
again, she ascribes the fact that girls liked to visit her house to her
generosity: "I was getting money from my mother ... she had enough
for me, such that when you're my friend and you don't have money
and you come to me ... I was able to provide – even as a child, you
knew that you needed to give the person something. So they used to
come to me more than I went to them."

Ameley naturalizes and reflects on her provider role not only
through a gendered language, but also by deploying age. I ask her:
"How do you mean you are the man in the relationship?" She replies:
"In everything there should to be a head." Reminding her of her past
dramatic relationship, I argue that her girlfriend might have been the
head. But Ameley passionately interrupts me: "She won't dare! She
can't be given that right. If she does that outside, then *fine*, but not
on my *side*." I insist: "How do you mean 'the head'? What does it
mean?" Ameley replies: "As we are sitting here, there should by all
means be an elder, there should be an elder amongst us."[19]

To mark role divisions, Ameley resorts to a negotiable junior/
senior – rather than masculine/feminine – binary and asserts that
every social situation, be it between lovers, among friends, or sitting
around a table in an interview, needs a leading head. Vested with
symbolic power, being an elder is both a privilege and a duty that
implies the capacity to take charge of others' well-being, give guidance, and make wise decisions under challenging economic circumstances. Ameley's boastful comment that her ex-girlfriend could
have only taken on an "elder" position vis-à-vis another lover "outside" their relationship indicates how relational and situational this

role is. It speaks to the possibility of having multiple lovers and being the senior in one relationship and the junior in another. As Ameley concedes, she has been with "big women" older and better off than herself, and simultaneously had lovers who were her juniors. The older Ameley grows, the more she is eligible to claim the senior role with which she identifies, even if she cannot provide.

Ameley's elaborations underpin how self-evident it is for "knowing women" to refer to social rather than physical aspects of masculinity. Portraying herself as committed to the provider role, she claims she stopped having "women friends" due to her monetary shortcomings – a statement she amended in a second interview, a year later. In fact, at the time of our first interview she was getting involved with her pastor's wife. Since this friend worked at the hospital, Ameley even allowed her to give "chop money" to her children to buy school lunches. Still, Ameley maintains that she would never ask a lover for money as doing so would undermine her sense of "being on the man's side."

Similarly, Janet speaks of herself as "the man" when she expounds on her courting strategies. "The man," she tells me, is "the one who first says 'I love you,'" the one who first articulates her love interest. The implications of such a declaration dawned on me when she introduced my assistant and me to a mature woman she adored. Janet was single at the time and we asked her why she would not propose to the woman who was the owner of a little saloon and a wife and mother of five. She explains: "Hey, you want me to be in trouble? If I go first to tell her I love her, then I will be the man and I will have to take care of her. I have to give her money and I don't have the money. So I was waiting for her to tell me she loves me, but she was not saying it ... At the end nobody told anybody anything and we are friends now."[20] Declaring love is tricky. It comes with expectations. The one who proposes is supposed to provide (love). Janet shies away from tapping into the ambiguous power of the spoken word and explicitly courting a woman who is more resourced. If she were to hastily disclose her erotic interest and make the first move, she would be taking on a role she could not live up to. As a "man" without money who is young, effusive, and not always discreet, it would be difficult to secure a respectable position.

Aware of the fact that she cannot afford to be "the man," Janet needs a woman who allows for her assertiveness without making monetary demands. This was the case with Sister Vida, mentioned at the beginning of this chapter. Even though Janet cannot learn "jobs that women do," she happily fulfilled a junior role with Vida, who was more established and more than ten years older than herself. As Vida was busy running her market stall all day, Janet performed domestic chores usually assigned to wives or children. She took it upon herself to get up at dawn, sweep their room and compound, prepare a bucket of warm water for Vida's shower, and iron Vida's dress; in the evening, she made sure dinner was ready and on Sundays she would do their laundry – washing even Vida's panties, an unmistakable sign of devoted love, as Janet emphasizes.[21] Vida, on the other hand, made it possible for Janet to complete an unpaid internship on the military campus by meeting the costs for food and transportation. Based on their mutual care, which corresponds with the Akan understanding of marital love – an understanding that thrives on a couple's reciprocal support rather than on pure romance – Janet considers her relationship with Vida a "true love," even though it eventually deteriorated. Vida claims they eventually separated because one night, when Vida had a male visitor, Janet insulted her in front of neighbours. Janet believes it was her incapacity to contribute financially to their household that made Vida pick a quarrel over the nocturnal visitor, whom Janet would have been willing to accept as genitor of the child Vida was after.

Janet's readiness to take on a "wifely" role highlights the structuring effect of age and the flexibility poverty requires. Both Janet and Ameley consider their stifling economic situation, rather than their sexed bodies, as a hindrance to the manliness they invoke. The primacy of socioeconomic status prompts women who are particularly keen to assume a dominant role to employ a variety of flirtatious strategies in order to smooth the gap between ideal and precarious reality. Their considerations resonate with the frustrations of non-salaried young men in West Africa, who struggle to compete with older and wealthier men. What they lack in economic stability, they attempt to make up through the mastery of the "modern" language of emotional intimacy (Masquelier 2009, 219). Similarly, Ameley knows how to sweet talk and relies on her verbal versatility when speaking love. Her identification with the initiator role and her charge to attend to her own and her lovers' intimate desires puts her in a vulnerable position, which is only partially veneered by the masculinity she lays claim to.

CONCLUSION

Many women I came across professed to striving to be relational men. But what they called the "man's side" in their same-sex relationships referred less to bodily styling than to the ideal of assuming a provider role. While this role may allude to erotic, social, and symbolic capital, it does not necessarily correlate with physical embodiments and visible insignias of masculinity. As Ameley conveys, passionate same-sex bonds are configured by constant negotiations over leadership that are not mediated or obfuscated through superficial understandings of dominance. Relationships emerge as sites of mutual care, but also as particularly dense transfer points of relational power beyond butch/femme representations.

Young women often lack the capacity to give "provider love," but have more leverage in transgressing gender boundaries and adapting globalized styles of youthful masculinity. Elizabeth Kennedy and Madeline Davis (1993) account for such a dynamic in working-class butch/femme constellation in the United States, where the younger partner with a more masculine appearance fulfilled domestic chores. While visible differences between butch and femme are often seen as structuring community and relationships, the roles I encountered among women in Ghana were not considered visual. The primacy of relational power that is generated by seniority curtailed the relevance of physical gender display.

Is it their readiness to articulate and act on their desires that makes Janet and Ameley "men"? Is it their endurance in pursuing female lovers and asserting "the erotic as power" that makes them knowing women? Whereas their physical appearance may not be read as butch, Ann Cvetkovich's understanding of being butch as an emotional style certainly applies to Ameley's and Janet's provider ideal and their passion to be in charge of their lovers' desires. Cvetkovich advocates for a notion of being butch that is not bound up and circumscribed by visible insignia of female masculinity. Instead, she suggests, "the relation between being butch and hypervisible styles of masculinity must remain unpredictable" (1989, 169). The styles and practices I came across shifting and unpredictable, and the very notion of a female masculinity looses its potency when difference is conceptualized along multiple metaphors of power. It seems relationality, rather than visibility, forms the butch identity of those who seek to be "the one who first says: I love you."

10

LGBTI Community and Citizenship Practices in Urban Ghana

KATHLEEN O'MARA

In June 2010 in Sekondi-Takoradi, twin port towns in Ghana's Western Region, "thousands of angry youth" marched in the "first ever anti-gay protests" (*Peace FM Online*, 4 June 2010). Organized by local Muslim imams, the march demonstrated public hostility to non-normative sexualities, but equally publicized the growth of social networks of the self-identified lesbians and gays who have founded small, vibrant communities in Accra, Kumasi, Takoradi, and elsewhere. Subsequently, in March 2012 in Accra, there was reported vigilante violence against perceived gays and lesbians (*Joy Online*, 13 March 2012). The violence was "incited" by a lesbian birthday party, at which the "celebrant and well wishers were gays and lesbians." In the subsequent days, "armed men" returned to "attack homes," leading nine of the suspected gays and lesbians to seek "refuge at a NGO" (*Joy Online*, 17 March 2012). Media reported that angry youth armed with chains, sticks, and cutlasses spoke about a "sexual cleansing exercise" (*Joy Online*, 31 May 2012), which underscored the effects of a rising tide of anti-gay rhetoric, public awareness of same-sex intimate or LGBTI networks in Ghana, and the politicization of sexuality.[1]

Though slower to become a topic of public discussion than in Southern or Eastern Africa, where politicians have employed anti-gay rhetoric since the early 1990s, public awareness has progressed since September 2006, when Ghana experienced its first "gay" moral panic (O'Mara 2007). That panic resulted from a Joy FM radio discussion of a sexual behaviour survey that morphed into a rumour of

a "forthcoming gay conference" (*BBC News*, 1 September 2006) that
incited weeks of condemnation in pulpits, newspapers, blogs, television, and radio, identifying gays as "unnatural, bestial, satanic, deviant and un-Ghanaian" (Ireland 2006). Subsequently, Ghana's media
regularly covered the topic in articles such as "Gays Raid Kids'
Butts" (*GhanaWeb*, 11 December 2006), "Male Prostitutes Practice
Openly in Accra," (*African Veil*, 14 October 2008), or "Gay Party in
Takoradi!" (*GhanaWeb*, 26 August 2009). Media called Accra, the
capital city, and Sekondi-Takoradi, with many foreign petrol industry workers, "Sodom and Gomorrah" (*Peace* FM *Online*, 4 June
2010; *GhanaWeb*, 11 December 2006). Despite this inflammatory
public discourse, the Takoradi march and the Accra assaults underlined reality, as one of my informants, Spiffy, said in a 2005 interview: "We have everything, everyone here, darling! But you cannot
see it." That is, Ghana contains sexual practices, LGBTI gathering
places, and communities comparable to other countries.

 The invisibility and silence Spiffy referenced was a social practice
of "don't ask, don't tell." In the past half-decade, mass media, religious and government officials – including health bureaucrats and
local and international NGO functionaries – and, increasingly, individual Ghanaians who identify as LGBTI have helped others
acknowledge their existence. This marks a shift from the perception
of homosexuality as an individual moral problem to a social phenomenon and major social problem detailed in sermons, official government pronouncements, popular videos about money-obsessed
young men selling their bodies and souls such as *The Dons of Sakawa*
(2011), and self-education manuals such as *Same-Sex Attraction:
Choice or Genetic?* (Akagbor 2007). In urban Ghana as elsewhere in
Africa, the "veil" that "obscured" same-sex sexual conduct in Sub-
Saharan Africa is being lifted by homosexual subjects, their states
and government actors, and individual and institutional agents who
construct connections between African LGBTI individuals and the
processes of globalization (Broqua chapter 11 in this volume).

 This chapter intersects with several others in this volume – Dankwa
and Broqua, notably – in examining social practices of same-sex intimate men and women in Accra as well as the discursive practices
that comprise some of their strategies to fashion self and community.
In the first section of this chapter, I discuss the sociopolitical and
juridical conditions that frame the emergence of LGBTI networks
and the conceptual scaffolding to understand them. In the second

section, I examine the social and discursive practices in constructing community. Finally, I discuss two incipient leaders who demonstrate the progress and character of community in Accra. I layer a discussion of Ghanaian ways of living same-sex intimate lives in an often hostile environment, the construction of community discursive and social practices, efforts through practice to realize (culturally and metaphorically) citizenship, and the impact of Global North cultures in shaping LGBTI communities.

FRAMEWORKS OF SEXUALITIES

Ghana's emergent communities reflect the intersection of conflicts embedded in discussions of sexualities elsewhere in Africa: a local (and colonial) reading of LGBTI persons as un-African, deviants created by Westerners, or victims of Global South human rights violations who need legal protection to "come out." As Nyeck discusses in chapter 8, the politicization of sexuality in general has escalated in Africa in the twenty-first century, with heightened fears about homosexuality, the perceived spread of Western homosexual identity, and the notion of sexual human rights connected to the work of international health NGOs, especially those dedicated to HIV/AIDS prevention. Religious institutions everywhere are central to this conflict, e.g., at its sixty-ninth synod in August 2010, the Global Evangelical Church (GEC) asked the government to condemn "cultures ... inimical to the spiritual and moral health of Ghanaians in the name of human rights" (GhanaWeb, 8 August 2010). LGBTI Ghanaians, like other Africans, struggle to stake a claim in society as ordinary citizens and to self-define and experience full social belonging. They do not, as studies of sexual minorities elsewhere in the developing world show, necessarily self-define with the dominant Western paradigm of a notion of individualized sexual subjectivity, expressed in coming out of the closet and claiming a fixed identity (Undie and Benaya 2006); indeed, such a benchmark portrays the developing world as the other and the West as normative. Rather, listening to and comprehending how Africans express same-sex intimacy and live and think about their sexuality and social lives should be read against Western – and indeed residual colonial – discourse. Reverend Zacc Kawalala of Word Alive Ministry referenced this in his response to foreign criticism of a male couple's arrest for marrying in Malawi: "The West ... wants to look at Africa and say, 'If you don't accept homosexuality, you are primitive'"(*New York Times*, 13 February 2010). It is not only the closet which is a discursive constraint for Ghanaians, for as Oyèrónké Oyéwùmí (2005, 99) and Maria Lugones (2008, 7–9) discuss, basic concepts such as gender and race are colonial constructs and part of the Euro-centred axis of modernity, and do not necessarily reflect indigenous notions of organizing social identity. Social debates in Ghana, as elsewhere in Africa, are framed by and react to colonial constructions of an African "deviant" or "underdeveloped" sexuality versus a "developed" Western one that critics such as Marlon Ross (2005, 181) urge researchers to reject and instead rethink theories of sexual identity of racialized and colonized groups in the West and Global South.

In Ghana as in Africa generally, homosexuality is perceived as a sign of Westernization that, in a nationalist reading, is inappropriate for a de-colonized subject position. The homosexual, as Foucault (1978), Katz (1990), and others argue, arose in the late nineteenth century West, a time that coincided with colonization in Africa. The category contains a history that camouflages the history of racialization and contempt of African sexualities and fails to reflect the diversity and complexity of African same-sex intimacies (Epprecht in this volume, among others). Modern, urban, sexually non-normative Africans implicitly contest this category as they assert their cultural authenticity. At one level, such assertion resists the West's notion of sexual identity as the core of modern subjectivity, and at the other, it resists the racialized colonial structure of power that inhabits the Enlightenment model of sexual progress – from tradition to modernity – and the diffusionist model of globalization – from North to South. This does not mean international or Western influences are absent, or that social developments, of gays, lesbians, and their myriad assemblages, do not resemble Western LGBTI historical community traits that, as Broqua (chapter 11 in this volume) argues for Bamako men, applies as well to men's networks in Accra.

African sexual practices provide a clearer understanding of indigenous cultural logics. Henriette Gunkel (2009, 208), in revising Eve Kosofsky Sedgwick's characterization of (Western) women's sexuality, argues that it is illuminating to consider African same-sex intimacies as positions on a continuum, rather than a binary between friendships and homosexual relations. Where individuals sit on the continuum at any moment is flexible, situational, and relational. Western ideology obscures those characteristics with regulation and surveillance: language and concepts of unnatural sex that serve to freeze the non-normative subject. In examining African resistance to a static identity and fashioning non-normative sexual expressions, this essay reflects Ross's appeal, as well as Carlos Decena's analysis of immigrant US Dominican gay men, who he found occupy a space both in and out of the closet in terms of being tacit subjects. That is, what is tacit is neither secret nor silent, but is understood or assumed. In speaking about their homosexuality as knowable in a tacit way to family and friends, such individuals also assume that some people have the necessary skills to "read" and decipher their behaviour.

In Ghana, as in northern Nigeria (Pierce 2007; Gaudio 2009) or southern Africa (Epprecht 2006), the Accra LGBTI interviewees[2] understood that while not everyone may be able to read the signs, some can apprehend their non-normative sexuality, i.e., their identification as those who know or, in local Akan terms, as *kodjo besia* or women in *supi* relationships, despite their efforts to conceal such identification from the population at large (Decena 2008, 340). This tactic (see Dankwa chapter 9 in this volume) equally reveals the complicities that frame their social relations and the ways they negotiate information about themselves within local homosocial practices that create space for ambiguity, such as homes, football pitches, and public baths. Cynthia, a twenty-two-year-old lesbian craft trader, acknowledged her mother and grandmother's unspoken acceptance of her relationship with her primary girlfriend: "She has a key to my room and stays when I am not there. My Mum calls her 'daughter.'" Using kin terms is one social tool, conveniently ambiguous, which carries different meanings to those in the know. She added that her girlfriend's family "love me so much ... her fiancé has called me ... to talk with me about her!" When an acquaintance of his suggested the two were *supi*, he inquired, and Cynthia said, "I told him, absolutely no." Similarly, Mike, like many men interviewed, lives in a house adjacent to his mother's, which necessitates much discretion, but believed his mother knew about his boyfriend.

In making an LGBTI community in Ghana, there was tension between alternative approaches to living as non-normative sexual citizens – between quietly building community versus publicly demanding human rights – contoured by Ghanaian customs of social discretion and suspicions that imported gay models of self-definition might undermine Ghanaian authenticity. The public debate on homosexuality in Ghana, especially since 2010, has undermined the former strategy. The influence of international gay organizations (e.g., ILGA, IGLHRC, Rainbow Coalition, Queer African Youth Network), and numerous health and HIV/AIDS NGOs has further eroded the possibility of under-the-radar community organizing. In particular, the lure of access to funds and information through NGO grants encourages emulation of global organizational models. That carries an additional cost, for example, the Gay and Lesbian Association of Ghana (GALAG), a singular small organization attached to the health and human rights NGO Centre for Popular Education Human Rights Ghana (CEPEHRG), has been the target, especially since 2006, of condemnatory statements.

Global LGBTI cultural influences are most evident in the realm of entertainment consumption choices and social activities used to fashion a shared sub-cultural community of practice, such as watching bootleg copies of the gay African American cable series *Noah's Arc*, Showtime's *The L Word*, Nigerian and Ghanaian homoerotic videos like *Girls Cot 2/3*, and African American gay male porn. Same-sex intimate men and women claimed public spaces such as bars, garden cafés, video clubs, and dance clubs as LGBTI spaces, not necessarily continuously but rather in rotating fashion or on special occasions during most of the 2000s, but public awareness has made some commercial establishments risky places and others, such as Henri's, a pub, have closed. In building a gay community, a domestication process is discernible and includes tactics such as adapting the discourse to Ghana, building LGBTI kin networks synchronized with local customs (gay daughters, lesbian senior brothers), and using knowledge of informal community organizing for group protection, recreation, and information dissemination. Thus, emerging LGBTI communities in Ghana raise questions about the social production of non-normative subjecthood and move interpretations away from assumptions about a Western model of liberation in which LGBTI identity is a necessity for social transformation; however, these strategies are indirectly and directly under ideological and material pressure to change, go public, and wage formal campaigns for human rights.

Christophe Broqua (chapter 11 in this volume), in describing global influences on Africa, argues for the similarity between "historic homosexuality" in the United States, as described by George Chauncey in *Gay New York* (1994), and homosexual practices among men in Bamako, Mali. Broqua stresses the dominance of the gender inversion model, particularly in language, but also the diversity of sexual role practices. The assemblages of men in Accra also reflect this diversity. Chauncey's (1994, 2–3) more useful discussion for this chapter is about community practices and refuting the myths about gay New York prior to the Second World War, such as that homosexual men were isolated and invisible, and internalized negative hegemonic ideas of homosexuality as sick and perverted. Rather, gay men constructed parallel non-normative communities through a variety of pedestrian actions such as birthday parties, rent parties, drag/costume balls, regular attendance on certain nights at dance or jazz clubs, pubs, restaurants, churches, parks, and cruising grounds. Like other aspects of US society, homosexual life was classed, gendered, and racialized though more cross group interactions than heterosexual life. In Accra and in Bamako, as Broqua details, the divide between heterosexuality and homosexuality is as porous as in *Gay New York*. Historically, the development of same-sex communities has required an urban milieu, a territory that required certain freedoms from rural and familial social strictures, especially spaces of anonymity, access to a large population, and possibilities for camouflaging social and sexual activities. Accra, a city of four million persons, similar to Bamako, Dakar, or Yaounde, provides the necessary *mise en scène* for individuals to forge a distinct parallel culture and, like cities of the Global North rather recently, to fashion community in a context of social hostility and draconian policing (Chauncey 1994, 4).

In this context of public condemnation and partial private tolerance, fall 2011 marked a watershed in international attention/intervention. On 10 October 2011, UK Prime Minister David Cameron publicly tied continued UK foreign aid to a change in African states' denial of LGBTI legal rights, beginning with a nineteen-million-pound cut in aid to Malawi after two men were sentenced to fourteen years hard labour (*New York Times*, 10 October 2011). Ghanaian President John Atta Mills publicly retorted, "I, as president, will never initiate or support any attempt to legalise homosexuality in Ghana," stressing that the country's "societal norms are different than the UK" (*BBC News*, 2 November 2011). A few weeks later, US Secretary of State Hillary Clinton also called for "progress," said "gay rights are human rights," and publicized a new policy which directed US government agencies to consider gay rights when making aid and asylum decisions (*BBC News*, 7 December 2011).

DISCURSIVE PRACTICES

The importance of discretion among Africans has been examined in several recent studies of same-sex intimacy by Epprecht (2006), Pierce (2007), Hoad (2007), Gaudio (2009), and Dankwa (2009).[3] As Dankwa notes in this volume and elsewhere (chapter 9; 2009, 193), silence is common for Ghanaian same-sex intimate or "knowing" women, and reflects indigenous preferences for discretion and indirect speech about sexual matters. It structures social and even erotic intimacy where body language often prevails over the spoken word (2009). Sylvia Tamale (2011, 14) points to silence and discretion as a prime example of "'African culture' viewing silence as being powerful and as empowering as speech," a position that evidence from Accra supports. Significantly, discretion as practice maintains spaces for ambiguous expressions of homosociality (Dankwa 2009 and in this volume) and hence for building alternative community. All the subjects for this project indicated that discretion was unquestioned; it prohibits public displays of affection or, in principle, discussion of sexual behaviour. Intergenerational discussions of sex are seen as inappropriate, though most subjects believe parents and siblings know. As Frank reported: "My mum would never ask, nor my sisters. Three years ago a man who was living with me stole money and clothes, then left, and my aunt found out from a neighbour. I am afraid to see her or her children." Norms of discretion and indirection are rooted in Ghana's dominant ethno-linguistic group, the Akan, but extend to other ethnicities (Yankah 1995, 50). While not everyone is able to read the signs, there are those who apprehend who is sex or gender non-normative, gay, or lesbian. Straddling the visible-invisible divide, Ghanaian LGBTI networks enact civic-minded ways of living as participatory citizens, as they build community and engage in a domestic rather than a global process. This approach includes adapting the discourse to Ghana and engaging in community social practices similar to those described in *Gay New York* or almost any other community where homosexuality is or was illegal or socially vilified, e.g., identifying sub-rosa community spaces, creating dress codes and a subcultural lexicon, and creating fictive kin – gay mothers, lesbian sons, eagle senior uncles, even multi-generational families. Api, a working deejay and corn miller in Tema, has created such a family and has provided a home over time to so many homeless, migrant LGBTI youth that some call him

Mama, while younger ones address him as Grandma, a quintessentially Ghanaian practice.

CONCEPTUAL FRAMEWORKS

In this chapter, I make use of particular underlying assumptions about sexual difference, such as that social identities are fluid and permeable (Butler 1990) and that "community" as constructed in discourse is also a social construction that largely exists in the minds of its members. As Mary Bucholtz and Kira Hall (2004, 505) assert, "gender does not have the same meanings across space and time, but is instead a local production, realized differently by different members of the community," as are various sexual practices. The men's and women's networks, articulated within a local neighbourhood community, are marked by a specific shared geography of safe spots within neighbourhoods, and links with peers in other neighbourhoods, both male and female, effectively creating an LGBTI circuit that runs from the West side of Accra to East of Tema (Greater Accra). The following analysis of LGBTI communities is informed by a "communities of practice" perspective that views identities as multiple and fluid and emerging through social and discursive practices (Wenger 1998). Sexual and/or social identities are produced in relation to specific material conditions and positions of power, including local social customs and stigma. In Ghana, a sense of LGBTI community forms around shared knowledge, individual and collective experiences, events, and strategies of in/visibility in everyday life, echoing Eckert and McConnell-Ginet's (1992, 463–4) point that "ways of doing things ... talking" emerge through mutual endeavour as participants move from "one identity to another ... meaning ... it is the result of a local production" (Bucholtz and Hall 2004, 505). In this way, *saso* ("buddy") or *eagle* ("husband, strong woman"), gay or lesbian identifications, intersect with other meaningful claims, namely ethnicity, gender, clan, and religion. The analytic tool Liz Morrish (Morrish and Sauntson 2007, 99–101) applies, Charles Clark's idea of concealment, also demonstrates that one can conceal something from one part of an audience and simultaneously reveal it to another by using a code that depends on mutual knowledge. The Accra men's networks employ this strategy and a small specialist lexicon in conjunction with disguisement (to deceive a listener) especially when speaking about fellow community members in risky spaces. For some LGBTI Ghanaians, such as religious or legal professionals, the tactic means concealing and revealing simultaneously, often in public spaces such as shrines, funerals, and courts. My Accra interviewees most often self-identified as gay or lesbian. None was wealthy or a member of an elite profession; a number worked in the hospitality industry in hotel management or restaurant service, and many were self-employed as tailors, hair stylists, craftsmen, and market vendors.

DISCURSIVE COMMUNITY FRAMEWORK

Gender binaries and Ghanaian cultural references inhabit the men's small lexicon, indigenizing and localizing group discourse and creating playful expressions. The female interviewees rarely incorporated such references, and so matched Anglo and Western women who also have few words for their sexual behaviours, erotic interests, and relationships (Morrish and Sauntson 2007, 130–6). In interviews, women referred to their partners or love interests most often as "dear" and, if they identified them in a commanding position, as "eagle" or "king." In describing fellow male community members, men spoke of *saso* ("buddy") or *yag* ("backslang"), though men with matronly appearances were called *Mami*. Rarely, leaders received the appellation *Yaa Asantewaa* ("queen"), though twice I heard men publicly hail someone they understood to be gay and found attractive with "*Yaa Asantewaa*!" invoking a subversive identity in a Butlerian (1990) reality. LGBTI people therefore use Ghanaian history to signify LGBTI identities, for example, referring to Yaa Asantewaa, the Queen Mother of Ejisu, who in 1900 and 1901 led a rebellion against the British occupiers of the Asante state, the most powerful precolonial nation within Ghana. In naming their own community leader after her, men dramatically align themselves with national culture and armed motherhood, the ultimate form of female power. Stephan Miescher (2005, 8, 12) argues that Akan societies possess a "long history of contested masculinity and femininity," with rival notions of masculinity, the ɔpanyin ("senior," a mediator with good advice) and ɔbirɛmpɔn (a big man, wealthy and generous) as alternatives to the warrior model, ideas that expanded under colonialism. This lexicon reveals two strategies of an evolving community of practice: the domestication and incorporation of nonnormative sexuality into local culture by inventing new expressions of it (Yankah 1991, 18), and a rhetoric of ambiguity that conceals from those who should not or do not want to know, yet reveals to those who do.

REGULATION AND THE POLITICS OF SEXUALITY

While individual sexual practices are personal and private, sexuality as a concept has become loudly political in Ghana, and its regulation reflects nationalist, anti-colonial, Christian, Muslim, ethnic, metropolitan, LGBTI, local, and global political agendas. Foucaultian concepts are useful in deciphering these politics. Of particular use is *governmentality*, or the processes, laws, and technologies of social regulation Foucault (1978) argues define the modern state, and which are subsumed within the conceptual triangle of sovereignty-discipline-government (Burchell et al. 1991). This is a multilevel approach to comprehending the interplay between formal institutions such as mass media, schools, churches, the state, and the processes that individual citizens employ in self-management of sexual conduct, or its opposite, resistance to social controls in constituting themselves as subjects. It is key to revealing how cultures and individuals within them consciously and unconsciously govern sexualities. Postcolonial states and societies, like others, produce what Ann Stoler (2004) calls "educating consent," or securing agreement by directing judgement and even pushing individuals to sever some affective relationships.

LEGAL AND ECONOMIC FRAMEWORK

Ghana is a postcolonial developing country that hit economic bottom in the late 1970s and 1980s during a structural adjustment period marked by Christian revivalism, which continues today through the many Charismatic and Pentecostal churches to contribute to a profoundly heteronormative culture (Gifford 89–128). Ghana is now a lower-middle-income developing nation with a per capita income of $1,210 in 2011 (Ghana Statistical Services 2011). However, income distribution varies extremely between regions and classes. Three quarters of the workforce is in the informal sector and most residents of Accra survive on less than two dollars per day (Ghana Statistical Services 2011). Legally, British colonial era anti-sodomy laws remain in force; notably, article 104 of the criminal code states that anyone "guilty of unnatural carnal knowledge of any person sixteen years or over without his consent shall be guilty of first degree felony, and liable on conviction to imprisonment for a term of not less than five years and not more than twenty five years." Further, "any person with his consent or of any animal, is guilty of a misdemeanor" (UNHCR 1961). The article lumps together rape, homosexuality, and bestiality, and discursively organizes public attitudes. Men and women have been prosecuted and imprisoned since 2000: in October 2011, three gay men were arrested in Sakumono, Accra (www.dailyguideghana.com); in August 2005, a young woman was charged in with practicing unnatural sex for "luring an 18 year old girl into lesbianism" (*Ghanaian Chronicle*, 22 June 2005); and in August 2003, four men were tried for "unlawful carnal knowledge" and "indecent exposure" and sentenced to two years' imprisonment for exchanging photos for money with a Norwegian man (Zachary, www.sodomylaws.org). Arrests do not necessarily result in convictions, but the public announcements of charges serve as warnings. Heightened public discourse of homosexuality has resulted in media debates over the sodomy law, and lawyers such as Ernest Kofi Abotsi, a law lecturer at KNUST, assert it is "almost impossible for the act of homosexuality to be considered criminal" in Ghana because the 1992 Constitution and the Criminal Offences Act, 1960 (Act 29) do not clearly state what homosexuality means (*Ghana News Now*, 17 June 2010).

Widespread extortion and even police entrapment reinforce messages for sexual self-management. The IGLHRC has reported both. Mac-Darling Cobbinah's chapter on Ghana in *Nowhere to Turn: Blackmail and Extortion of LGBT People in Sub-Saharan Africa* (2011) also reports that the victims attributed the ubiquity of blackmail against MSM to the "illegality" of homosexuality, the standard interpretation of the sodomy law. Alex, Kofi, Jacob, Isaac, Frank, and others all emphasized the continuous threat of extortion and increased assaults, as did many of my female interviewees. Mercy, a self-employed thirty-year-old craft artist, told me that she struck a man with a broom and bloodied his nose because he "cursed me, calling me lesbian, evil" outside a market. She was jailed for two weeks, until her stepfather collected "several hundred cedi" so the police would release her. Several women said that they and their partners try to live in compounds with other lesbian" (her term), but nonetheless are harassed by neighbours who call them *supi*. Ama, a fish seller, claimed she often verbally fought back with, "I play football! I like to dress this way." She was hospitalized in 2011, though, when her girlfriend's ex-boyfriend viciously attacked her and broke her nose, cheekbone, wrist, and several teeth. Most victims of assault and blackmail know the perpetrators. Caroline, a young footballer, described how her girlfriend's brother turned her in to the police: the "CID arrested me" and "I had to borrow one hundred twenty Ghana cedi" to pay them and "give her brother my laptop." Family and public abuse, blackmail, and police bribery all comprise elements of the surveillance regime that shapes LGBTI subjecthood in Ghana. It is a strategy of control secured by penetrating the individual's consciousness with the threat of surveillance, and thus nudges the person to adhere to cultural norms.

Technology, especially the Internet, aids a regime of surveillance and economic exploitation. Nii, who offered blackmail prevention trainings from 2007 to 2009, claimed: "There are so many cases ... I know men who have gone into hiding ... some who pay and pay and fear for their life." Alex described a Nigerian friend of his who met an email date at the airport, but was "robbed, left naked and bloody a mile from the airport." Women face blackmail primarily in private, while men face assault and extortion in many public places (Thoreson and Cook 2011, 4–14). Cynthia's narrative, echoed with minor variation by a number of women in their twenties, reflected a pattern of exploitation by neighbours, fellow parishioners, and co-workers: "This girl ... I go to church with her ... She wanted to watch a movie with me ... She wants me to hold her, so it came to a point where we were making out. Later she called me ... said she needs money ... her boyfriend said he'd tell people I'm lesbian ... wanted about 150 Ghana cedi. I was afraid. I sold my TV, got 130 cedi ($90). I gave it to him." As Cobbinah (2011) details, men who were blackmailed in Accra and dared to report the issue to police did not always receive help, such as "K.K. (who was) raped multiple times" and was advised by police that his "attacker was a wanted criminal," but they did not know where to find him. Fearful, he left his job and neighbourhood (Thoreson and Cook 2011, 67). NGOS collect data on blackmail – for example, CEPEHRG began to do so in late 2007 – but most women's and men's networks focus on creating alternative modes of communication, such as texting when in trouble, and sharing information about people and places to avoid at house parties, sporting events, and gay-owned venues. Media scare tactics on homosexuality and Sunday morning sermons have increased awareness of LGBTI youth in particular and have resulted in many working, urban, poor, young lesbians and gays arguing that Accra has grown more dangerous. Blakk Rasta, a radio deejay on Joy FM, rarely permits a week to pass without condemning "batty boys" (Jamaican slang) and freely stating that they should die.

Creating alternate community constitutes resistance to the system of regulating sexuality and, as noted above, employs multiple tactics, including a domestication and incorporation of non-normative sexuality to local culture through inventing new expressions of it (Yankah 1991, 18) and a rhetoric of ambiguity that conceals the truth from those who should not or do not want to know, yet reveals to those who do. The majority of the LGBTI individuals I interviewed adopted a stance as tacit subjects: they viewed their homosexuality as assumed or understood clearly enough by family and friends to make revelation redundant. Venita, in his early thirties, is typical: he lives in a house on his family property, where his mother welcomes his fictive kin and community. He notes: "My Mum likes my friends and they like her," and adds, "We go out for drink-ups." His parents never pushed him to marry and at his father's funeral, the close friends who comprise his community sat adjacent to his family, reflecting on their connection, alongside nephews who call Venita "auntie."

In this way, Venita and his extended "family" are complicit in nurturing a non-normative community which he leads: "I bring people together to arrange social affairs ... birthday parties, weddings, funerals, all yag or eagle affairs." A helper and social fixer, he connects gay or MSM friends with tailors to make clothes for birthday parties, funerals, and engagements or "marriages." He refers community members to hair stylists, doctors, nurses, clinics, lawyers, pastors, prophets, police, shrine priests, and information technology specialists. Carrying two or three cell phones with different address books in each, he both connects members and "give counselling to this eagle" who had a "fight with her wife over a woman she made love to." He refers community members to traditional religious personnel, prophets, and Christian pastors for spiritual and material help, including "for some friends to get [unofficially] married ... I know a gay pastor." Socially connected with individuals across Accra, LGBTI and otherwise, and in other cities in Ghana, Venita is one hub of an elaborate circuit of contacts with nodes across the city. There are others, each with their own circuit, which intersect not unlike electric wires with a junction box. The junction position carries risks and undermines the strategy of invisibility and silence. Venita's activities and that of the men (and handful of women) with whom he works, however, demonstrate that there is a parallel community and subculture available to those "in the know."

Adai, also known as Nii Korley, is one of Venita's female equivalents, but her field of operation is local and less extensive. Although her father and twenty-something daughter tacitly accept her partner as kin, they do not discuss her sexual orientation and she accommodates them by toning down her dress and self-expression in their presence, i.e., she "wear(s) loose shirts" and "speaks like a woman ... in higher voice." Short and stocky with nearly shaved hair, on the street Adai passes as a man, which makes everyday life both easier and more complicated: she faces few male challengers and a few more questions when she volunteers as a football coach for teenage girls. Her partner's family, in old Accra, accepts her as a "son-in-law" and urged the couple to marry, which they did unofficially in fornt of 130 guests in late 2010, demonstrating a level of acceptance that Adai claims "only the Ga of Bukom" would confer. In our interviews, she indirectly positioned herself as a "big woman," similar to several of Dankwa's (chapter 9) subjects, and a habit that Akyeampong (2000) and Clark (1999) note in strong, successful Asante market women called *obaa barima* ("manly, brave"), who achieve financial independence and commanded respect. Adai relayed how she had built her own house, brick by brick, on land her father owned. She proudly displayed her thirty hutches of rabbits, which she breeds and sells, and also kills and skins for customers. She no longer works construction due to health problems, but her resourcefulness in providing and caring for her partner is manifest in Esther's domestic role and recognition of Adai as the one in command. Adai described her own sexual prowess in more than one interview, and indicated that women, even strangers, find her erotically irresistible, that her lovemaking led women to exclaim, "I love so much the way you make me feel!" and that she rejects any partner's reciprocity – in American parlance, she is a stone butch, but she had no term for it and instead stressed that her skill is "very good." Contradicting norms of discretion, she confides in and entertains close gay male friends with her open descriptions of sexual needs and conquests. Silence and indirectness, then, is neither necessarily concealment of sexual practice nor protection against hostility, but a social protocol about what it means to be visible or invisible within normative sites like the family, church, or community. To some extent, Adai also meets the characterization of the coastal Ga as more indiscreet than the dominant Asante.

Venita and Adai, in particular, reveal how a community of practice can form through combining a tacit understanding of sexual practices, a small lexicon (for men), claiming particular public spaces, constructing self-help networks, and bestowing recognition on network leaders. Another tactic for cultural authentication of LGBTI communities is to locate and incorporate same-sex intimate spiritual and healing professionals, *won hegbemei,* traditional mediums and healers, and Christian prophets and pastors into networks. Ghanaian cultural practices include quotidian attention to spirits and spiritual forces that requires the employment of religious professionals. It is worth examining the intersections between traditional non-normative social identities outside the Western gender regime, *won hegbemei,* since these occupations exist in other African countries and have historically created spaces for gender and sexual alterity (see Nkabinde 2009).

SPIRITUAL LEADERSHIP

Several interviewees who identify as same-sex loving were forthcoming about their spiritual work with the community. Nate, a short, muscular *wontse* ("diviner/healer") who self-identifies as *kodjo besia* and lives and works in James Town, provides spiritual guidance, diagnosis, and treatment to same-sex intimate clients. Raised Anglican, he recounted that in his late teens an unidentified spirit, later diagnosed as twin personalities, filled him: the female goddess called Mami Wata, a well-known West African deity associated with commodities and destructive forces, and a male god called Bentum, who lives under the sea. Nate claimed he can cure most diseases, such as hypertension, diabetes, and depression, and also treats the loss of or desire for a partner. He described a medicine fabricated from wood, charcoal, and hair from an ex-lover's comb, with which he brought a lover back to his client. Pattey, a shrine priest from Tema whose god is Dantu, predominantly interacts with and serves LGBTI networks. Pattey is resistant to gender expectations, never heterosexually married, and never produced a child or raised a partner's child: "Everyone knows ... that I am eagle. I was born with [an] interest in women." A physically large woman who exudes confidence, she claimed: "Neighbours have come to me and said, 'If you are an eagle, then I want to be one,' though they use the word *supi*. I am so strong, they want that strength." Both Pattey and Nate live in densely occupied urban neighbourhoods, are respected for their spiritual powers, and service Ga cultural and social affairs. Same-sex identified prophets, such as Okai, also diagnose health problems, but communicate with Elijah to address social injustice and restore order in individual patient's lives, whether through the return of a lover, the cure for an illness, or the restoration of a job. Okai, a tall, thin man in his mid-forties with a soft-spoken, sweet, pastoral manner, works out of his one-room house west of downtown Accra, nearly always with his male partner in attendance. Gender non-normative in body language, he neither is harassed by neighbours nor short of clients who use his spiritual interventions which requires a trek to hills beyond Accra for days of prayer and collecting plants to make potions.

COMMUNITY LEADERSHIP

The LGBTI domestication process is apparent in recognizing certain lay community leaders. Lartey is one such leader, and is referred to as *Yaa Asantewaa*, an honour he acknowledged by asserting that his sexual orientation is "a gift from God ... God created me to become somebody." Lartey modeled himself after the widely admired King Bennett, who died in 2005, and positioned himself as a new ɔ*panyin*, a man of reputation good at mediation and offering advice, until 2009 when chronic illness forced him to withdraw from active community membership. His message to others is: "I tell how it is to be gay, even to the chief ... God gave it to us, we have to give it back."

Lartey's social withdrawal and Venita's active life demonstrate that an LGBTI community, like any other, must socially replicate to survive and evolve. As the other men once did, Viola performs at times as *ókyeame*, the indigenous "linguist" between the king and the people whose rich oratory is valued in discussions of sensitive topics (Yankah 1995, 51), though this role has become an intermediary in a triad between government offices and community. The dominant position of men in Ghanaian society creates opportunities for Lartey or Venita that women cannot find as easily. Men recount extensive contacts with different "gay" professionals. Women are more reluctant to assume leadership beyond a small circle, though pairs of women, including Adai/Nii Korley and Gifty, who live on the coast east of James Town, have developed self-help and community service networks with other eagles and lesbians to conduct outreach beyond their neighbourhood boundaries using football matches, health education forums, birthday and cultural festival parties, and *susus* (rotating savings associations). Female leaders share scarce funds and social knowledge, provide emotional and "kin" work to others, and build a sense of unity for neighbourhood networks. In 2011, Gifty began to share skills and knowledge with a small group of LGBTI deaf friends who have since formed their own self-supporting community.

Venita and Lartey recognized that women find it more difficult to make connections, and so in 2008 they helped various neighbourhood women's groups meet over several months to form Sister to Sister for Social Justice and Empowerment (SSSJE), a registered NGO and small human rights organization, as an LGBTI group could be dangerous and impractical (see Gueboguo 2009). SSSJE draws together six neighbourhood networks to promote unity and social improvement of women regardless of age, religion, ethnicity, sexuality, or occupation through outreach on health, sports, and sex education. These women, who choose *dears*, have found unity harder to forge than occasional collaboration and funding impossible to obtain. Their willingness to reach out to international NGOs, though, is evidenced by their collaboration with a QAYN survey in 2011 (QAYN 2011, 3). In 2010, Venita and his colleagues recognized that an organization opened possibilities for international funding on MSM health issues and education and established an NGO, Brother to Brother in Unity and Diversity. In 2011, it received funding for MSM education. As in other African states, international agencies structure foreign influence, and specifically HIV funding, and so organizations have incentives to bureaucratize sexual difference, the intersection of the global and local, and Western and African gay men (see Nguyen 2005). There are also incentives to adhere to a Western notion of human rights in HIV organizations' policies, as Cameron and Clinton discussed in autumn 2011. Many health NGOs receive American funding and are conduits for USAID, legitimizing accusations that American and British governments are trying to force their values on Africans, as President Atta Mills inferred above. This process removes agency from grassroots groups that come to depend on external funding and find themselves incorporated into the nexus of a global human rights NGO system and positioned as victims of human rights violations.

CITIZENSHIP CLAIMS

Building alternative community raises questions not only of rights, but also of belonging and citizenship. While there is no standard definition of sexual citizenship, most theorists agree that the construct depends on a perception of sexual minorities as second class because citizenship confers certain rights, such as freedom from discrimination or the right to serve in the military (Richardson 2001, 153). Writing about the West, Richardson (1998, 83) and other scholars describe LGBTI individuals as "partial citizens" who must "remain in the private sphere" and not seek "public recognition or membership in the political community." In the West homosexuality has been and continues to be described by opponents as a threat to the nation, reflecting behaviours that undermine traditional institutions and ways of life, and indeed the health of the body politic. Concepts of citizenship, however, have evolved from notions of civil, political, and social rights to include "intimate spheres of life," how to raise children, be an erotic person, and more (Plummer 2001), and many theorists emphasize the social and cultural claims to citizenship – even metaphorical claims that arguably the Accra communities described above exemplify. They expose the need to construct meaningful categories of belonging, and reveal that the Foucaultian argument that citizenship has a disciplinary function is convincing, but also that as Carl Stychin argues, the discipline is "resistable." Hence, citizenship (sexual, racial, cultural) is a claim for a "right to spaces for subcultural life" and to "undermine the fixity of boundaries which contain a categorization" (Stychin 2003). The Ghanaian citizens described here may, indeed, be denied rights not specifically protected in law, but they are individuals who exercise their claims to cultural and social citizenship, concealing difference and revealing it, in daily practice, whether through enacting neighbourliness, connecting friends to jobs or partners, raising funds for a LGBTI compatriot's funeral plans for a parent, or mobilizing voters for an election.

CONCLUSIONS

The growth of Ghana's LGBTI communities clarifies several aspects of social change in Africa today. On the one hand, the people described above confirm Judith Butler's assertion that the "foundationist reasoning of identity" politics is off the mark; that is, "that an identity must be in place for ... political action to take place." Rather, the subjectivity of the "doer" is "constructed in and through the deed" (1990, 142). This is a process of repetition in serving the community: discursively constructing community with kin terms, indigenizing their lexicon, incorporating practices and personnel of local cosmologies into activities, linking LGBTI city networks through celebrating birthdays and attending funerals, linking women's football teams for matches, advocating for those in legal trouble or in need of health care, and in general providing support. Claiming citizenship is enacted by being good Ghanaians, and by recoiling at assaults such as those in March 2012 in James Town. Those events came as no surprise, as both Venita and Alex commented right after the Cameron-Clinton policy announcement, "We are the ones who will pay for this!"

Claiming a form of patriotism and making it non-normative – for example, Venita often remarks, "Oh, I *love* Ghana, so much!" when passing a handsome man – demonstrates a playful form of social belonging. After he was publicly threatened with death, Prince asserted, "I am Ghanaian. I do not want to live anywhere else." Gifty speaks about deaf LGBTI friends as part of her community. With civic consciousness and action, they tacitly challenge heteronormativity, instate intragender love as indigenous, and claim community and citizenship. Sexual identity is no mere individualized subjectivity, but is intertwined with gender, community, and nation, a strategy that disrupts the colonial and Christian argument that same-sex intimate relationships are a Western import, upends the Western narrative of "coming out" with its emphasis on the individual, and culturally legitimizes LGBTI communities as exemplars of national pride and identity through practices of cultural authentication.

11

Male Homosexuality in Bamako: A Cross-Cultural and Cross-Historical Comparative Perspective

CHRISTOPHE BROQUA

Translated by Michael Bosia

After many decades of silence, the question of same-sex sexuality in Sub-Saharan Africa began to emerge as a topic for research during the 1980s and 1990s (see for example Gay 1986; Shepard 1987; Murray and Roscoe 1998; Teunis 2001).[1] This developed primarily through a variety of studies in history and ethnography, and through investigations initiated as a result of the concern over the spread of HIV/AIDS and the risks associated with sexual practices between men (see for example Niang et al. 2003; Epprecht 2006; 2008; Nguyen 2005; Gueboguo 2006; Lorway 2006; 2008; Gaudio 2009; Tucker 2009). These studies of sexual expression have become part of the larger renaissance of work on sexuality and the construction of gender and other identities in Africa (see for example Arnfred 2004; Reid and Walker 2005; Bhana et al. 2007).

This chapter is a reflection on this larger movement as well as a product of it. Based on the results of ethnographic research I conducted between 2003 and 2008 in Bamako,[2] the capital of Mali, I respond to a certain blind spot in the analysis of sexual practices between men in Sub-Saharan Africa and reveal the link that binds homosexuality to the process of globalization. This chapter is also part of a comparative approach that counters an evolutionary tendency underlying the dominant conception of homosexuality in Africa.[3]

HOMOSEXUALITY, GLOBALIZATION, AND THE EVOLUTIONARY TENDENCY

Anthropology has explored various forms of same-sex sexual expression outside the West, ones that rarely conform to the social construction of modern homosexuality and indeed where the category of *homosexual* does not exist. Briefly, there are two general forms, sometimes combined (Herdt 1997; Murray 2000): one is based on gender differentiation, such that one partner is associated with a masculine gender and the other partner is associated with a feminine gender, or where one partner identifies with neither masculine nor feminine but with a "third gender"; the other is based on age, and refers to sexual practices or unions between persons of the same sex but different generations. Both forms are often observed in Sub-Saharan Africa. A third form of homosexuality, often called *egalitarian*, in which partners do not exhibit differences in age or gender, constitutes the currently dominant model in the West, but can also be found in other regions or historic periods.

After the expansion of comparative research and case studies since the 1980s in and outside the West, a new agenda appeared when scholars focused on the links between homosexuality and globalization to examine the influence of the Western model on other regions of the world. If it is possible to reproach gay and lesbian studies, and queer theory, for ethnocentrism, the first works on globalization and homosexuality tended to analyze this phenomenon in terms of the homogenization and Americanization of a global homosexual identity (Altman 1996).[4] Nevertheless, this work led the way to a rapidly developing literature and a transnational turn in gay and lesbian studies during the 1990s (Povinelli and Chauncey 1999).

In order to avoid a globalizing approach, empirically anchored in the West, by default different scholars choose to analyze the effects of globalization as a part of local studies in the Global South. The greater share of these analyses focus on Asia (e.g., Johnson 1998; Jackson 2000; Johnson et al. 2000; Boellstorff 2003), where the diversity of sexual identities is more visible than in Sub-Saharan Africa. This research shows that the specific sexual identities of each country, forged across the long term, are articulated today through the forms of identity close to those of "modern" Western homosexuality. From Africa, on the other hand, works that address the links between homosexual identity and globalization are still rare (Phillips 2000; Hoad 2007).

The principle critique of these works is their tendency to reason in terms of homogenization. But scholars have also reproached them for subscribing to an evolutionary concept that at the same time is the subject of a debate between essentialist and constructivist approaches. At the heart of anthropology, the notion of evolution is considered an outmoded framework from a century ago, a closed case, with no place in theory today. But it finds a way into the literature in history and anthropology when considering homosexuality. The topic is often posed in such terms (for example, Roberts' [1995] "gay identity formation"), which suggests that the risk of evolutionary thought undermines the scholarship of researchers who study non-Western societies. But the notion of evolution equally and more frequently can be found far from the field of the social sciences, in particular in the realm of homosexual activism linked to human rights and public health. Joseph Massad (2002) controversially describes this as the "Gay International" and denounces it as a new form of Western imperialism.

The temptation to fall for an evolutionist explanation not only touches those who have far-fetched and inadequate knowledge about same-sex relations in Africa, but also threatens to affect those who have more accurate and complete knowledge. Anthropology has revealed different models of same-sex sexual behaviour in Africa that belong generally to the past (Epprecht in this volume). These behaviours can be distinguished as either recognized as legitimate (for example, by spirit possession) or admitted as mistakes or crimes, though they are strongly regulated in both cases. From the point of view of their social significance, they are often invoked to justify and legitimize the existence of contemporary homosexual behaviour. Yet the observable forms of same-sex sexual behaviour in Africa today often are more distanced from local historical models than they are from models that existed in the countries of the Global North. To be more specific, contemporary same-sex sexuality in Bamako more closely resembles previous forms of homosexuality in the West than it does traditional forms of sexuality in Africa. In effect, the situation of men who practice same-sex sexual expression in Bamako, as in other African urban areas, resembles those of Western homosexuals during the decades that preceded the liberation movements. As a result, this revelation invites a comparative approach that is not only transcultural, but also transhistoric – it is concerned with both the present and the history of the society under study.[5]

In the following, I will first evoke several of these similarities between contemporary same-sex sexuality in Bamako and the homosexuality of the historic past in the West. Next, I will contextualize these first considerations with particular attention to transactional sex, secrecy, and the widespread practice of maintaining official heterosexual relationships while living a double life as homosexuals. I conclude with reflections on cultural homogenization in the transformation of male homosexuality in Africa today.

THE DOMINANT CONCEPTION
OF HOMOSEXUAL BEHAVIOUR IN BAMAKO

The first similarity concerns the dominant model of sexuality between same-sex loving persons in Bamako today and the West in the past. In his work *Gay New York*, which focuses on the period from 1890 to 1940, historian George Chauncey (1994) shows that homosexuality was conceived as an inversion of gender, opposing "normal man" against the effeminate man. While customary at the start of the twentieth century in New York, this idea was progressively replaced by the binary of "homosexuality/heterosexuality." Concerning the character of the "fairy," Chauncey (1994, 48) explains that among the men of the working class, "the fundamental division of male sexual actors ... was not between 'heterosexual' and 'homosexual' men, but between conventionally masculine males, who were regarded as men, and effeminate males, known as fairies or pansies, who were regarded as ... members of a 'third sex' that combined elements of the male and female." In this model, the criterion of gender precedes the criterion of sexuality. According to Chauncey, the 1930s give rise to the transition between a system of gender and one of sexual orientation.[6]

In Bamako, it appears that sexual expression between men conforms to a model founded on a differentiation of gender (where one partner manifests feminine attributes and is supposed to be receptive in sexual relations, while the other manifests masculine attributes and plays the insertive partner) that anthropological studies, along with *Gay New York*, describe with regard to numerous societies.

One of the most common terms for designating men who engage in sexual conduct with men reveals the importance of gender: it is a term borrowed from Wolof, *gor-jigeen*, which literally signifies "man-woman" (see Nyanzi chapter 4 in this volume). Likewise, in

Bambara, expressions often associated with male to male sexual conduct include *cɛtɛmùsotɛ*, which can be translated as "neither man nor woman," and *cɛmùsoman*, a "man as woman." Often in a relationship between two men, one partner is a *yossi* (derived from Wolof), that is to say, a man with a masculine appearance thought to play the insertive role in sex, and the other is a *qualité* (derived from French), a man with a feminine appearance considered to be sexually receptive. Men also speak of their companions as "my wife." Another example is evident in a 2005 anecdote from my fieldwork that shows Bamakans do not necessarily categorize the individual by presumed sexual orientation but by gender identity. After a French visitor to the city began a relationship with an effeminate African, a young Malian neighbour who visited the French man one day said, "I understand. That boy is your wife!" Other nonspecific terms, with which men who engage in sexual practices with men can identify themselves, still designate men according to their sexual role and their gender identity: *soungourouba*, which signifies "slut" in the sense of an "easy woman," signifies an individual known for playing the sexually receptive role, while *kamelemba*, or "cruise," is associated with an insertive role.[7]

Finally, the principle pejorative term for homosexuality in Bambara, *sa*, does not suggest "homosexual" but "snake," in reference to the serpent's undulating motion; this term therefore does not connote a sexual meaning but, because of cultural associations, one of gender, and it is used just as much to denigrate a man who does not demonstrate sufficient virility as it is to specify a man who has sex with other men. This term points to what disturbs the categories of gender more than sexuality. In such a context, men who conform to traditional masculinity to a certain degree can engage in sexual conduct with other men without fearing they will be identified by their activities.[8]

Gender difference is not the only aspect of the dominant conception of homosexuality present in both New York at the dawn of the twentieth century and Bamako at the debut of the twenty-first; the two also share a type of sexual conduct that rests on age differentiation. In New York, while a man who conformed to the masculine norm and had relations with "fairies" was called a *trade*, a *wolf* was a masculine homosexual who had relations with younger partners (Chauncey 1994). In Bamako, the generational difference also structures an important aspect of sexual practices or relationships between men, starting with a period of initiation during which

– putting to one side those who might meet up with adolescents from time to time – a youth will couple with an older adult, often from his own circle or family.

Another set of striking resemblances resides in the logic of construction through dominant norms that, though not directly contested, are diverted sufficiently to make same-sex sexual expression possible within the "normal" (heterosexual) world.

In *Gay New York*, Chauncey (1994) insists on homosexuals' capacity to invent a parallel world, founded on the quotidian but invisible to the general population, in a way that relates to Michel de Certeau's notion of *tactic* to qualify these "popular procedures" that "manipulate the mechanisms of discipline and conform to them only in order to evade them" (De Certeau 1990 [1980], xiv [tr 1984]). This same phenomenon was manifest in relationships between women in Victorian England as analyzed by Sharon Marcus (2007, 27), who uses the expression "play of the system" to "conceptualize the yield and elasticity built *into* systems. Play signifies the *elasticity* of systems, their ability to be stretched without permanent alteration of their size or shape; it thus differs from *plasticity*, which refers to a pliability that allows a system or structure to acquire a new shape and be permanently changed without fracture or rupture." In Bamako, such tactics or plays of the system are evident in many ways. For example, just as friendship in Victorian England allowed women to explore more intimate liaisons, the practice of two young men (or two unmarried men) sleeping in the same bed does not provoke concern about the possible development of a sexual relationship.

More generally, men who engage in sexual conduct with men in Bamako can use the dominant social logic to underwrite their relative freedom of action, if they can master that logic and possess the artistry to thwart it. As in *Gay New York*, the principle tactic here resides in the strategic use of secrets, silence, and double entendre, a language with two meanings where only the initiated understand the second (Weeks 1977; Chauncey 1994). The use of the term *gay* in New York at the start of the twentieth century (previously, it did not have a specialized signification) corresponds to *branché* ("plugged in") or *milieu* ("scene") in Bamako. These terms are at the same time inexplicit and non-specific, a point Jeay (1991, 66) reveals in her analysis of Bambara men's choice of terms to describe specific erotic acts, for example, *reposer le corps* and *se détendre* ("relax the body" and "loosen up"). For men who engage in sexual practices with other men, these linguistic tactics are the first condition for getting together under the rubric of heteronormative conventions of masculinity in the social spaces of daily existence (for example, streets, discos, bars, or groups who come together for tea), and permit them to develop a particular sociability often without those around them being conscious of the nature of their relationship. Such forms are imposed in a context in which intimacy is limited and social control is exercised without fail, as the majority of individuals live with their families until marriage. As an extreme but evocative example, public same-sex weddings are sometimes organized such that those outside the group are not aware of the reason for the event, which makes it an open secret under the cover of an unspecified celebration.

The logic of construction through dominant norms appears equally through the principle of the "double life" that prevails among men who engage in sexual behaviour with other men, in Bamako as in *Gay New York*.[9] First, such practices are often transitory. Second, those who engage in same-sex sexual expression also have sexual experiences or relationships with partners of the opposite sex. Here, conforming to heterosexual conjugality is not only a social obligation from which it is difficult to escape, but also a means to indulge in same-sex practices without becoming a target of the judgments or worries that attach to single men after a certain age (even without suspicions of homosexuality, bachelorhood raises concerns in the family about, for example, possession by a malevolent spirit). Heterosexuality is a possibly crucial condition for the practice of homosexuality. Other tactics similar to those Chauncey (1994) describes include, for example, participation in social spaces (such as those related to the practice of spirit possession) or professions (such as being a dry cleaner or hair dresser) in which it is possible to accept and even recognize homosexuality, or at least to juggle identity and modulate behaviour and dress according to context.

The last similarity is the constant preoccupation of persons who have same-sex relations with the threats of exposure, blackmail, or legal consequences that hover over them in most African countries. In France, Britain, or the United States, blackmail was an everyday practice in the mid-twentieth century. In Mali, the question of sex between men appears nowhere in the law and is therefore not illegal. However, even if it does not carry a legal risk, a forced outing can expose men to the social risks associated with stigmatization and rejection.

In Bamako, the fear of exposure forces many men who engage in sex with other men to denigrate and flee from the company of others whose behaviour or dress might reveal their sexual orientation and who are judged to be too "open," according to the term that designates them. The same fear existed in Montreal during the 1950s, according to the results of one of the first sociological studies on Western homosexuality (Leznoff and Westley 1956). That study showed a strong hostility combined with fear that closeted men had developed with regard to men who were open about their homosexuality.

THE EVOLUTIONARY PERIL

Among Western observers, these various similarities sometimes nurture the idea that Africans who engage in homosexual practices will experience a fate comparable to that of homosexuals in the West (implicitly positioned at the summit of the hierarchy), which leads to the evolutionary analysis that several approaches in the literature present. One critique by Neville Hoad (2000, 148) of an extract of the first work of Jeffrey Weeks (1977) sums up the evolutionary concept of homosexuality in Africa while abusing the notion: "The rest of the world is understood as equivalent to the past of the now dominant form of male homosexuality in the western metropolis: we were like them, but have developed; they are like we were and have yet to develop. Space is temporalised and difference hierarchised, with the modern male homosexual taking the place of the normative white male heterosexual in an uninterrogated replication of the old evolutionary narrative." The classic question therefore becomes one of how to think of the effect of globalization on the evolution of social forms with regard to same-sex sexuality in Sub-Saharan Africa while avoiding the double pitfall of an evolutionary concept and analysis in terms of the homogenization of global sexual culture.

From here, I will indicate why the evolutionary concept is not justified by showing that the evocative resemblances across historic space are accompanied by important differences. Note that the first peril of evolutionary thought is its anachronism: the aspects of the situation in Bamako today that are similar to those of the West in the historic past bring out those elements which, in the West, are themselves out of temporal sequence. As Epprecht (2012b) notes in his observation of young black "queens" (their term) in the main Zimbabwean gay rights association, performance of effeminity was "often more reminiscent of Doris Day than any recognisable African femininity."

The main difference between the situation in the West at the dawn of the twentieth century and that of Bamako today is clear. For all those who now in engage sexual expression with partners of the same sex, and for everyone, a reference model (whether positive or negative) is available. This was not the case for Western homosexuals before the liberation movements, and this reference is precisely the "modern" model of Western homosexuality.

This model functions as a negative reference for the great majority of Malians, who consider it to be a symptom of the decadence of Western countries. But it can function as well as a positive reference for many people who engage in homosexual practices in the construction of their sexual identity, even if the majority of this group does not intend to imitate Western identities in an African context. The existence of the reference model therefore makes it impossible for anthropological studies to focus on the forms of homosexuality in Bamako (and more generally in urban Africa) independent of the processes of globalization through which an understanding of these other ways of life is made legible.

However, this process is not entirely new, as the representation of Western homosexuality penetrated the borders of African countries quite a long time ago, which explains the vivid hostility that it inspires. This hostility is in fact and in many ways a Western import: during the colonial period, the West exported its conception of homosexuality to the colonies (Bleys 1995; Epprecht 2006), notably through the repression of sexual acts judged to be immoral followed by the installation of legal devices that left the criminalization of homosexuality in many African countries (and elsewhere in the world) as their legacy. The paradox is that, in most cases, these laws are protected and defended precisely with the goal of sheltering Africa from Western influences such as harmful forms of sexual expression. Later, in light of the consecutive liberation movements in the countries of the North, the visible and political homosexuality that has developed in the West could appear to be a Western specificity and so reinforce many Africans' hostility towards it. This process, equally evident in other regions, has led some to write that the globalization of homophobia has known greater success than that of homosexual identity (Binnie 2004, 77).

Colonial powers imposed their own negative judgment of homosexuality on Africans, and so Africans now read those societies as lax and morally decadent. Hostility to homosexuality in African countries therefore is not particularly constructed against an endogenous social category, since the category in question does not exist and, moreover, those who engage in such sexual practices are not generally visible. Instead, it is contra a category of behaviour considered to be specific to the West. If, in many African countries, homosexuality has become the symbol of the West, it has also become the object of a broader discourse in public or private that often gives weight to a binary between Africa or Islam and the Western world. From this point of view, and as several contributors in this volume attest, the conception and the treatment of homosexuality in Africa regularly appear as an avatar of the relationship with former colonial powers.

Today, Malians's awareness of the Western model of homosexuality draws not only from this history, but also from links and exchanges between African and European or North American countries. With regard to migration, for example, Malians are the largest community of Africans living in France. In addition, television contributed to the diffusion of representations of Western homosexuality in Africa and specifically in Mali, where many people followed the debates over legal recognition for same-sex couples in France. At the same time, this diffusion of Western representations can feed the hostility towards those who are more open about a way of life now public, when same-sex sexual practices in African countries often remain in the domain of private life and so unspoken. Thus, the conception of homosexuality in Bamako depends on globalization and, at the same time, on the history that links the country to France.

A COMBINATION OF DIFFERENT MODELS OF HOMOSEXUALITY

One of the principle similarities between Bamako today and New York of the historic past concerns the dominant conception of homosexuality as an inversion of gender. However, in Bamako, though the model of homosexuality based on a gendered differentiation appears hegemonic in the discourse of most such men, the sexual roles theoretically associated with such categories – presupposed by the model – are in fact variable. They are determined, for example, by the character of the financial transactions related to everyday sexuality in Bamako.

The social organization of homosexuality is constituted by a combination of three principal models of homosexuality that cross history and culture. These three models include gendered differentiations between partners, generational differentiations between partners, and egalitarian structures between partners, the model of homosexuality dominant in the West.

Moreover, in Bamako sexuality between men is sometimes associated with a desire for a homosexual identity that develops in reference to, though not in imitation of, the Western model. A detour by way of language aids in understanding: homosexuals in Bamako (as well as in other francophone African cities) use the term *milieu* ("scene") to designate not only the places they gather (such as favoured bars and discos), but also, just as it is in French or translated into American English, the population they form. Language also creates and certifies the feeling of sharing a social category when these men designate themselves by the term *branché* ("plugged in" or "in the know"). There is, therefore, a *milieu* in Bamako composed of those who are *branché*, even if their visibility and desire for visibility is weak.

It might appear that a transition is in process between a system based on gender and one based on sexual orientation, like that described in *Gay New York*. To me, this is unjustified. In an interview published ten years after his book, Chauncey (2004) expresses doubt that the change he marked out after the 1940s was produced in its entirety: "I no longer believe that the binary hetero-homosexual should be imposed as a universal future, in New York and in all American society. I am more and more struck by the considerable variety of models, not only according to social class, but also according to race and ethnicity." This optic helps to conceptualize homosexual behaviour in Bamako in the form of a plurality of combined models. Different systems of norms coexist and link up, and at the same time return to the traditional forms of sexual practice and to contemporary Western homosexuality.

Though there are several models in the North and the South, the diverse social forms of homosexuality are not becoming the same everywhere, as they depend strongly on social, political, and cultural contexts. I will use examples from specific locales in Bamako that show the relationship between sexuality and money, the social use of silence, and the disassociation of sexuality from reproduction to illustrate this diversity. My concern here is not to determine exclusive cultural traits related to homosexual activities in Bamako that make the transformation of sexual practices impossible in some essential way. Instead, local specificities are relevant in tactics that depend on a social and cultural context (as do all tactics, by definition). It is a fundamental aspect of my argument that I do not merely describe cultural particularities; more importantly, I reveal the gestures that are without a doubt universal. In all similar cases where homosexuality exists as a category of stigmatization, these gestures are tactics to thwart hostility, not mere cultural artefacts. In other words, there is not a specific cultural form of same-sex sexuality, but there are processes of adaptation to the constraints and risks of local stigmatization, which are simultaneously anthropologically universal and always modeled by a specific cultural context.

First, in Mali, as in many countries of Sub-Saharan Africa, sexuality is often associated with financial or material support. Certainly, scholars have analyzed the logic of "transactional sexuality" in terms of relations of gender, based on a postulate that views women's sexuality as a commodity that men can market or buy. More recently, scholars have considered this commodification of sexuality as a tool that women use to reinforce their autonomy and agency more than as an effect of domination. This remuneration of sexuality appears equally in the case of sexual expression between persons of the same sex (Broqua 2009), which differs from the forms of homosexuality in the West (even if the remuneration of sex was present in gay New York at the start of the twentieth century).

Such a commodification of same-sex sexual expression reveals a logic that aligns these practices with the dominant model – not only of heterosexual relations, of which the transactional dimension is today constitutive, but also of ordinary social conventions that presuppose a payment for services rendered. The introduction of money in sexual relations between men confers a sensibility through which such relations insert themselves into the general economy of social relations in Bamako, where sexual relations proceed from a logic of exchange such that money or gifts condition the ensemble of social relations. Money is equally a means to reduce the transgressive significance of socially prohibited forms of sexuality because its expression is thought to have a single motivation. Transactional sex, then, is a specific type of tactic composed through the dominant order modeled by local sexual culture.

Second, in Bamako, a seal of secrecy marks same-sex sexuality. The most current vocabulary reveals this desire to conceal, since it is both inexplicit (invoking homosexuality only for the initiated) and non-specific (employed to designate those who share in the group); *milieu* and *branché* to indicate those who engage in same-sex sexual expression, and *contre* ("against") for homophobes. Some replace even this lexicon with other terms, adding a second layer of encoding; for example, one of my informants uses the word *truc* ("thing") to indicate "homosexual."[10]

Dissembling as a tactic of language refers more generally to the role of silence in the management of identity and of social relations among Bamakans. Silence about homosexual behaviour does not prevent outing, nor does it only function to maintain the secret. Instead, it primarily aims to empty such behaviour of all social recognition. In being unspoken, these practices do not acquire the status of a reality that could be debated in the presence of the person concerned. More often, the logic of social relations forbids all commentary on the same-sex sexuality of an acquaintance or intimate who strives to keep quiet about it – there is an implicit rule that requires people to accept someone's homosexuality if they do not articulate it.

Those who advocate tactics of non-verbalization are opposed to the principle of visibility that gay activists in Northern and certain African countries advocate and that serves as the basis for collective mobilization. However, the silence of "shame" that visibility seeks as its opponent, with the goal of promoting acceptance, is not the silence of Bamako respect, as for them, silence is a way to receive acceptance.

The organization and social meaning of homosexuality in Bamako are thus rooted in context: the public revelation of homosexuality is rarely considered as a path to fulfillment, conforming instead to a context where the performative force of language, and moreover of silence, is crucial.[11] There is a long distance between this model of experience in Africa and the politics of homosexuality in the West, where a revelation or public disclosure is the key moment in the course of socialization or mobilization.

Third, though the margins of individual manoeuvre in the Malian capital are larger than in rural settings, it remains difficult to resist a number of social exigencies. First are those concerning marriage and children, even if people are getting married for the first time later in life. It is often impossible to resist social pressure, and so by custom men organize their sexual lives in great part alongside their married reproductive lives, knowing that Mali is a Muslim country and polygyny is widespread.

Norms related to same-sex sexuality have adapted to the specificity of Malian culture. Among men who engage in sexual relationships with other men, homosexual behaviour, including identity, is not considered to be opposed to the dominant conception of parenthood and reproduction. Most such adult men are married and have children in a way that is both obligatory and largely consensual, but they are not compelled to cease their same-sex activities nor relationships. During the period of sexual expression before marriage, many combine several forms of relationships and sexual engagements. Though some homosexual couples are exclusive, the great majority also engage in sexual relationships with women and, often simultaneously, keep up an official heterosexual relationship (and not as pretence), living another part of their sexuality alongside it.

This logic of a so-called double life is not only the product of a will to camouflage same-sex sexuality under the cover of conjugal heterosexuality, but also corresponds to a cultural model characterized by a strong dissociation between reproductive conjugality and recreational sex. The inverse of Western gay men and lesbians who demand the rights of parenthood, Malian men separate the reproductive and pleasurable aspects of sexuality, and consider it possible to construct a minority sexual identity and at the same time respect the dominant order of parenthood and reproduction. Moreover, the secondary socialization as homosexual, where it exists, does not presuppose coming out publicly as it often does in the West. The majority of the men concerned lack the will (more than the contextual opportunity) to activate a homosexual identity formed through public demands, even if collective mobilization is developing on the African continent.

CONCLUSION: RECONSIDERING THE TRANSFORMATION OF MALE HOMOSEXUALITY IN AFRICA

Within the arena of research on same-sex sexual expression, the risk is double: casting certain forms of homosexuality as a-historic; or, just as erroneous, dedicating research to an evolutionary notion written in advance on a presumed historical linearity (notably, toward liberation).

As Chauncey (1994) demonstrates with regard to New York City, the dominant mode of homosexuality in a given society is not immutable but is in fact susceptible to self-transformation. However, this evolution of dominant models is not linear but discontinuous. For example, Chauncey (1994) and Florence Tamagne (2004) describe homosexual social spaces that were abundant and visible during the years between the two world wars, but disappeared as the result of a vast repression that was part of the Second World War. Such was the case in New York as well as in Berlin, London, and Paris. A similar transformation occurred in the double category of butch/femme in the United States, which the liberation movement stigmatized nearly to the point of extinction in the 1970s, but which reappeared later (Faderman 1992).

It would be particularly incongruous to deny a similar potential for self transformation in the model of sexuality between persons of the same sex observable in Bamako (or elsewhere in Sub-Saharan Africa), just as it would be absurd to think these individuals will necessarily evolve in the sense of a movement towards liberation such as that imagined by an ideal that forces (implicitly at least) the modes of accommodation or resistance into a hierarchy.

The question of which factors contribute to the evolutionary model of sexuality proves crucial at this point, but the answer is complex and subject to contradictory debates. Among historians of American homosexuality, there remains contention over whether the phenomenon of urbanization is more important than the development of capitalism in the emergence of gay and lesbian identities (Maynard 2004).[12] Likewise, according to Chauncey (1994), the passage from a simple and prohibited sexual behaviour to the constitution of a social category and form of identity in the West – or a *species*, according to the celebrated formulation of Michel Foucault (1990 [1978], 43) – is not solely the product of categorizations imposed from "outside," as would be those from the field of medicine. More importantly, and without a doubt, the change is the product of how the individuals concerned live and evolve these categories.

As I have shown in this chapter, it can be fruitful to cross-examine the historical comparison (retracing the evolution of models in a single place) and transcultural comparison (considering the existing models in different places in the same moment). It remains to compare the factors that contribute to the evolution of the same model in different contexts.

In South Africa, for example, the political context and a legal device have affected the transformation in the forms of same-sex sexuality. In the wake of the political upheavals of the 1990s, some homosexual activists pressured the ANC to state its commitment to sexual rights, and the party quickly embraced their cause. In 1996, after the election of Nelson Mandela as president, South Africa became the first country to prohibit all forms of discrimination based on sexual orientation in its constitution (Croucher 2002; Cock 2003). The phenomenon of liberation that accompanied political change also introduced a progressive transition between two forms of homosexuality through a process comparable to the one Chauncey (1994) describes: the passage from a model based on the differentiation of gender to one where an egalitarian homosexuality unites two same-sex partners, with both models in coexistence from then on (Donham 1998, 11–12; De Vos 2000; Nkabinde 2009). Carving a principle of non-discrimination into the constitution had another major consequence. As the result of a suit against existing marriage laws filed by two women who charged that the laws were discriminatory and unconstitutional, South Africa became the first African state to legalize same-sex marriage in November 2006. Briefly, the transition between two models of homosexuality was rendered possible by political and legal transformations, themselves concurrent with homosexual collective action.

Beyond the social, cultural, and political particularity, numerous countries in Sub-Saharan Africa recently benefited from international aid programs that serve those who engage in same-sex sexual expression and were founded principally to address HIV/AIDS. The precondition of the dominant donors that links public health to human rights opens up the possibility of collective action on the basis of homosexuality, though only the future will determine whether it constitutes a determinant factor in any transformation of the dominant model of homosexuality. But at the same time, superior forces – such as state or religious authorities, or, on a transnational scale, those who apply pressure from outside on HIV/AIDS related programs to promote abstinence or fidelity while demonizing condoms – push in the opposite direction. The events of 2008 in Senegal show that any tolerance on the part of state authorities for HIV/AIDS-related programs that target men who have sex with men does not efface strategies of sexual repression (Kasse 2013).

From this point of view, the similarities between homosexuals in the historic West and in contemporary Bamako can be understood as well as a consequence of the fact that in different societies and different historic periods, confrontation over the same problem can lead to comparable responses: when the transgression of sexual or gender norms inspires hostility, the reaction of guardians of public morality consists of thwarting and resisting. Only the modality of this response varies as a function of different contexts. However, recognizing that the same causes can produce the same effects is not equivalent to adopting evolution as a mode of analysis or essentializing homosexuality; to the contrary, it is a way to consider homosexuality as a social construction dependent on context.

In diverse regions of the world, the influence of Western homosexuality on non-Western forms of homosexuality is visible.[13] Such influence often seems to extend across numerous countries where collective action is developing, and so might appear to be the revelation of a process of globalization. However, the tendency to consider this course as the final stage in the domination of one part of the world by another is seriously flawed. The amplification of transnational exchanges and the development of communication systems do not seem to produce the dreaded effects of cultural homogenization. They instead seem to recompose, even in certain cases harden, cultural traits or localized societies.

Thus, in Sub-Saharan Africa as in the West, at least in the urban zones, there are plural models of homosexuality. This plurality reflects the variety of specific equilibriums manifested through local particularities. It excludes, therefore, a scheme where the phenomenon is solely an evolutionary one, but also challenges the presumption of homogenization. In other words, local or cultural particularities condition not only specific forms of homosexuality, but also specific arrangements between different models of homosexuality that coexist. These arrangements, which are produced by history, are never immutable but are always susceptible to change. At the same time, they are conditioned by social and cultural contexts that do not offer infinite latitude for immediate transformation, even if outside forces encourage it.

The Politics of Sexual Diversity:
An Afterword

SYLVIA TAMALE

Sexual Diversity in Africa: Politics, Theory, and Citizenship comes at a time when Africa has been placed under the global spotlight of sexual conservatism accompanied with the systemic oppression of those who do not conform to dominant heterosexual ideologies of femininity and masculinity. Indeed, the continent has come under scathing attack – largely from Western governments, funding agencies, international NGOs, and media – for repressive and regressive regimes that discriminate against individuals who espouse same-sex orientation and non-conforming gender identities. Unfortunately, most of these critiques occur outside the context of a well-grounded understanding of the historical, socio-economic, cultural, and political forces that have fuelled global hegemonies, and the structural inequalities they reflect. Hence, they often "otherize" the phenomena of homophobia and transphobia. In other words, the geopolitical differentials of race, power, and economics that dominate the global stage have found their way into contemporary debates on sexual orientation and gender identity on the African continent – from the deployment of aid conditions tied to expanding LGBTI protections to the hypocritical selective double standards of accountability and responsibility (e.g., supporting African leaders that are tainted with rigged elections, detentions-without-trial, corruption, abuse of media freedoms, etc.).

The launch of the International Resource Network for Africa (IRN-Africa) to deepen the understanding of sexualities and further the intellectual discussion of this supposedly taboo subject is a welcome development. Indeed, IRN-Africa is in line with earlier efforts, including the publication of the collection *African Sexualities: A Reader*, which I edited in 2011. For example, those engaged with sexual politics on the continent would greatly benefit from reading the first part of *Sexual Diversity in Africa: Politics, Theory, and Citizenship*, which deals with the intricate context of African sexualities. The essays in part 1 examine past and contemporary imperial and fundamentalist influences in constructing the dominant sexual scripts, criminalizing and legislating "unnatural" sexualities out of legal protection, preaching dogma, and stifling LGBTI expression. Such appreciation is crucial in raising awareness about the global nature of the struggle against sexual and gender repression and in erasing the "us/them" mentality with which most critics approach the subject matter. Equally important is the recognition of the agency of African activists and scholars in the regional and international struggles against sexual/gender apartheid and the interlocking, intersectional mechanisms of oppression.

The burgeoning scholarship on non-conforming sexualities and gender identities in Africa is simultaneously pushing the boundaries of African feminisms and challenging the exclusionary democratic and constitutional paradigms. It has led to complex explorations of methodological and epistemological issues that challenge orthodox constructions of knowledge in the wider quest for postcolonial justice. This research has illuminated the intricate links between sexuality, gender, power, and politics. Even then, it has only excavated the surface and has yet to uncover the full liberatory and transformative potential of the phenomenon of sexuality. Arguably the last bastion of essentialized subjectivity and legitimized discrimination, homophobia, and transphobia must be viewed within the wider democratic struggles around the world.

It is against the backdrop of these developments that my country – Uganda – has become the locus *par excellence* of homophobia. This is largely thanks to the infamous Anti-Homosexuality Bill that was tabled in the Ugandan parliament in 2009 and reintroduced in 2012. The draconian bill, which dangles like the sword of Damocles over the heads of all Ugandans, seeks to tighten the noose around the necks of homosexuals and transgendered individuals and those who advocate their rights. Its primary objective is to deal a final blow to what its proponents describe as "un-African" abominable acts that offend culture and threaten the institution of the traditional

Ugandan family. The bill also seeks to protect Uganda's children from what it describes as a massive "recruitment campaign" into homosexuality. There are several disturbing parallels between such unfounded accusations in Uganda and those from the Cold War McCarthy era and current conservative Christian accusations in the United States. State moral panics have always served as an effective decoy to distract attention from the more significant socio-economic and political crises that afflict society. This was as true of Adolf Hitler's Nazi regime that targeted Jews and homosexuals as it is of the current economic woes in most Western countries being attributed to foreign migrants. Just as Nazi Germany created a phalanx of laws and regulations that targeted homosexuality, Western governments today churn out new and ever more intricate regimes of discrimination in immigration, dresscodes (e.g., the Islamic veil), and religion (e.g. the controversy over Islamic minarets in Switzerland). By creating these artificial scapegoats, the political elite dislocates social anxieties while further entrenching themselves in power.

Homophobic sentiments and intolerance of sexual and gender diversity are not the exclusive bane of Africa or non-Western societies. The current trend that seeks to reinvent Africa as a heterosexual continent and Europe as the heart of sexual democracy is dangerous and divisive. Indeed, the homophobic laws that currently exist on the continent were a direct import from former European colonial powers. Increasingly, research and scholarship show that sexuality in pre-colonial Africa was more complicated than the idealized heterosexuality that contemporary African leaders have sought to colonize and reinterpret as African tradition. Attempts by the political and religious elite to construct African models of sexuality are designed to facilitate control and regulation. Thus the claim that same-sex erotic activity is un-African simply becomes a metaphor for the propagation of conservative oppressive agendas.

In the Global North, even as the domino effect of the decriminalization of homophobic laws has swept across Europe in the last few decades, the United States is still very much engaged in the struggle to eradicate homophobic and transphobic attitudes. Moreover, this struggle even in Europe has proved much more challenging than the success of legal reform. Even as US politics on sexual diversity continue to evolve, there are many examples of legal reform in non-Western countries (albeit fraught with contradictions and tensions), including South Africa, Brazil, Argentina, India, and Nepal, from which the West could cull a few lessons. Nyeck and Epprecht's anthology demonstrates that a nuanced multidisciplinary theorizing of sexual diversity in Africa is essential for the wider project of engendering transformative change and building a peaceful and sustainable continent. We all look forward to a future when sexual diversity is unconditionally celebrated around the world.

Contributors

OLAJIDE AKANJI has a PhD in political science. He is a senior research associate in African diplomacy and foreign policy in the Faculty of Humanities at the University of Johannesburg.

CHRISTOPHE BROQUA holds a PhD in social anthropology (EHESS, Paris). He is researching AIDS and homosexual mobilizations in Mali, Côte d'Ivoire, and Senegal.

CHERYL COOKY is an assistant professor with a joint appointment in health and kinesiology and women's studies at Purdue University.

SERENA OWUSUA DANKWA is a doctoral candidate in social anthropology and gender studies at the University of Bern, affiliated with the University of Ghana.

MARC EPPRECHT has a PhD in history (Dalhousie). He is a professor in the departments of global development studies and history at Queen's University.

MELISSA HACKMAN is the Louise Lamphere visiting assistant professor of gender studies in the Department of Anthropology at Brown University.

NOTISHA MASSAQUOI is the executive director of women's health at Women's Hands Community Health Centre in Toronto. She is currently completing her PhD in sociology and equity studies at the University of Toronto/Ontario Institute for Studies in Education.

CRYSTAL MUNTHREE is currently employed as a researcher in National Department of Tourism, South Africa. She holds a masters degree in population studies from the University of KwaZulu-Natal.

STELLA NYANZI is a medical anthropologist based at Makerere University. Her research explores sexualities, culture, health, and law in Uganda and the Gambia.

S.N. NYECK holds a PhD from the University of California, Los Angeles. She is assistant professor in political science at Clarkson University and a fellow at the Institute for Humane Studies.

KATHLEEN O'MARA has a PhD in African history (Columbia). She is currently the chair of the African and Latino Studies Department at the State University of New York at Oneonta.

VASU REDDY is deputy executive director at the Human Sciences Research Council (South Africa) and an honorary professor at the University of KwaZulu-Natal.

AMANDA LOCK SWARR is an associate professor of gender, women, and sexuality studies at the University of Washington, Seattle. She has worked in South Africa since 1997.

LISA WIEBESIEK is a researcher at the Human Sciences Research Council in South Africa, and a PhD candidate at the University of KwaZulu-Natal.

Notes

INTRODUCTION

1 See, in particular, African Activist (www.africanactivist.org), the Coalition of African Lesbians (www.cal.org.za), African Men for Sexual Heath and Rights (amsher.net), and numerous local associations.

CHAPTER ONE

1 See the website of the International Gay and Lesbian Human Rights Commission (www.iglhrc.org), which monitors the status of sexual minority rights and legal rulings around the world; Amnesty International (2008); and the International Commission of Jurists (2011). The Naz case has particular resonance for Africa since the law struck down is the exact law applied under British colonialism in places like Uganda. See also Sircar and Jain (2012). Thank you to Sibongile Ndashe for her insightful comments on a draft of this chapter.

2 The pertinent MDGs are: to achieve universal education, gender equality, maternal health, and child health, and to combat HIV/AIDS (United Nations 2012, http://www.un.org/millenniumgoals/bkgd.shtml).

3 See also an analysis and links from one of the international donors, Partnership Africa Canada (http://www.pacweb.org/programs-african-peer-e. php).

4 See also the website of African Men for Sexual Health and Rights (AMSHeR, www.amsher.net), a Johannesburg-based NGO established in 2009 with a mandate "to address the vulnerability of gay and bisexual men, male-to-female transgender women and other MSM, to HIV."

CHAPTER TWO

1 Victor subsequently returned to Uganda along with Kenyan activist
   Yvonne Oyoo and successfully sued the government for the raid.
2 The original motion was withdrawn, but at the time of writing has been
   reintroduced with the provision for the death penalty removed.
3 Since Teresa de Lauretis introduced it in 1991, the term *queer theory* set out
   to encompass new histories of gays and lesbians (Goldman 1996). Queer
   theory was seen as having the ability to problematize what it meant to be
   and live as lesbian and gay. I see queer theory as the vehicle of desirous utopian imagination as in the style of Warner (1993), fighting for both equality
   while claiming difference, demanding political representation while insisting
   on its material and historical specificity. According to Samuels (1999), *queer*
   celebrates the diversity of subjects who experience heterosexist oppression
   without essentializing identity, but at the same time acts as an umbrella term
   for all those who are marginalized because they transgress the heterosexual
   norm (Kyatt 2002). Queer theory then becomes a useful tool for making
   visible how some subjects pass as normal and others are rendered dysfunctional. Without a doubt, *queer* can be seen as a term that negatively erases
   difference, but I hold on to the utopian use of the term that is theoretically
   structured around the concept of intersecting identities, allowing me to begin
   the exploration of a queer African framework that looks at the multiple
   positions of gender, race, ethnicity, culture, and geography (Walcott 2005).
4 See Walcott (2005) for an exploration of methodology that inspired me.
5 The sponsoring institution for this study is the department of Sociology
   and Equity Studies at the University of Toronto/Ontario Studies in Education. I met all ethical requirements in accordance with the University of
   Toronto's institutional guidelines.
6 A variety of terms used across various African communities to connote
   same sex desire.

CHAPTER THREE

1 Critical studies of intellectual and artistic origins of various stereotypes
   about Africa include Miller (1985), Brantlinger (1992), Bleys (1995),
   Lyons and Lyons (2005), Thomas (2007), Cole and Thomas (2009), and
   Epprecht (2006, 2007, 2008, 2009, and 2013 – errors in the first volume
   are corrected with an update on the situation in Uganda in Epprecht 2013).
   I am deeply indebted to Edward Said (1979, 2003), and would like to suggest parallels in this study to an important interpreter of Said in Africa,

Joseph Massad (2007). Among many effective critiques of the Caldwell thesis and of the ethnography upon which it is based are Ahlberg (1994) and Stillwaggon (2003). The diversity of HIV prevalence in Africa also somewhat undermines the thesis, ranging as it does from the highs of southern Africa to Niger (adult seroprevalence 0.8 per cent) or Senegal (0.9 per cent, which compares to Estonia at 1.2 per cent). Madagascar, with its large cotier (black African) minority, has an adult seroprevalence of 0.2–3 per cent, a third to half of that in the United States (UNAIDS 2010).

2 These, and other debates and developments in the struggle for sexual rights in Africa, are reported on the website of the International Gay and Lesbian Human Rights Commission (www.iglhrc.com).

3 Some of the most egregious public homophobia in Africa is fomented by non-Africans, particularly missionaries from the US Christian right (Kaoma 2009; Hackman, chapter 6 in this volume).

4 I discuss breakthrough studies of African sexualities in history below, but several were especially helpful for formulating my own research questions: White (1990), Jeater (1993), Arnfred (2004), Morgan and Wieringa (2005), Boddy (2007), and Gaudio (2009). These studies contest naturalistic essentialisms or assumptions of a static dichotomy between heterosexuality and homosexuality, often taking the work of Michel Foucault (1978) as jumping-off point to understanding the mutability and diversity of sexualities over time. I discuss film, fiction, memoirs, and activist writing below.

5 Foundations of my understanding of feminist theory, the historiography of gender and sexuality, and critical men's studies in Africa include McFadden (1992), Morrell (2001), Ouzgane and Morrell (2005), and Setel (1999), in addition to works cited in the previous note. Queer theory has also been proposed as an effective approach to sexuality research, and I respect the intentions as elaborated, for example, by Riggs (2006) and Massaquoi (chapter 2 in this volume). I do note problems, however, in the way queer theory has been practiced in African studies. See, for example, Murray's (2009) withering critique of, primarily, obtuse writing and lack of grounding in historical or ethnographic research, or the debates around queer imperialism discussed in the introductory chapter to this volume. Similar problems undermine certain articulations of Africentric or Africana womanist theory such as those by Oyéwùmí (1997) and Thomas (2007). See Matory (2005) for a powerful caution regarding these approaches, which Nyeck (chapter 8 in this volume) also alludes to. I also note that the focus here is on published scientific work and that I only indirectly capture a sense of discourses coming out of the performative and visual arts. Early critical analysis of the latter does suggest strong parallels (e.g., Azodo and Eke 2007).

6 Senegal San Luis, accessed 4 December 2009, http://www.senegalsanluis. org/spip.php?article72.

7 Crawford (2007) and the essays in Canaday (2009) overview the rich historiography of these processes, while Stoler (2002) and Bederman (1995) explain aspects of European and American imperialisms in the nineteenth century.

8 Lyons and Lyons (2005) provide a fair discussion both of Burton's racism and of his impact on sexuality debates in Europe.

9 Note that Evans-Pritchard published his disquisition on the topic thirty years *after* his fieldwork. That said, several important publications in this period mention same-sex and other non-normative sexuality, though they rarely flag it as an issue worth further investigation. Herskovits (1967 [1938]) and Maquet (1961) are unusual for suggesting their subjects' erotic lives might be more complicated than generally assumed.

10 For their part, gay rights activists tended to keep a low profile in these years to avoid attracting further stigma. Gay rights and AIDS activists in the West colluded in the promotion of heterosexual "African AIDS" as a persuasive tool in their anti-homophobia work (see, for example, Zackie Achmat cited in Epprecht 2008, 126).

CHAPTER FOUR

1 I maintain the word *homosexual* when referring to participants' own use of the label. However, because of the ambivalences and ambiguities of this word, I use *alternative sexualities* or the acronym LGBTI (lesbian, gay, bisexual, transgender, and intersex people) elsewhere in the paper.

2 Local newspapers, including the *Daily Observer*, *Freedom Newspaper* (31 May 2008), *Wow Gambia* (13 June 2008), and the *Point Newspaper*, carried several varying accounts of this story.

3 Amory (1997, 9) also refers to these outlets as "not 'respected' academic journals, but popular feminist and lesbian newsletters." Reportedly, even renowned anthropologist Evans-Pritchard first published his findings about same-sex marriage among Azande warriors and young men in a "relatively obscure journal" long after his fieldwork ended (see Murray and Roscoe 1998, xii). Epprecht (2008 and this volume) also discusses factors that limit academic research of same-sex relationships in African scholarship.

4 In retrospect, and with the emerging high-quality scholarship in the field, these fears seem overstated.

5 My doctoral studies, the basis for the bigger ethnographic study, were based at the London School of Hygiene and Tropical Medicine, an institute

that prizes public health, biomedicine, epidemiology, and statistics. Human sexuality studies were largely premised upon the biological approach in which the body is central to understanding individual sexual behaviour. Many explanatory models (e.g., the theory of reasoned action) were largely essentialist and heterosexist.

6 These problems of higher education in Uganda and other similar sub-Saharan African countries include under-stocked libraries, overworked or absentee professors, over-crowded classes, rote pedagogical approaches, multiple university closures due to demonstrations by staff or students, underfunding by public budgets, and static curriculum and course modules that are not responsive to student needs. For example, my interest in sexuality studies was not met at either an undergraduate or post-graduate level at the time I attended Makerere University.

7 Set in Côte d'Ivoire, the characters in this film elaborate that a *woubi* is a man who chooses to play the role of a wife in a relationship with another man. A *yossi* is a bisexual man, perhaps married, who accepts the role of a *woubi*'s husband. A *toussoubakari* is a lesbian. *Controus* are homophobes who oppose the *woubi* lifestyle.

8 For example, Pickering et al. (1992, 77–8) write: "Informal discussion with prostitutes and men in the bars had established that sexual contact was almost invariably confined to straight-forward vaginal intercourse, with little in the way of manual stimulation or other preliminaries. Only twice did we hear of anything different being demanded: one of the rare European clients had two girls at the same time and on one occasion a young local man wanted manual stimulation only."

9 Jammeh's schizophrenic relationship with the death penalty is detailed in the literature. For example, Wiseman (1997, 267) discusses how the president moved from a position of publicly stating "we abhor the death penalty" in 1994 to reintroducing it as a necessity in August 1995. Wiseman (1997) also discusses Kandeh's (1996, 395) assertion: "For one thing, the AFPRC was opposed to the death penalty. In the words of Jammeh: 'We abhor the death penalty as much as any other Gambian. And let nobody fear, we are not going to set up any military tribunal. We have only suspended the constitution but the judiciary will not be suspended. And all due process will take place without interference'" (*West Africa*, 14 August 1994).

10 The constitution does not identify a state religion. Furthermore, some Gambians are non-Muslims. It is also important to note that the Muslim population in the Gambia is not heterogeneous. As discussed earlier in the chapter, there are various Muslim sects. In addition, in their day-to-day

practice, Gambian Muslims synchronise diverse African traditional religions and Islamic practice (Darboe 2004).

11 Islamic jurisprudence and law based on scholarship and interpretation of the Qur'an and Sunnah of the prophet Muhammad in the hadith by Ulama (Muslim jurists). Some Islamic scholars distinguish between *shari'a*, the principle, and *fiqh*, the inferences of scholars.

12 "In addition to this Constitution, the laws of The Gambia consist of a) Acts of the National Assembly made under this Constitution and subsidiary legislation made under such Acts; b) Any orders, rules, regulations or other subsidiary legislation made by a person or authority under a power conferred by this Constitution or any other law; c) The existing laws including all decrees passed by the Armed Forces Provisional Ruling Council; d) The common law and principles of equity; e) Customary law so far as concerns members of the communities to which it applies; f) The shari'a as regards matters of marriage, divorce and inheritance among members of the communities to which it applies." (article 7)

13 Darobe (2004, 74) writes: "Islamism is understood as the organised efforts by believers in the Islamic faith to influence national politics along Islamic precepts ... In their aspirations to modify society, Islamists ... use politics in the interest of their religion and its followers, while politicians use Islamic symbols or rationale to gain or maintain political power."

14 Wiseman (1997, 125) elaborates: "To attempt to explain this supposed absence of corruption by depicting Jammeh as a 'devout Muslim with an abiding sense of mission and empathy for the poor' is to take purely at face value the calculatingly invented public image of the military leader which the latter is anxious to project for political reasons. Around six months after the coup pin-up pictures of Jammeh dressed in battle fatigues, which had been widely available on the streets of Banjul, were replaced by new ones depicting him as a holy man at prayer."

15 Niang et al. (2003) report that some women with male partners sometimes have anal sex, and so anal sex is not practiced by same-sex couples exclusively.

16 Yahya Jammeh allied with the Wahhabis, who were initially Gambian graduates of Arabian Islamic studies who completed state-sponsored studies in Saudi Arabia, converted to the orthodox fundamentalist Sunni sect of Wahhabi, returned home, and started to teach fundamentalist Islam. According to Darboe (2004, 77), with the state support of the president (who built a mosque on the state house grounds and appointed Imam Fatty, a Wahhabi, as his spiritual guide), these Wahhabi scholars campaigned to rid "Gambian Islam of all corrupting Western influences." They

launched an aggressive program of Friday sermons on national television and radio, which broadcast "open and harsh anti-American rhetoric by the fundamentalist group. It was not unusual to hear anti-American sentiments and criticisms of U.S. foreign policy and the U.S. relationship with Islam at funerals, naming ceremonies, weddings, or other social gatherings at which the Wahhabis were present" (Darobe 2004, 77).

17 This twenty-four-hour ultimatum was no mere threat. Jammeh summarily expelled or deported high-ranking diplomats for crossing him. For example, he expelled a Zimbabwean UNDP official for questioning his claimed ability to cure HIV/AIDS using a miracle concoction of herbs, Qur'anic verses, prayer, and massage (see Nyanzi 2012 for details).

CHAPTER FIVE

1 While much of our focus in this chapter is on conscription and not recruitment (only white men were conscripted into the military, while other races and women could volunteer), we have included the narratives of two women in our analysis as men were not the only victims of the aversion program.

2 Although, see Hackman in chapter 6 of this volume for a discussion of the "treatment" and "rehabilitation" of so-called ex-gays in post-apartheid Cape Town outside the framework of Christian nationalism.

3 Foucault has written extensively about the body in several texts (e.g., 1977; 1984; 1986; 1989). See also Antonio Campillo's "On War: The Space of Knowledge, Knowledge of Space" (in Miguel-Alfonso and Caporale-Bizzini 1994, 277–99). On the border war, see Price (1989), Cawthra, Kraak, and O'Sullivan (1994), and Evans and Phillips (1988).

4 For the international scholarship, see Appy (1993), Bourke (1996), D'Amico and Weinstein (1999), Feinman (2000), and Enloe (2000), for example.

5 This film does not feature in our analysis, but it does also focus on victims' testimonies that reconstruct the aversion program. Directed by Gerald Kraak, the film, including unedited footage, is available at the archives at Gay and Lesbian Memory in Action (GALA) archives.

6 Holmes (1996, 161–80) addresses the discourse of homophobia in her discussion of the Winnie Mandela trial for public kidnapping and assault in 1991, also a focus of concern during the TRC hearings. See TRC *Report* (volume 2 [1998], 554–82).

7 Other events in history equally demonstrate how queer identities take shape in events that pathologize the homosexual. See John D'Emilio's

(1992, 57–73) excellent analysis of the politics of sexuality in Cold War America, especially his analysis of the McCarthy Era witch-hunts and climate of persecution that provide a context for the radical origins of the gay movement in the United States. D'Emilio's discussion of what he terms the homosexual menace forms an interesting parallel here with the aversion program in the SADF.

8 The reference team is listed in van Zyl et al. (1999). The methodology entailed in-depth semi-structured interviews with survivors of abuse, friends and family of survivors, and workshops with relevant institutions, also explained in *The Aversion Project*.

9 These concepts are highly technical and have particular meanings in the discipline of psychology and psychiatry. Reber (1995, 244) explains "electrotherapy" as a treatment that uses "mild, brief electrical stimulation." Electroconvulsive therapy (ECT) uses electroconvulsive shock (a brief electrical shock applied to the head that produces full-body seizure, convulsions and usually loss of consciousness (Reber 1995, 243). ECT, according to Reber (1995, 243), "produces a period of drowsiness, temporary confusion and disorientation, and a variety of memory deficits, some of which the patient recovers over time, although gaps may remain." Reber also explains that there has been a significant decline in use of this technique, and that its current therapeutic use is restricted "in the treatment of cases of severe depression that have proven intractable to antidepressant drugs" (1995, 243).

10 "Ego-dystonic homosexuality" derives from the concept *ego-dystonic*, which Reber (1995, 240) explains as: "Descriptive of wishes, dreams, impulses, behaviours, etc. that are unacceptable to the ego; or, perhaps more accurately, unacceptable to the person's ideal conception of self. Hence, an ego-dystonic idea is one that seems to have invaded consciousness, to have come from 'outside' the self." According to Reber, "ego-dystonic sexual orientation" refers to a "condition where the individual's sexual orientation is not in doubt but he or she is unhappy with it and wishes to change it."

CHAPTER SIX

1 The names of the ministry, church, and people are pseudonyms.
2 The Wenner-Gren Foundation for Anthropological Research supported the research for this chapter. I thank Carolyn Martin Shaw and Kate Wilkinson for their thoughtful responses to this chapter and the people at HRM and the Church of the Reborn for allowing me into their lives.

3 I use self-referential racial terms throughout this chapter. During apartheid, South Africans were categorized as white, coloured, or black.
   Afrikaans people are white.

4 *Moffie* directly translates from Afrikaans as sissy. It is also often used to
   say someone is gay in a demeaning way and men in HRM understand it to
   mean faggot. Some South Africans have reclaimed the term *moffie* as positive, similar to how many in the United States have reclaimed queer.
   Adrian means *moffie* negatively here.

5 The question asked was, "Do you think it is wrong or not wrong for two
   adults of the same sex to have sexual relations?" Possible answers were
   "always wrong, almost always wrong, wrong only at times, [and] not
   wrong at all." The percentages per year answering "always wrong" were
   84 per cent (2003), 83 per cent (2004), 85 per cent (2005), 83 per cent
   (2006), and 82 per cent (2007) (Roberts and Reddy 2008, 2).

6 Durban and Johannesburg also had gay communities and political/social
   groups during apartheid. During the 1980s and early 1990s, changes in
   black townships led to the emergence of new models for same-sex sexuality. Before this time, male individuals were understood as *isitabane*, hermaphrodites, and were socially reinscribed as women. The sexual identity
   of the "homosexual" or "gay" person sometimes replaced and sometimes
   existed alongside prior models for same-sex activity (Epprecht 2006).

7 Gayle is not the only "gay language" in South Africa. There is also *ising-
   quomo*, township gay slang, which is heavily Zulu based and thought to
   have originated in Durban (McLean and Ngcobo 1995).

8 There are documented cases of gay sex and relationships across racial lines
   during apartheid (e.g., Gevisser 2006; Achmat 1995).

9 Statistics on the type of Christian affiliation were not collected in the 2011
   census. Census information can be found on Statistics South Africa's website (www.statssa.gov.za).

10 I almost never heard HRM members use the term "gay" to refer to
    themselves.

11 It also believes that it has demonic causes.

12 I am not interested in critiquing or commending the commission here. My
    focus is on how the commission popularized new ideas about trauma and
    healing (see Ross 2008 for a critique of the commission). Although TRC
    trauma discourses were not universally embraced, they caught on much
    more with urban than rural citizens, and they are well known throughout
    the country.

13 Apartheid was supported by the Afrikaner Christian theologies of the
    Dutch Reformed Church and also resisted by anti-apartheid Christian

activists across race and ethnicity, who used their faith for social justice work (Moodie 1975; Anderson and Pillay 1997; Balia 1989).

14   There are over 250 twelve-step groups based on AA's structure.

15   American ex-gay leaders also travel internationally to teach that homosexuality can be "cured." Exodus International leaders Scott Lively and Don Schmierer ran ex-gay workshops in Kampala, Uganda in 2009. One month later, a member of the Ugandan Parliament came up with the "Anti-Homosexuality Bill," which proposed that people should be imprisoned and even killed for being gay (Muskin-Pierret 2010). For more information and interviews with ex-gay leaders, see the Rachel Maddow Show's (2009) "Uganda Be Kidding Me" series. For a more in depth discussion of the influence of the American religious right in Uganda see Kaoma (2009a, 2009b), and on homosexuality in Uganda see Sadgrove et al. (2012).

16   Youth With a Mission begun in 1960 and is an international volunteer mission organization that people of any age can participate.

17   I am referring to the AIDS denialism that marked the Mbeki administration.

18   I was unable to find statistics or studies on how widespread faith-based counselling is in South Africa.

19   The "healing of memories" is the same idea and process as the "healing prayer" or "listening prayer."

CHAPTER EIGHT

1   I use the word *homosexual* exclusively in this chapter because it is the commonly used label for queer sexuality in Cameroonian media.

2   Although I focus on "discourse" as the primary site of analysis, I acknowledge discourse only captures a fraction of social realities and perceptions.

3   "Corruption Perceptions Index 1995–2005," Transparency International, accessed April 2007, http://www.transparency.org/policy_research/surveys_indices/cpi/previous_cpi__1/1998.

4   Also see the final report of multi-donor governance and anti-corruption mission to Cameroon (OECD, accessed March 2010).

5   Unless otherwise stated, all translations are mine.

6   I deal with this issue elsewhere with reference to a wide range of political theory (Nyeck 2011). The Romanian philosopher E.M. Cioran (1968, 33, 66) once formulated the "problem" with the ways in which nations imagine their immaculate conception in terms of an appeal to a "historical role as a metaphysical career" in a paradoxical manner that does not entail "ownership of the nations' rise and fall." According to Cioran, the abnormal

evolution of some countries often confuses people's minds by forcing them to "pose themselves as a unique problem" (65). The problem identified here often occurs during the developmental phases of the national self, which circumstantial singularity and characteristics may force people to generate essential interrogations as well as "series of anomalies on the miracle or the significance of their fate" (67). If Cioran is right, and if there is a moral and economic malaise in Cameroon, the argument for the (neo)colonial origin of homosexuality frames sexuality as a question that one could "answer only by a constant mortification" (70) with no possibility to own one's corruption and decadence. The impossibility to own one's decadence means perpetual search for causes that are solely exogenous or metaphysical.

7 N'gouo Woungly-Massaga, a former guerrilla combatant against the French administration in Cameroon after the Second World War, coined the word *homocracy* after the publication of the lists in 2006 and defined it as "gay power."

8 Also see my analysis of Cameroonian novelist Calixthe Beyala's satiric representation of women, eroticism, and same-sex desire in Nyeck (2004).

9 The controversy in the colonies was heated in France under the Vichy government determined to hunt down freemasons and Jews (Coy 2008).

10 My translation. The spelling of "Kamerun" dates back to the era of German administration (1882–1917) of the territory, a time when it included land now part of Nigeria, Congo and Gabon, and Central African Republic. Nationalists and members of the UPC often use it to affirm the political unity of the populations of Cameroon. It implies irredentist ambitions and possible nostalgia for German (masculinist) rule.

11 Afko Dock, accessed 5 May 2007, http://www.afkodock.net/?page=show &menu=12&id=92.

12 The doctor was not denounced in media. It is not clear whether the state retaliated against him for his defiance of a court order.

CHAPTER NINE

1 An earlier version of this article was first published in *Ghana Studies* 14 (2011). For their comments on different drafts of this paper I thank Dominique Grisard, Andrea Hungerbühler, Yv E. Nay, Patricia Purtschert, and Talya Zemach-Bersin. I am grateful to Judith J. Halberstam for entrusting me with the English version of her introduction to Masculinidad Femenina (2008). For their enabling financial support, I thank the Swiss National Science Foundation and the Swiss Commission for Research Partnerships with Developing Countries.

2 I have changed the names of all my respondents.

3 In Akan society, youthful masculinity in its junior, subordinate status implies that young men are less constrained in their moral comportment than women. It allows them to be impetuous, stagy, and exuberant, and to voice emotions associated with women.

4 Janet herself never explicitly mentioned this dramatic event, which according to gossip must have destabilized her for quite a while.

5 I gathered the main data between 2006 and 2012 in a market town in the Eastern Region and the Greater Accra Region. My research included sixty-two in-depth narrative interviews, half of which I conducted with my research assistant Josephine Enyonam Agbenozan.

6 For a discussion of what Amadiume considered a neocolonial appropriation on Lorde's behalf, see Evelyn Blackwood and Saskia Wieringa (1999, 4).

7 Since titles were awarded based on economic success, women took titles much less often than men. A woman's duties as the head of the matrifocal unit of her husband's or father's compound made it arduous to accumulate capital. Her cash turnover went back into the subsistence economy and household needs, which hampered her capacity to a acquire titles and subsequently occupy senior masculine roles (Amadiume 1987, 39).

8 Oyéwùmí's contentious claim that "Yorùbás don't do gender" has been refuted by scholars who consider her linguistic and ethnographic evidence selective (Bakare-Yusuf 2004). While Africanist feminists critique her disregard of the difference between ideological formations and women's factual constraints, her claims are nonetheless widely referenced and have become somewhat paradigmatic.

9 The Akan consist of a dozen regional sub-groups that exhibit considerable linguistic and cultural differences. They used to be part of the Asante kingdom, founded in 1701.

10 I use womanhood to signify female adulthood, associated with motherhood and maturity, and reserve femininity for globally pervasive images of femininity associated with youthful ideals of urban femininity.

11 Accounts on the ambivalent positions of queen mothers and female elders suggest that matriliny effectively translates into male gerontocracy transmitted through the female line (Akyeampong and Obeng 1995). Historians further show that patriarchal tendencies were buttressed during the colonial period when governors and missionaries privileged men as their political partners. Today, men access public power and accumulate wealth more directly and more overtly than women.

12 If not specifically referenced, all quotes in this section are taken from an interview I conducted with Janet Aidoo in English (20 February 2006).

13 Female friendships forged on the pitch are a vital force in the life histories of adolescent women who do pursue football as a career. As I watched training sessions and matches and overheard comments by coaches and audiences, I was amazed by the gendered jester's license that youthful female players enjoy in Ghana.

14 This manifests in popular rumours about men losing their sexual organs due to evil magic.

15 Although Ghanaian women are known for their autonomy and mobility as long-distance traders, the driving and repairing of motorized vehicles has remained a masculine field. Women occasionally conduct state-owned public buses, but I never met a female taxi or *trotro* ("minibus") drivers.

16 Further, strong matrikin bonds coupled with separate properties make divorce relatively easy and frequent (Adomako Ampofo 1997, 178).

17 *Obaa barima* is composed of *obaa* ("woman") and *obarima* ("man"), turned into the adjective *barima*. See Clark (1999, 721–2) for a discussion of the less frequent transfer of core female traits, such as showing economic motherliness and being an *obaatan* ("nursing mother") onto men.

18 This is a literal translation from an interview conducted together with Josephine Enyonam Agbenozan in Ga, Ameley Nortey's first language. Words in italics were originally uttered in English. All the following quotations in this section come from this interview.

19 To answer my subsequent question of who then was the elder among the four of us, she did not point to herself, the chronologically oldest, or to me or my assistant, the interviewers, but to the chronologically youngest in the group, who had introduced us to Ameley and insisted on being present througout the interview.

20 Field note, 20 April 2007. Josephine Enyonam Agbenozan conducted this conversation in Twi and recorded it from memory.

21 I heard other junior, masculine-styled women talking about "working for love" when doing house chores for a senior lover who sustained them.

CHAPTER TEN

1 In this chapter, I use LGBTI as an umbrella term for same-sex intimate persons of various gender identities who by and large see this aspect of themselves as ongoing and social. I do not use it to include all MSM or WSW.

2 The data for this paper draw from twenty-three semi-structured retrospective life history interviews, as described by Paul Thompson (2000), gathered in separate series of interviews once or twice per year from 2005 to 2010. I gathered the subjects, daisy-chain fashion, and conducted and

244   Notes to pages 195–208

transcribed the interviews (with assistance in two early interviews from an African American gay male assistant). In several cases, Nii Richie Cudjoe and Tei Moncar provided translations. My location as outsider – *obruni* ("white/foreign") – was a limiting factor, but one perhaps tempered by my insider status as LGBTI/queer.

3 African (homo)sexualities are quite under-examined with the exception of South Africa, where a specific racialized national history and economic development differ from the rest of Africa south of the Sahara. For that nation, William Leap (1997; 2003) has studied the gay geography of Cape-town and its imbrication with race and class, and Gevisser and Cameron's (1994) anthology *Defiant Desire* covers apartheid (and anti-apartheid South African history), demonstrating the intersections of anti-apartheid resistance with the rise of gay and lesbian activism. More recently, Morgan and Weiringa's (2005) *Tommy Boys, Lesbian Men and Ancestral Wives* highlights women's testimony on their same-sex practices in southern Africa. Murray and Roscoe's (1998) anthology *Boy Wives and Female Husbands* typifies research on sexualities south of the Sahara, and demonstrates that same-sex patterns of behaviour in Africa are diverse and may employ distinct language to describe non-normative masculine and feminine behaviour. Wieringa and Blackwood's (2002) *Female Desire* includes discussions of women's same-sex relationships in Southern and Eastern Africa within a global study. Arnfred's (2004) anthology *Rethinking Sexualities in Africa* is a groundbreaking work, a decolonial feminist anthology that includes empirical studies of local practices from a grassroots perspective. Earlier researchers on African (homo)sexualities described alternative genders or indigenous "third sex" categories, such as *ghanith/xanith*. Murray and Roscoe claim that the African inventory of same-sex patterns lacks an identity and "lifestyle" in which homosexual relationships are primary and not necessarily based on socially dominant ideas of gender differences.

CHAPTER ELEVEN

1 An important part of the research published over the last fifteen years concerns South Africa (more than a dozen books after the start of the 1990s), where the situation is markedly different from that in the other African countries (see in particular Gevisser and Cameron 1994).

2 I conducted the study in Bamako primarily through ethnographic observation over a period that totalled three years spread over different stays between 2003 and 2008 (see Broqua 2007, 2009, 2010). Parallel to these observations, I participated in a study involving interviews coordinated by

the group Arcad-sida (Sylla et al. 2007). The men we met in these two settings were all residents of Bamako and were generally from very modest
economic and social backgrounds.

3 Recognizing the deficiency of a maladapted vocabulary, I use the term
homosexual when considering practices in the West, or to facilitate understanding when other terms might cause confusion. *Men who have sex with
men* or *same-sex sexuality* signify sexual practices and relationships outside the West, despite the limits that such a definition presents. There is a
vibrant semantic critique of these notions, and while it might be continued
infinitely while the vocabulary available remains trapped, my choice here
is to set aside such debate.

4 See the recent text by the same author on the subject, Altman (2004).

5 Acknowledging that by its nature, the limited perspective that "classic"
anthropology offers about same-sex sexuality in Sub-Saharan Africa is as
much historical artefact as it is anthropological. The famous article of
Evans-Pritchard (1970) is a flagrant example, in that it is based on data
from forty years prior, revealed through oral history, and rests on facts
that had disappeared by the time the anthropologist began his investigation, so that today they are nearly a century old.

6 Chauncey has his critics, and for the sake of argument, I have somewhat
simplified the historiography.

7 The same thing can be observed among women. On "relational masculinity" within female same-sex relations, see Serena Owusua Dankwa in
chapter 9 of this volume.

8 In other respects, there is a "traditional" representation of homosexual
behaviour in Africa according to which those concerned inhabit a double
and opposed sex (see Nkabinde 2009 for a South African case). The existence of this representation in Bamako is evident in the strong presence
of homosexuals at the heart of *jiné-don* spirit possession cults, where the
recourse to ritual trance aims to take charge of the disorder born from
the work of genies or their doubles; but it seems to play a limited role in
the ordinary representation of homosexuality. See also Gaudio (2009)
for reflections on the *bori* cult and homosexuality among Hausa men
of northern Nigeria.

9 At the start of the twentieth century, the passage from a system based on
gender to one based on sexual orientations accompanied a transition
between the logic of the "double life" to that of the "closet." In the first,
one can engage in homosexual practices as long as one conforms to a masculine role; in the second, one must camouflage these practices or risk
being categorized as a homosexual.

10 The terms *milieu, branché,* or *truc* as markers for persons who engage in
    same-sex sexuality are also found outside Mali, in Africa and beyond.

11 On the "nonsensical" nature of coming out for certain groups of men out-
    side the West (or of origins outside the West) and who engage in sexual
    relations with men, see for example Manalansan (2003, 27–35).

12 Neville Hoad (2000, 152) affirms the influence of capitalism on the emer-
    gence of homosexual collective action in the countries of the South: "The
    emergence of small yet vocal and visible gay rights movements predomi-
    nantly among the urban classes in many Latin American, Asian and
    African countries testifies to the effect of capitalist penetration on the
    emergence of lesbian and gay identity, even though these identities are
    inflected by local 'traditions' and gender and class variables."

13 For a clarifying example with regard to Turkey, see Bereket and Adam
    (2006).

Works Cited

Abou-Rihan, F. 1994. "Queer Marks/Nomadic Difference: Sexuality and the Politics of Race and Ethnicity." *Canadian Review of Comparative Literature* 21 (1/2): 255–63.

Abwa, Daniel. 2005. *Ngouo Woungly-Massaga Alias Commandant Kissamba: "Cameroun, Ma Part de Vérité."* Paris: Minsi.

Achebe, Nwando, and Bridget Teboh. 2007. "Dialoguing Women." In *Africa After Gender?*, edited by C.M. Cole, T. Manuh, and S.F. Miescher, 63–81. Bloomington: Indiana University Press.

Achmat, Zackie. 1993. "'Apostles of Civilised Vice': 'Immoral Practices' and 'Unnatural Vice' in South African Prisons and Compounds, 1890–1920." *Social Dynamics* 19 (2): 92–110.

– 1995. "My Childhood as an Adult Molester: A Salt River Moffie." In *Defiant Desire: Gay and Lesbian Lives in South Africa*, edited by Mark Gevisser and Edwin Cameron, 325–41. New York: Routledge.

Adhikari, Mohamed. 2005. *Not White Enough, Not Black Enough: Racial Identity in the South African Coloured Community*. Cape Town: Double Storey Books.

Adomako Ampofo, Akosua. 1997. "Costs and Rewards – Exchange in Relationships: Experiences of Some Ghanaian Women." In *Transforming Female Identities: Women's Organizational Forms in West Africa*, edited by E.E. Rosander, 177–94. Uppsala: Nordiska Africa Institute.

African Women's Development Fund. 2009. "In Solidarity: Statement by South African Feminists – Caster Semenya and Gender Discrimination – the 'Elephant in the Room.'" http://africanwomensdevelopmentfund. blogspot.com.

Ahlberg, Beth Maina. 1994. "Is There a Distinct African Sexuality? A Critical Response to Caldwell." *Africa* 64 (2): 220–4.

Ahmadu, Fuambai. 2007. "'Ain't I a Woman Too?' Challenging Myths of Sexual Dysfunction in Circumcised Women." In *Transcultural Bodies: Female Genital Cutting in Global Context*, edited by B. Shell-Duncan and Y. Hernlund, 278–310. NJ: Rutgers University Press.

Ajen, Nii. 1998. "West African Homoeroticism: West African Men Who Have Sex with Men." In *Boy-Wives and Female Husbands: Studies in African Homosexualities*, edited by Stephen O. Murray and Will Roscoe, 129–38. New York: St Martin's Press.

Akagbor, Sena. 2007. *Same-Sex Attraction: Choice or Genetic?* Tema, Ghana: Seal Press.

Aken'ova, Dorothy. 2011. "International Centre for Sexual Health and Reproductive Rights (INCREASE), Nigeria: Battling the Proposed Bill on the Prohibition of Sexual Relationships and Marriage Between People of the Same-Sex, 2006." *Feminist Africa* 15: 135–48.

Akoto, E.S. 2005. "Lesbian on C10 Million Bail." *Behind the Mask*, August 1. http://www.mask.org.za.php.id=260.

Akyeampong, Emmanuel K. 2000. "'Wopentam Won Peba' ('You Like Cloth but You Don't Want Children') Urbanization, Individualism and Gender Relations in Colonial Ghana, C. 1900–39." In *Africa's Urban Past*, edited by D.M. Anderson and R. Rathbone, 222–34. Oxford: James Currey.

Akyeampong, Emmanuel K., and Pashington Obeng. 1995. "Spirituality, Gender, and Power in Asante History." *International Journal of African Historical Studies* 28 (3): 481–508.

Alfredsson, Gudmundur. 1998. "Minority Rights: International Standards and Monitoring Procedures." *Latvia Human Rights Quarterly* (5/6): 9–28.

Allen, Danielle. 2000. *The World of Prometheus: The Politics of Punishing in Democratic Athens*. Princeton: Princeton University Press.

Allen, Jafari S. 2012. "Introduction: Black/Queer/Diaspora at the Current Conjuncture." *GLQ: A Journal of Lesbian and Gay Studies* 18 (2–3): 212–48.

Allman, Dan, Sylvia Adebajo, Ted Myers, Oludare Odumuye, and Sade Ogunsola. 2007. "Challenges for the Sexual Health and Social Acceptance of Men Who Have Sex with Men in Nigeria." *Culture, Health and Sexuality* 9 (2): 153–68.

Allman, Jean, and Victoria Tashjian. 2000. *"I Will Not Eat Stone": A Women's History of Colonial Asante*. Portsmouth, NH: Heinemann.

Altman, Dennis. 1996. "Rupture or Continuity? The Internationalization of Gay Identities." *Social Text* 14 (3): 77–94.

– 1997. "Global Gaze/Global Gays." *GLQ: A Journal of Lesbian and Gay Studies* 3 (4): 417–36.

– 2001. *Global Sex*. Chicago: University of Chicago Press.

– 2004. "Sexuality and Globalization." *Sexuality Research and Social Policy: Journal of NSRC* 1 (1): 63–68.

Amadiume, Ifi. 1987. *Male Daughters, Female Husbands: Gender and Sex in an African Society*. London: Zed Books.

Amnesty International. 2008. *Love, Hate and the Law: Decriminalizing Homosexuality*. London: Amnesty International Publication. http://www.amnesty.org.

Amoah, Elizabeth. 1991. "Femaleness: Akan Concepts and Practices." In *Women, Religion and Sexuality*, edited by J. Beecher, 129–53. Philadelphia: Trinity Press International.

Amory, Deborah P. 1997. "'Homosexuality' in Africa: Issues and Debates." *Issues: A Journal of Opinion* 25 (1): 5–10.

Anderson, Allan H, and Gerald J. Pillay. 1997. "The Segregated Spirit: The Pentecostals." In *Christianity in South Africa: A Political, Social, and Cultural History*, edited by Richard Elphick and T.R.H. Davenport, 227–41. Berkeley: University of California Press.

Ankerberg, John, and John Weldon. 1994. *The Facts on Homosexuality*. Eugene: Harvest House.

Ansolabehere, Stephen, and Iyengar Shanto. 1995. *Going Negative: How Political Advertisements Shrink and Polarize the Electorate*. New York: The Free Press.

Appy, Christian G. 1993. *Working-Class War: American Combat Soldiers and Vietnam*. Chapel Hill: University of North Carolina Press.

Arac de Nyeko, Monica. 2007. "Jambula Tree." In *African Love Stories*, edited by Ama Ata Aidoo, 164–77. Banbury: Ayebia Clarke Publishing.

Arendt, Hannah. 1970. *On Violence*. New York: Harcourt Brace.

Arnfred, Signe. 2004a. "African Sexuality/Sexuality in Africa: Tales and Silences." In *Re-thinking Sexualities in Africa*, edited by Signe Arnfred, 59–76. Uppsala: Nordiska Afrikainstitutet.

– ed. 2004b. *Re-thinking Sexualities in Africa*. Uppsala: Nordiska Afrikainstitutet.

– 2011. *Sexuality and Gender Politics in Mozambique: Rethinking Gender in Africa*. Uppsala: Nordiska Afrikainstitutet.

Arthur, J. 2000. *Invisible Sojourners: African Immigrant Diaspora in the United States*. Westport, Connecticut: Praeger.

Association for Women's Rights in Development. 2011. *Towards a Future Without Fundamentalisms: Analyzing Religious Fundamentalist Strategies and Feminist Responses*. Toronto: Association for Women's Rights in Development. http://awid.org/content/download/107116/1229707/ file/Towards%20a%20Future%202012%20PDF.pdf.

Atsenuwa, A. 1999. "Human Rights Protection of Vulnerable and Marginalized Group." In *Text for Human Rights Teaching in Schools*, edited by A.O. Obilade, 209–54. Lagos: Constitutional Rights Project.

Auerhahn, Nanette, and Dori Laub. 1990. "Holocaust Testimony." *Holocaust and Genocide Studies* 5 (4): 447–62.

Austin-Broos, Diane J. 1997. *Jamaica Genesis: Religion and the Politics of Moral Orders*. Chicago: University of Chicago Press.

Awondo, P. 2010. "The Politicisation of Sexuality and the Rise of Homosexual Mobilisation in Postcolonial Cameroon." *Review of African Political Economy* 37 (125): 315–28.

Azodo, Ada Uzoamaka, and Maureen Ngozi Eke, eds. 2007. *Gender and Sexuality in African Literature and Film*. Trenton, NJ: Asmara: Africa World Press.

Azuah, Unoma N. 2005. "The Emerging Lesbian Voice in Nigerian Feminist Literature." In *Versions and Subversions in African Literatures I: Body, Sexuality and Gender*, edited by Flora Veit-Wild and Dirk Naguschewski, 129–41. Amsterdam: Rodopi.

Bâ, Mariama. 1985. *Scarlet Song*. New York: Longman.

Bagnol, Brigitte, and Esmeralda Mariano. 2008. "Elongation of the Labia Minora and Use of Vaginal Products to Enhance Eroticism: Can These Practices Be Considered FGM?" *The Finnish Journal of Ethnicity and Migration* 3 (2): 42–53.

Bakare-Yusuf, Bibi. 2004. "Yorubas Don't Do Gender: A Critical Review of Oyeronke Oyewumi's *The Invention of Women: Making An African Sense of Western Gender Discourses*." In *African Gender Scholarship: Concepts, Methodologies, and Paradigms*, edited by Signe Arnfred, 61–81. Dakar: CODESRIA.

Balia, Darryl. 1989. *Christian Resistance to Apartheid: Ecumenism in South Africa 1960–1987*. Braamfontein, South Africa: Skotaville Publishers.

Banda, Fareda. 2005. *Women, Law, and Human Rights: An African Perspective*. Oxford: Hart Publishing.

Bannerji, H. 2000. *The Dark Side of the Nation*. Toronto: Canadian Scholars' Press.

Bartels, Larry. 2002. "Beyond Running Tally: Partisan Bias in Political Perceptions." *Political Behavior* 24 (2): 117–50.

Bederman, Gail. 1995. *Manliness and Civilization: A Cultural History of Gender and Race in the United States, 1880–1917*. Chicago: University of Chicago Press.

Bell, B., and J. Binnie. 2000. *The Sexual Citizen: Queer Politics and Beyond*. Cambridge: Polity Press.

Bennett, Jane. 2011. "Subversion and Resistance: Activist Initiatives." In *African Sexualities: A Reader*, edited by Sylvia Tamale, 77–100. Cape Town: Pambazuka Press/Fahamu Books.

Bereket, Tarik, and Barry D. Adam. 2006. "The Emergence of Gay Identities in Contemporary Turkey." *Sexualities* 9 (2): 131–51.

Berger, Jonathan. 2008. "Getting to the Constitutional Court on Time: A Litigation History of Same-Sex Marriage." In *To Have and To Hold: The Making of Same-Sex Marriage in South Africa*, edited by Melanie Judge, Anthony Manion, and Shaun de Waal, 17–28. Auckland Park, South Africa: Fanele.

Bérubé, A. 2001. "How Gay Stays White and What Kind of White It Stays." In *The Making and Unmaking of Whiteness*, edited by Birgit Brander Rasmussen, 234–65. Durham: Duke University Press.

Beyala, Calixthe. 1996. *Your Name Shall Be Tanga*. Portsmouth, NH: Heinemann.

– 2003. *Femme Nue, Femme Noire*. Paris: Albin Michel.

Beyrer, Chris, Andrea Wirtz, Damian Walker, Benjamin Johns, Frangiscos Sifakis, and Stephan D. Baral. 2011. *The Global HIV Epidemics among Men Who Have Sex with Men*. Washington: World Bank.

Bhana, Deevia, Robert Morrell, Jeff Hearn, and Relebohile Moletsane, eds. 2007. "Sexualities in Southern Africa." *Sexualities* 10 (2): 131–9.

Binnie, Jon. 2004. *The Globalization of Sexuality*. London: Sage Publications.

Birrell, Susan, and C.L. Cole. 1990. "Double Fault: Renee Richards and the Construction and Naturalization of Difference." *Sociology of Sport* 7: 3.

Blackwood, Evelyn. 2010. *Falling into the Lesbi World: Desire and Difference in Indonesia*. Honolulu: University of Hawai'i Press.

Blackwood, Evelyn, and Saskia E. Wieringa, eds. 1999. *Female Desires: Same-Sex Relations and Transgender Practices across Cultures*. New York: Columbia University Press.

Bleys, Rudi C. 1995. *The Geography of Perversion: Male-Male Sexual Behaviour outside the West and the Ethnographic Imagination, 1750–1918*. New York: New York University Press.

Blier, Suzanne. 1993. "Truth and Seeing: Magic, Custom, and Fetish in Art History." In *Africa and the Disciplines: The Contributions of Research in Africa to the Social Sciences and Humanities*, edited by R. Bates, V.Y. Mudimbe, and J. O'Barr, 139–66. Chicago: University of Chicago Press.

Boddy, Janice. 2007. *Civilizing Women: British Crusades in Colonial Sudan*. Princeton: Princeton University Press.

Boellstorff, Tom. 2003. "Dubbing Culture: Indonesian Gay and Lesbi Subjectivities and Ethnography in an Already Globalized World." *American Ethnologist* 30 (2): 225–42.

– 2005. *The Gay Archipelago: Sexuality and Nation in Indonesia.* Princeton: Princeton University Press.

Bongmba, Elias. 2001. "African Witchcraft from Ethnography to Critique." In *Witchcraft Dialogues: Anthropological and Philosophical Exchanges,* edited by Georges C. Bond and Diane Ciekawy, 39–79. Ohio: Ohio Center for International Studies.

Borer, Tristan Anne. 1998. *Challenging the State: Churches as Political Actors in South Africa, 1980–1994.* Notre Dame: University of Notre Dame Press.

Bosch, Tanja. 2008. "Online Coloured Identities: A Virtual Ethnography." In *Power, Politics, and Identity in South African Media,* edited by Hadland Hadland, Eric Louw, Simphiwe Sesanti, and Herman Wasserman, 184–203. Cape Town: HSRC Press.

Bourdieu, Pierre. 1985. *Sozialer Raum und "Klassen"; Leçon Sur La Leçon. Zwei Vorlesungen.* Frankfurt: Suhrkamp.

Bourke, Joanna. 1996. *Dismembering the Male: Men's Bodies, Britain and the Great War.* London: Reaktion Books.

Brah, A. 1996. *Cartographies of Diaspora: Contesting Identities.* London: Routledge.

Brandes, Stanley H. 2002. *Staying Sober in Mexico City.* Austin: University of Texas Press.

Brantlinger, Patrick. 1985. "Victorians and Africans: The Geneology of the Myth of the Dark Continent." *Critical Enquiry* 12 (Autumn): 166–203.

Broni, Y. 2006. "Joy FM Had a Homosexual on a Program and My Oh My." *Accra Mail,* August 29. http://allafrica.com/stories/200608291000.html.

Brooks, George E. 1980. "Artists' Depictions of Senegalese Signares: Insights Concerning French Racist and Sexist Attitudes in the Nineteenth Century." *Genève-Afrique* 18 (1): 75–89.

Brooks, Philip, and Laurent Bocahut. 1998. *Woubi Chéri.* Paris and Abidjan: ARTE France.

Broqua, Christophe. 2007. "Compositions Silencieuses avec les Normes Sexuelles à Bamako." *Terroirs: Revue Africaine de Sciences Sociales et de Philosophie* 1–2: 33–47.

– 2009. "Sur les Rétributions des Pratiques Homosexuelles à Bamako." *Canadian Journal of African Studies/Revue Canadienne D'études Africaines* 43 (1): 60–82.

– 2010. "La Socialisation du Désir Homosexuel Masculin à Bamako." *Civilisations: Revue Internationale D'anthropologie et de Sciences Humaines* 59 (1): 37–57.

Bruce, Toni. 2009. "Winning Space in Sport: The Olympics in the New Zealand Sport Media." In *Olympic Women and the Media: International Perspectives*, edited by Pirkko Markula, 150–67. London: Palgrave Macmillan.

Brusco, Elizabeth E. 1995. *The Reformation of Machismo: Evangelical Conversion and Gender in Colombia*. Austin: University of Texas Press.

Bryk, Felix. 1964. *Voodoo-Eros: Ethnological Studies in the Sex-Life of the African Aborigines*. New York: United Book Guild.

Bucher, Nathalie Rosa. 2009. "South Africa: Law Failing Lesbians on 'Corrective Rape.'" *Inter Press Service*, August 31. http://www.ips.org.

Bucholtz, Mary, and Kira Hall. 2004. "Theorizing Identity in Language and Sexuality Research." *Language in Society* 33: 469–515.

Bujra, Janet. 2000. "Targeting Men for a Change: AIDS Discourse and Activism in Africa." *Agenda* 44: 6–23.

Burchardt, Marian. 2009. "Subjects of Counselling: Religion, HIV/AIDS and the Management of Everyday Life in South Africa." In *AIDS and Religious Practice in Africa*, edited by Felicitas Becker and P. Wenzel Geissler, 333–58. Leiden: Brill.

Burchell, Graham, Colin Gordon, and Peter Miller. 1991. *The Foucault Effect: Studies in Governmentality, with Two Lectures by and an Interview with Michel Foucault*. Chicago: University of Chicago Press.

Burton, Richard. 1885. *A Plain and Literal Translation of the Arabian Nights' Entertainments, now Entitled: The Book of the Thousand Nights and a Night, with Introduction, Explanatory Notes on the Manners and Customs of Moslem Men and a Terminal Essay upon the History of The Nights*. London: Burton Club.

Butchart, Alexander. 1998. *The Anatomy of Power: European Constructions of the African Body*. New York: Zed Books.

Butler, Judith. 1990. *Gender Trouble: Feminism and the Subversion of Identity*. New York: Routledge.

– 1993. *Bodies that Matter: On the Discursive Limits of "Sex."* New York: Routledge.

– 2003. "Critically Queer." *GLQ: A Journal of Lesbian and Gay Studies* 1: 17–32.

– 2008. *Gender Trouble: Feminism and the Subversion of Identity*. New York: Routledge

– 2009. "Wise Distinctions." *London Review of Books Blog*. http://www.lrb.co.uk/blog.

Byfield, J. 2000. "Introduction: Rethinking the African Diaspora." *African Studies Review* 43 (1): 1–9.

Cage, Ken. 2003. *Gayle: The Language of Kinks and Queens – A History and Dictionary of Gay Language in Southern Africa*. Houghton, South Africa: Jacana Media.

Cahn, Susan. 1994. *Coming on Strong: Gender and Sexuality in Twentieth-Century Women's Sport*. Cambridge: Harvard University Press.

Caldwell, John C., Pat Caldwell, and Pat Quiggin. 1989. "The Social Context of AIDS in Sub-Saharan Africa." *Population and Development Review* 15 (2): 185–233.

Camara, Mohammed. 1997. *Dakan*. Conakry: ArtMattan.

Canaday, Margaret. 2009. "Thinking Sex in the Transnational Turn: An Introduction." *American Historical Review* 116 (5): 1250–7.

Case, S. 2002. "The Emperor's New Clothes: The Naked Body and Theories of Performance." *Substance* 31 (2/3): 186–200.

Castilhon, J.L. 1993. *Zingha, reine d'Angola, Histoire Africaine*. Edited by Patrick Graille and Laurent Quilerie. Bourges: Ganymede.

Cavanagh, Sheila L., and Heather Sykes. 2006. "Transsexual Bodies at Olympics: The International Committee's Policy on Transsexual Athletes at the 2004 Athens Summer Games." *Body & Society* 12: 75–102.

Cawthra, Gavin, Gerald Kraak, and O' Sullivan, eds. 1994. *War and Resistance: Southern African Reports, Struggle for Southern Africa as Seen by "Resister" Magazine*. London: Macmillan.

Centre for Human Rights, University of Pretoria. 2010. "African Commission Should Reconsider Decision on Coalition of African Lesbians: Statement to the 48th Session of the African Commission on Human and Peoples' Rights, November 2010, Banjul, The Gambia." *Pambazuka News*, 506: Special Issue: African Commission blocks LBGTI human rights edition. http://www.pambazuka.org/en/issue/506.

De Certeau, Michel. 1990. *L'invention Du Quotidien. I: Arts de Faire*. Paris: Éditions Gallimard – Folio Essais.

Chabal, Patrick, and Jean-Pascal Daloz. 1999. *Africa Works: Disorder as Political Instrument*. Bloomington: Indiana University Press.

Chanock, Martin. 1986. *Law, Custom and Social Order: The Colonial Experience in Malawi and Zambia*. Cambridge: Cambridge University Press.

Che-Riboud, Barbara. 2003. *Hottentot Venus*. New York: Doubleday.

Chauncey, George. 1994. *Gay New York: Gender, Urban Culture, and the Making of the Gay Male World, 1890–1940*. New York: Basic Books.

– 2004. "De l'autre côté du placard (interview)." *Vacarme* 26. http://www.vacarme.org/article424.html.

Chetty, Dhianaraj. 1995. "A Drag at Madame Costello's: Cape Moffie Life and the Popular Press in the 1950s and 1960s." In *Defiant Desire: Gay and Lesbian Lives in South Africa*, edited by Mark Gevisser and Edwin Cameron, 115–27. New York: Routledge.

Cioran, E.M. 1968. *The Temptation to Exist*. Chicago: Quadrangle.

Clark, Gracia. 1999. "Mothering, Work, and Gender in Urban Asante Ideology and Practice." *American Anthropologist* 101 (4): 717–29.

– 2001. "Gender and Profiteering: Ghana's Market Women as Devoted Mothers and 'Human Vampire Bats'." In *"Wicked" Women and the Reconfiguration of Gender in Africa*, edited by D.L. Hodgson and S.A. McCurdy, 293–311. Oxford: James Currey.

Cock, Jacklyn. 1991. *Colonels and Cadres: War and Gender in South Africa*. Cape Town: Oxford University Press.

– 2001. "Gun Violence and Masculinity in Contemporary South Africa." In *Changing Men in South Africa*, edited by Robert Morrell, 43–55. London: Zed Books.

– 2003. "Engendering Gay and Lesbian Rights: The Equality Clause in the South African Constitution." *Women's Studies International Forum* 26 (1): 35–45.

– 2005. "Engendering Gay and Lesbian Rights: The Equality Clause in the South African Constitution." In *Sex and Politics in South Africa*, edited by Neville Hoad, Karen Martin, and Graeme Reid, 188–209. Cape Town: Double Storey Books.

Cock, Jacklyn, and Lawrie Nathan, eds. 1989. *War and Society: The Militarization of South Africa*. Cape Town: David Philip.

Cohen, Cathy. 1999. *The Boundaries of Blackness: AIDS and the Breakdown of Black Politics*. Chicago: University of Chicago Press.

Cohen, Jean L. 2002. *Regulating Intimacy: A New Legal Paradigm*. Princeton: Princeton University Press.

Cole, Cheryl L. 2000. "One Chromosome Too Many?" In *Olympics at the Millennium: Power, Politics and the Game*, edited by K. Schaffer and S. Smith, 128–46. New Brunswick: Rutgers University Press.

Cole, Jennifer, and Lynn M. Thomas. 2009. *Love in Africa*. Chicago; London: University of Chicago Press.

Colvin, Christopher. 2000. "The Angel of Memory: 'Working Through' the History of the New South Africa." In *Between the Psyche and the Polis: Refiguring History in Literature and Theory*, edited by Anne Whitehead and Michael Rossington, 157–73. Burlington, VT: Ashgate.

– 2008. "Trauma." In *New South African Keywords*, edited by Nick Shepherd and Steven Robins, 223–34. Johannesburg: Jacana Media.

Converse, Philip. 1962. "Information Flow and the Stability of Partisan Attitudes." *The Public Opinion Quarterly* 26 (4): 578–99.

Cooky, Cheryl, and Shari Dworkin. Forthcoming. "Running down What Comes Naturally: Gender Verification and South Africa's Caster Semenya." In *Fallen Sports Heroes, Media, and Celebrity Culture*, edited by Lawrence Wenner. New York: Peter Lang.

Cooky, Cheryl, Ranissa Dycus, and Shari Dworkin. 2012. "'What Makes a Woman a Woman?' vs. 'Our First Lady of Sport': A Comparative Analysis of US and South African Media Coverage of Caster Semenya." *Journal of Sport and Social Issues* (in press).

Cooper, Emily J. 2010. "Gender Testing in Athletic Competitions – Human Rights Violations: Why Michael Phelps Is Praised and Caster Semenya Is Chastised." *The Journal of Gender, Race, and Justice* 14: 233–64.

Correa, Sonia, and Rosalind P. Petchesky. 1994. "Reproductive and Sexual Rights: A Feminist Perspective." In *Population Policies Reconsidered: Health, Empowerment, and Rights*, edited by Gita Sen, Adrienne Germain, and Lincoln C. Chen, 107–23. Boston: Harvard Centre for Population and Development Studies.

"Country Profiles." 2005. *Behind the Mask*. www.mask.org.za.

Coy, Jean-Louis. 2008. *Forces occultes: Le complot judéo-maçonnique au cinéma*. Paris: Véga.

Crawford, Katherine. 2007. *European Sexualities, 1400–1800*. Cambridge: Cambridge University Press.

Croucher, Sheila. 2002. "South Africa's Democratisation and the Politics of Gay Liberation." *Journal of Southern African Studies* 28 (2): 315–30.

Crowder, Michael. 1959. *Pagans and Politicians*. London: Hutchinson.

Csordas, Thomas J. 2002. *Body/Meaning/Healing, Contemporary Anthropology of Religion*. New York: Palgrave Macmillan.

Currier, Ashley. 2007. "Transgender Inclusion in the Namibian and South African LGBT Movements." Annual Meeting of the American Sociological Association: New York. http://www.allacademic.com/meta/p183017_index.html.

Cvetkovich, Ann. 1998. "Untouchability and Vulnerability: Stone Butchness as Emotional Style." In *Butch/Femme: Inside Lesbian Gender*, edited by S.R. Munt, 159–69. London: Cassell.

D'Amico, Francine, and Weinstein, eds. 1999. *Gender Camouflage: Women and the U.S. Military*. New York: New York University Press.

Dallas, Joe, and Nancy Heche. 2009. *The Complete Christian Guide to Understanding Homosexuality*. Eugene, OR: Harvest House Publishers.

Dankwa, Serena O. 2009. "'It's a Silent Trade': Female Same-Sex Intimacies in Post- Colonial Ghana." *NORA (Nordic Journal of Feminist and Gender Research)* 17 (3): 192–205.

Darboe, Momodou. 2004. "ASR Focus: Islamism in West Africa – Gambia." *African Studies Review* 47 (2): 73–82.

Davies, Bob. 1998. *History of Exodus International: An Overview of the Worldwide Growth of the Ex-Gay Movement*. Seattle: Exodus International – North America.

Davies, Bob, and Lori Rentzel. 1993. *Coming out of Homosexuality: New Freedom for Men and Women*. Downers Grove, IL: InterVarsity Press.

Davis, Laurel R., and Linda Delano. 1992. "Fixing the Boundaries of Physical Gender: Side Effects of Anti-Drug Campaigns in Athletics." *Sociology of Sport Journal* 9: 1–19.

Davison, Patricia. 1993. "Human Subjects as Museum Objects: A Project to Make Life-Casts of 'Bushmen' and 'Hottentots,' 1907–1924." *Annals of the South African Museum* 102: 165–83.

Decena, Carlos Ulises. 2008. "Tacit Subjects." *GLQ: A Journal of Lesbian and Gay Studies* 14 (23): 340–59.

Dellenborg, Liselott. 2004. "A Reflection on the Cultural Meanings of Female Circumcision: Experiences from Fieldwork in Casamance, Southern Senegal." In *Re-thinking Sexualities in Africa,* edited by Signe Arnfred, 79–96. Uppsala: Nordiska Afrikainstitutet.

Denzin, Norman K., and John M. Johnson. 1993. *The Alcoholic Society: Addiction and Recovery of the Self*. New Brunswick: Transaction Publishers.

Dickinson, Barry D., Myron Genel, Carolyn B. Robinowitz, Patricia L. Turner, and Gary L. Woods. 2002. "Gender Verification of Female Olympic Athletes." *Medicine & Science in Sports & Exercise* 34: 1539–42.

Dieke, Peter U.C. 1994. "The Political Economy of Tourism in the Gambia." *Review of African Political Economy* 21 (62): 611–27.

Diop, Cheikh Anta. 1960. *L'Afrique Noire Précoloniale*. Paris: Présence Africaine.

Donham, Donald L. 1998. "Freeing South Africa: The 'Modernization' of Male-Male Sexuality in Soweto." *Cultural Anthropology* 13 (1): 3–21.

Douglas, Stacey, Suhraiya Jivraj, and Sarah Lamble. 2011. "Liabilities of Queer Anti-Racist Critique," *Feminist Legal Studies* 19 (2): 107–18.

Dubel, Ireen, and André Hielkema. *A Report by HIVOS Netherlands*. HIVOS Netherlands.

Dubow, Saul. 1995. *Scientific Racism in Modern South Africa*. Cambridge: Cambridge University Press.

Dunton, Chris. 1989. "Wheything Be Dat?: The Treatment of Homosexuality in African Literature." *Research in African Literatures* 20 (3): 422–48.

Dworkin, Shari, and Cheryl Cooky. 2012. "Sport, Sex Segregation, and Sex Testing: Critical Reflections on This Unjust Marriage." *American Journal of Bioethics* 12: 21–3.

Dworkin, Shari, and Faye Linda Wachs. 2009. *Body Panic: Gender, Health and the Selling of Fitness.* New York: New York University Press.

Dynes, Wayne. 1982. "Homosexuality in Sub-Saharan Africa: An Unnecessary Controversy." *Gay Books Bulletin* 9: 20–1.

Ebron, Paulla A. 2007. "Constituting Subjects through Performative Acts." In *Africa after Gender?*, edited by C.M. Cole, T. Manuh, and S.F. Miescher, 171–90. Bloomington: Indiana University Press.

Eckert, Penelope, and Sally McConnell-Ginet. 1992. "Think Practically and Look Locally: Language and Gender as Community-Based Practice." *Annual Review of Anthropology* 21: 461–90.

Edie, Carlene J. 2000. "Democracy in the Gambia: Past, Present and Prospects for the Future." *Africa Development* 25 (3–4): 161–99.

Ekine, Sokari, and Hakima Abbas, eds. 2013. *Queer African Reader.* Oxford: Pambazuka Press.

Ekine, Sokari, and Mia Nikasimo. 2010. "Are We Not Human?" *Pambazuka News*, 506: Special Issue: African Commission blocks LBGTI Human Rights Edition. http://www.pambazuka.org/en/issue/506.

Ekins, Richard. 1997. *Male Femaling: A Grounded Theory Approach to Cross-Dressing and Sex-Changing.* London and New York: Routledge.

Ekins, Richard, and Dave King, eds. 1996. *Blending Genders: Social Aspects of Cross-Dressing and Sex-Changing.* London and New York: Routledge.

Elbl, Ivana. 1996. "'Men Without Wives': Sexual Arrangements in the Early Portuguese Expansion in West Africa." In *Desire and Discipline: Sex and Sexuality in Premodern West*, edited by Jacqueline Murray and Konrad Eisenbichler, 215–28. Toronto: University of Toronto Press.

Eldredge, John. 2001. *Wild at Heart: Discovering the Secret of a Man's Soul.* Nashville, TN: T. Nelson.

Eldredge, John, and Stasi Eldredge. 2005. *Captivating: Unveiling the Mystery of a Woman's Soul.* Nashville: Nelson Books.

Enloe, Cynthia. 2000. *Maneuvers: The International Politics of Militarizing Women's Lives.* Berkeley: University of California Press.

Epprecht, Marc. 1998. "The 'Unsaying' of Indigenous Homosexualities in Zimbabwe: Mapping a Blindspot in an African Masculinity." *Journal of Southern African Studies* 24 (4): 631–51.

– 2006. *Hungochani: The History of a Dissident Sexuality in Southern Africa.* Montreal: McGill-Queen's University Press.

– 2007. "The Marquis de Sade's Zimbabwe Adventure: A Contribution to the Critique of African AIDS." *Sexualities* 10 (2): 241–58.

– 2008. *Heterosexual Africa? The History of an Idea from the Age of Exploration to the Age of AIDS.* Athens and Scottsville: Ohio University Press and University of KwaZulu-Natal Press.

– 2009a. "Same-Sex Marriage Is African." *Global South* 5 (4): 36–8.
– 2009b. "Sexuality, History, Africa." *American Historical Review* 116 (December): 1258–72.
– 2012a. "Sexual Minorities, Human Rights and Public Health Strategies in Africa." *African Affairs* 111 (443): 223–43.
– 2012b. "Transnationalism in Sexuality Studies: An 'Africanist' Perspective." In *Understanding Global Sexualities – New Frontiers*, edited by Peter Aggleton, Richard Parker, Paul Boyce, and Henrietta L. Moore, 186–202. New York: Routledge.
– 2013a. "Preface to the Second Edition," *Hungochani: The History of a Dissident Sexuality in Southern Africa*. Montreal and Kingston: McGill-Queen's University Press.
– 2013b. *Sexuality and Social Justice in Africa*. London: Zed Books.
Erzen, Tanya. 2006. *Straight to Jesus: Sexual and Christian Conversion in the Ex-Gay Movement*. Berkeley: University of California Press.
Essien, Kwame, and Aderinto Saheed. 2009. "'Cutting the Head of the Roaring Monster': Homosexuality and Repression in Africa." *African Study Monographs* 30 (3): 121–35.
Evans, Michael, and Mark Phillips. 1988. "Intensifying Civil War: The Role of the South African Defense Force." In *State, Resistance and Change in South Africa*, edited by P. Frankel, N. Pines, and S. Mark, 117–45. Johannesburg: Southern Book Publishers.
Evans-Pritchard, Edward E. 1970. "Sexual Inversion among the Azande." *American Anthropologist* 72 (6): 1428–34.
Ezeh, Peter-Jazzy. 2003. "Integration and Its Challenges in Participant Observation." *Qualitative Research* 3 (2): 191–205.
Faderman, Lillian. 1992. "The Return of Butch and Femme: A Phenomenon in Lesbian Sexuality of the 1980s and 1990s." *Journal of the History of Sexuality* 2 (4): 578–96.
Fairbairn, B. 2005. "Gay Rights Are Human Rights: Gay Asylum Seekers in Canada." In *Passing Lines: Sexuality and Immigration*, edited by B. Epps, K. Valens, and B.J. Gonzalez, 237–54. Cambridge: Harvard University Press.
Fanon, Frantz. 1967. *Black Skin, White Masks*. New York: Grove Press.
Fausto-Sterling, Anne. 1985. *Myths of Gender: Biological Theories about Women and Men*. New York: Basic Books.
– 2000. *Sexing the Body: Gender Politics and the Construction of Sexuality*. New York: Basic Books.
Feinman, Ilene R. 2000. *Citizenship Rites: Feminist Soldiers and Feminist Antimilitaries*. New York: New York University Press.

Fisher, A.V., and Benno Torgler. 2006. "Does Envy Destroy Fundamentals? The Impact of Relative Income Position on Social Capital." *The Social Science Research Network*. Working Paper Series. http://papers.ssrn.com/sol3/papers.cfm?abstract_id=880089.

Fisiy, Cyprian. 1998. "Containing Occult Practices: Witchcraft Trials in Cameroon." *African Studies Review* 41 (3): 143–63.

Forces Favourites. 1987. Johannesburg: Taurus

Foucault, Michel. 1978. *The History of Sexuality: An Introduction*. Translated by Robert Hurley. New York: Pantheon

– 1984. *The History of Sexuality: Use of Pleasure*. Translated by Robert Hurley. Harmondsworth: Penguin.

– 1986. *The History of Sexuality: The Care of the Self*. Translated by Robert Hurley. Harmondsworth: Penguin.

– 1989. *Foucault Live: Interviews, 1966–1984*. Translated by John Johnston. Edited by. Sylvère Lotringer. New York: Columbia University Press.

Frederiksen, Bodil Folke. 2008. "A 1930s Controversy over African and European Female Sexuality: Jomo Kenyatta, Marie Bonaparte and Bronislaw Malinowski on Clitoridectomy." *History Workshop Journal* 65 (Spring): 23–48.

Fried, Susana, T, and Ilana Landsberg-Lewis. 2000. "Sexual Rights: From Concept to Strategy." In *Women's Human Rights Reference Guide*, edited by K. Askin and D. Koeing, 91–122. New York: Transnational Press.

Gandhi, Leela. 2006. *Affective Communities: Anticolonial Thought, Fin-de-Siècle Radicalism, and the Politics of Friendship*. Durham: Duke University Press.

Gasa, Nomboniso, ed. 2007. *Women in South African History: They Remove Boulders and Cross Rivers/basus'iimbokodo, Bawel'imilambo*. Cape Town: HSRC Press.

Gastaldo, D., A. Gooden, and N. Massaquoi. 2005. "Transnational Health Promotion: Social Well Being Across Borders and Immigrant Women's Subjectivities." *Wagadu: Journal of Transnational Women's and Gender Studies* 2 (Summer): 1–16.

Gaudio, Rudolf. 1997. "Not Talking Straight in Hausa." In *Queerly Phrased: Language, Gender and Sexuality*, edited by A. Livia and K. Hall, 416–29. New York: Oxford University Press.

– 2001. "White Men Do It Too: Racialized (Homo)sexualities in Postcolonial Hausaland." *Journal of Linguistic Anthropology* 11 (1): 36–51.

– 2009. *Allah Made Us: Sexual Outlaws in an Islamic African City*. Chichester: Wiley-Blackwell.

Gay, Judith. 1986. "Mummies and Babies and Friends and Lovers in Lesotho." In *The Many Faces of Homosexuality: Anthropological Approaches to Homosexual Behavior*, edited by Evelyn Blackwood, 97–116. New York: Harrington Park Press.

van der Geest, Sjaak. 2006. "'It Is a Tiresome Work': Love and Sex in the Life of an Elderly Kwahu Woman." In *Sex and Gendering in an Era of* AIDS: *Ghana at the Turn of the Millennium*, edited by C. Oppong, M.Y.P.A. Oppong, and I.K. Odotei, 211–32. Accra: Sub-Saharan Publishers.

Gerber, Lynne. 2011. *Seeking the Straight and Narrow: Weight Loss and Sexual Reorientation in Evangelical America*. Chicago: University of Chicago Press.

Geschiere, Peter. 1997. *The Modernity of Witchcraft: Politics and the Occult in Post-Colonial Africa*. Charlottesville: University Press of Virginia.

– 2008. "Homosexuality in Cameroon. Identity and Persecution." In *Urgency Required: Gay and Lesbian Rights Are Human Rights*, edited by Ireen Dubel and André Hielkema, 126–31. HIVOS: The Hague.

Gevisser, Mark. 1995. "A Different Fight for Freedom: A History of South African Lesbian and Gay Organisations from the 1950s to the 1990s." In *Defiant Desire: Gay and Lesbian Lives in South Africa*, edited by Mark Gevisser and Edwin Cameron, 14–86. New York: Routledge.

– 2006. "Inheritance." In *Beautiful/Ugly: African and African Diaspora Aesthetics*, edited by Sarah Nuttall, 204–23. Durham: Duke University Press.

Gevisser, Mark, and Edwin Cameron, eds. 1994. *Defiant Desire: Gay and Lesbian Lives in South Africa*. Johannesburg: Ravan.

Gibb, H.A. 1983. *Ibn Battuta: Travels in Asia and Africa, 1325–1354*. Translated by H.A. Gibb. London: Routledge.

Gibbon, Edward. 1925. *The Decline and Fall of the Roman Empire*. Vol 4. London: Methuen.

Gifford, Paul. 2004. *Ghana's New Christianity: Pentecostalism in a Globalising African Economy*. London: Hurst.

Gill, Lesley. 1990. "'Like a Veil to Cover Them:' Women and the Pentecostal Movement in La Paz." *American Ethnologist* 17 (4): 708–21.

Gilman, Sander. 1985. *Difference and Pathology: Stereotypes of Sexuality, Race, and Madness*. Ithaca: Cornell University Press.

Gilroy, P. 1995. "Roots and Routes: Black Identity as an Outernational Project." In *Racial and Ethnic Identity*, edited by Herbert W. Harris, 15–30. London: Routledge.

Glass, James. 1985. *Delusion: Internal Dimensions of Political Life*. Chicago: University of Chicago Press.

Global Commission on HIV and the Law. 2012. *HIV and the Law: Risks, Rights and Health*. New York: United Nations Development Program.

Goldman, R. 1996. "Who Is that *Queer* Queer?" In *Queer Studies: A Lesbian, Gay, Bisexual and Transgender Anthology*, edited by Brett Beemyn and Mickey Eliason, 169–82. New York: New York University Press.

Goodman, Tanya. 2009. *Staging Solidarity: Truth and Reconciliation in a New South Africa*. Boulder: Paradigm Publishers.

Goodwin, Jeff. 1997. "Libidinal Constitution of High-Risk Social Movement." *American Sociological Review* 62(1): 53–69.

Goren, Paul. 2005. "Party Identification and Core Political Values." *American Journal of Political Science* 49 (4): 882–97.

Gorman, Ben-David, Barr Anthony Hanson, Brucer Robertson, and Caleb Green. 1997. "Speed, Sex, Gay Men and HIV: Ecological and Community Perspectives." *Medical Anthropology Quarterly* 11 (4): 505–15.

Gray, Mary L. 2009. *Out in the Country: Youth, Media, and Queer Visibility in Rural America*. New York: New York University Press.

Greenberg, E. David. 1988. *The Construction of Homosexuality*. Chicago: University of Chicago Press.

Green-Simms, Lindsey. Forthcoming. "Occult Melodramas: Spectral Affect and West African Video-Film." *Camera Obscura*.

Grinker, Roy Richard. 2000. *Into the Arms of Africa: The Life of Colin M. Turnbull*. New York: St. Martin's Press.

Grunebaum, Heidi. 2011. *Memorializing the Past: Everyday Life in South Africa After the Truth and Reconciliation Commission*. New Brunswick, NJ: Transaction Publishers.

Gueboguo, Charles. 2006. *La Question Homosexuelle en Afrique: Le Cas du Cameroun*. Paris: Éditions L'Harmattan.

– 2009. "Penser les 'droits' des homosexuels/les en Afrique: du sens et de la puissance de l'action associative militante au Cameroun." *Canadian Journal of African Studies* 43 (1): 130–50.

Gunkel, Henriette. 2009. "'What's Identity Got To Do with It?' Rethinking Intimacy and Homosociality in Contemporary South Africa." *NORA (Nordic Journal of Feminist and Gender Research)* 17 (3): 206–21.

Haddawy, Husain. 1992. *The Arabian Nights*. New York: Albert P. Knopf.

Halberstam, Judith. 1998. *Female Masculinity*. Durham: Duke University Press.

– 2002. "An Introduction to Female Masculinity: Masculinity Without Men." In *The Masculinity Studies Reader*, edited by R. Adams and D. Savran, 355–74. Oxford: Blackwell.

– 2008. "Introduction to the Spanish Edition of Female Masculinity." In *MasculinidadFeminina*. Unpublished English version, courtesy of the author. Barcelona: Egales Editorial.

Hall, S. 2003. "Culture Identity and Diaspora." In *Theorizing Diaspora*, edited by Jana Braziel and Anita Mannur, 233–47. Oxford: Blackwell Publishing.

Hanry, Pierre. 1970. *Érotisme Africain: le comportement sexuel des adolescents guinéens*. Paris: Payot.

Hanson, Ebenezer. 2007. "No Room for Gays and Lesbians." *Public Agenda*, May 21. http://allafrica.com/.

Hardin, Russell. 1995. *One for All: The Logic of Group Conflict*. Princeton: Princeton University Press.

Harding, Susan Friend. 2000. *The Book of Jerry Falwell: Fundamentalist Language and Politics*. Princeton: Princeton University Press.

Hargreaves, Jennifer. 1997. "Women's Sport, Development, and Cultural Diversity: The South African Experience." *Women's Studies International Forum* 20: 191–209.

– 2000. *Heroines of Sport: The Politics of Difference and Identity*. New York: Routledge.

Harries, Patrick. 1994. *Work, Culture and Identity: Migrant Laborers in Mozambique and South Africa, C. 1860–1910*. Portsmouth, NH: Heinemann.

Hayes, Patricia. 1996. "'Cocky' Hahn and the 'Black Venus': The Making of a Native Commissioner in South West Africa, 1915–46." *Gender and History* 8 (3): 364–92.

Helle-Valle, J. 2004. "Understanding Sexuality in Africa: Diversity and Contextualized Dividuality." In *Re-thinking Sexualities in Africa*, edited by Signe Arnfred, 195–211. Uppsala: Nordiska Afrikainstitutet.

Hendricks, Muhsin. 2008. "A Way Forward Through Ijtihad: A Muslim Perspective on Same-Sex Marriage." In *To Have and To Hold: The Making of Same-Sex Marriage in South Africa*, edited by M. Judge, A. Manion, and S. de Waal, 219–27. Auckland Park, South Africa: Fanele.

Hendricks, Pepe, ed. 2009. *Hijab: Unveiling Queer Muslim Lives*. Cape Town: African Minds Publisher.

Herdt, G. 2009. *Moral Panic, Sex Panic: Fear and the Fight over Sexual Rights*. New York: New York University Press.

Herdt, Gilbert. 1997. *Same Sex, Different Cultures: Gays and Lesbians Across Cultures*. Boulder: Westview Press.

Herskovits, Melville J. 1967. *Dahomey: An Ancient West African Kingdom*. Evanston: Northwestern University Press.

Herwitz, Daniel. 2003. *Race and Reconciliation: Essays from the New South Africa*. Minneapolis: University of Minnesota Press.

Herzfeld, Michael. 1997. *Cultural Intimacy: Social Poetics in the Nation-State*. New York; London: Routledge.

Herzog, Don. 1998. *Poisoning the Minds of the Lower Orders*. Princeton: Princeton University Press.

Hoad, Neville. 2000. "Arrested Development on the Queerness of Savages: Resisting Evolutionary Narratives of Difference." *Postcolonial Studies* 3 (2): 133–58.

– 2007. *African Intimacies: Race Homosexuality and Globalization*. Minneapolis: University of Minnesota Press.

– 2010. "'Run, Caster Semenya, Run!' Nativism and the Translations of Gender Variance." *Safundi: The Journal of South African and American Studies* 11 (4): 398.

Hoad, Neville, Karen Martin, and Graeme Reid, eds. 2005. *Sex and Politics in South Africa*. Cape Town: Double Storey Books.

Hofstadter, Richard. 1965. *The Paranoid Style in American Politics and Other Essays*. Cambridge: Harvard University Press.

Holmes, Rachel. 1997. "Queer Comrade: Winnie Mandela and the Moffies." *Social Text* 52–3: 161–80.

Hosken, Fran P. 1979. *The Hosken Report: Genital and Sexual Mutilation of Females*. Lexington, MA: Women's International Network News.

HRM. 2004. *Life Matters: Ministering into Sexual and Relational Brokenness*. Cape Town: HRM.

Hughes, Arnold. 1992. "The Collapse of the Senegambian Confederation." *Journal of Commonwealth and Comparative Politics* 30 (2): 200–22.

Hughes, Arnold, and David Perfect. 2006. *A Political History of The Gambia: 1816–1994*. New York: University of Rochester Press.

Human Rights Watch. 2009. "Burundi: Gays and Lesbians Face Increasing Persecution." http://www.hrw.org.news.

Human Rights Watch. 2008. *Nigeria: 2008 Country Reports on Human Rights Practices*. Human Rights Watch Report. http://www.hrw.org.news.

Human Rights Watch. 2005. "Letter to the Minister of Justice of Cameroon Regarding 11 Men Detained on Suspicion of Homosexual Activity." December 1. http://www.hrw.org/news/2005/11/30/letter-minister-justice-cameroon-regarding-11-men-detained-suspicion-homosexual-acti.

Hunter, Mark. 2010. *Love in the Time of AIDS: Inequality, Gender, and Rights in South Africa*. Bloomington and Indianapolis: Indiana University Press.

– 2012. "Rights Amidst Wrongs: The Paradoxes of Gender Rights-Based Approaches towards AIDS in South Africa." In *Understanding Global Sexuality – New Frontiers*, edited by Peter Aggleton, Paul Boyce, Henrietta L. Moore, and Richard Parker, 66–74. New York: Routledge.

IGLHRC. 2006. "United Nations Group Finds Detention of Men in Cameroon on the Basis of Sexual Orientation to be a Violation of Human Rights." October 11. http://www.iglhrc.org/site/iglhrc/section.php?id=5&detail=685.

ILGA. 2009. "UN General Assembly Statement Affirms Rights for All." http://www.ilga.org/ilga/en/article/1211.

– 2009. "Victor Mukasa at the UN Speaking on Grave Human Rights Violations against LGBT People." 10 December. http://www.iglhrc.org/cgi-bin/iowa/article/pressroom/multimediaarchives/1073.html.

Illouz, Eva. 2003. *Oprah Winfrey and the Glamour of Misery: An Essay on Popular Culture*. New York: Columbia University Press.

The Inner Circle. 2009. *Hijab: Unveiling Queer Muslim Lives*. Cape Town: The Inner Circle.

International Commission of Jurists. 2011. *Sexual Orientation, Gender Identity and Justice: A Comparative Law Casebook*. Geneva: ICJ. http://www.icj.org/dwn/database/Sexual%20Orientation,%20Gender%20Identity%20and%20Justice-%20A%20Comparative%20Law%20Casebook%5B1%5D.pdf.

Ireland, Douglas. 2006. "Ghana: Media Leads Anti-Gay Witch-Hunt." *ZMag*, September 21. http://www.zmag.org/content/showarticle.cfm?ItemID=1106.

IRIN. 2009. "Senegal: Jailing Gay Activists Sets back AIDS Fight." http://www.plusnews.org.

Isaack, Wendy. 2010. "The Fallacy of Human Rights at the African Commission." *Pambazuka News* 506: Special Issue: African Commission blocks LBGTI Human Rights Edition. http://www.pambazuka.org/en/issue/506.

Jackson, Frederick. 1930. *Early Days in East Africa*. London: Edward Arnold.

Jackson, Peter A. 2000. "An Explosion of Thai Identities: Global Queering and Re-Imagining Queer Theory." *Culture, Health and Sexuality* 2 (4): 405–24.

Jeater, Diana. 1993. *Marriage, Perversion and Power: The Construction of Moral Discourse in Southern Rhodesia, 1890–1920*. Oxford: Clarendon.

Jeay, Anne-Marie. 1991. "Homosexualité et SIDA au Mali: variations sur l'étrange et l'étranger." In *Homosexualités et SIDA*, edited by Michael Pollak, Rommel Mendès-Leite, and Jacques Van dem Borghe, 60–8. Lille: Cahiers Gai-Kitsch-Camp.

Jewkes, Rachel, Yandisa Sikweyiya, Robert Morrell, and Kristin Dunkle. 2008. *Understanding Men's Health and Use of Violence: Interface of Rape and HIV In South Africa*. Cape Town: Medical Research Council.

Johnson, Cary A. 2007. *Off the Map: How HIV/AIDS Programming Is Failing Same Sex Practicing People in Africa*. New York: IGLHRC.

Johnson, Mark. 1998. "Global Desirings and Translocal Loves: Transgendering and Same-Sex Sexualities in the Southern Philippines." *American Ethnologist* 25 (4): 695–711.

Johnson, Mark, Peter Jackson, and Gilbert Herdt. 2000. "Critical Regionalities and the Study of Gender and Sexual Diversity in South East and East Asia." *Culture, Health and Sexuality* 2 (4): 361–75.

Johnston, Harry H. 1904. *The Uganda Protectorate*. Vol. 2. London: Hutchinson.

Jolly, Susie. 2000. "Queering Development: Exploring the Link between Same-Sex Sexualities, Gender and Development." *Gender and Development* 8 (1): 78–88.

Jordaan, Eduard. 2006. "Inadequately Self-Critical: Rwanda's Self-Assessment for the African Peer Review Mechanism." *African Affairs* 105 (420): 333–51.

Jung, Carl F. 1963. *Memories, Dreams, Reflections*. London: Collins.

Junod, Henri. 1911. *Zidji: étude de mœurs sud-africaines*. St Blaise: Foyer Solidariste.

– 1962. "Unnatural Vice in the Johannesburg Compounds." In *The Life of a South African Tribe*. Vol. 1. New York: University Books.

Kandeh, Jimmy D. 1996. "What Does the 'Militariat' Do When It Rules? Military Regimes: The Gambia, Sierra Leone and Liberia." *Review of African Political Economy* 23 (69): 387–404.

Kane, Mary Jo. 1995. "Resistance/Transformation of the Oppositional Binary: Exposing Sport as Continuum." *Journal of Sport and Social Issues* 19 (2): 191–218.

Kaoma, Kapya. 2009a. *Globalizing the Culture Wars: U.S. Conservatives, African Churches, and Homophobia*. Somerville, MA: Political Research Associates.

– 2009b. "The U.S. Christian Right and the Attack on Gays in Africa." *Public Eye Magazine*

Karkazis, Katrina, Rebecca Jordan-Young, Georgiann Davis, and Silvia Camporesi. 2012. "Out of Bounds? A Critique of the New Policies on Hyperandrogenism in Elite Female Athletes." *American Journal of Bioethics* 12: 3–16.

Kasse, Tidiane. 2013. "Mounting Homophobic Violence in Senegal." In *Queer African Reader*, edited by Sokari Ekine and Hakima Abbas, 262–72. Oxford: Fahamu Books.

Katz, Jonathan Ned. 1990. "The Invention of Heterosexuality." *Socialist Review* 20: 7–14.

Kennedy, Elizabeth Lapovsky, and Madeline D. Davis. 1993. *Boots of Leather, Slippers of Gold: The History of a Lesbian Community*. New York: Routledge.

Kenyatta, Jomo. 1961. *Facing Mount Kenya*. London: Mercury Books.

Khayatt, D. 2002. "Toward a Queer Identity." *Sexualities* 5 (4): 487–501.

Kristeva, Julia. 1982. *Powers of Horror: An Essay on Abjection*. New York: Columbia University Press.

Krouse, Matthew, ed. 1993. *The Invisible Ghetto: Lesbian and Gay Writing from South Africa*. Johannesburg: COSAW.

Kunzel, Regina G. 2002. "Situating Sex: Prison Sexual Culture in the Mid-Twentieth Century." *GLQ: A Journal of Lesbian and Gay Studies* 8 (3): 253–70.

Laburthe-Tolra, Philippe. 1985. *Initiations et sociétés secrètes au Cameroun: essai sur la religion beti*. Paris: Karthala.

Lahiri, Madhumita. 2011. "Crimes and Corrections: Bride Burners, Corrective Rapists, and Other Black Misogynists." *Feminist Africa* 15: 121–34.

Leap, William. 2005. "Finding the Centre: Claiming Gay Space in Cape Town." In *Performing Queer: Shaping Sexualities 1994–2004*, edited by Mikki Van Zyl and Melissa E Steyn, 236–64. Roggebaai, South Africa: Kwela Books.

Lewis, Bernard. 1990. *Race and Slavery in the Middle East: An Historical Enquiry*. New York: Oxford University Press.

Leznoff, Maurice, and William A. Westley. 1956. "The Homosexual Community." *Social Problems* 3 (4): 257–63.

Li, P. 2003. *Destination Canada: Immigration Debates and Issues*. Don Mills: Oxford University Press.

Lidstone, R. 2006. "Refugee Queerings: Sexuality, Identity and Place in Canadian Refugee Determination." Thesis, Simon Fraser University.

Lindberg, Staffan. 2006. *Democracy and Elections in Africa*. Baltimore: The John Hopkins University Press.

Lockhart, Chris. 2002. "Kunyenga, 'Real Sex,' and Survival: Assessing the Risk of HIV Infection among Urban Street Boys in Tanzania." *Medical Anthropology Quarterly* 16 (3): 294–311.

Loos, Jackie. 2004. *Echoes of Slavery: Voices from South Africa's Past*. Claremont, South Africa: David Philip.

Lorde, Audre. 1984. *Sister Outsider: Essays and Speeches*. Trumansburg, NY: Crossing Press.

Lorway, Robert. 2006. "Dispelling 'Heterosexual African AIDS' in Namibia: Same-Sex Sexuality in the Township of Katutura." *Culture, Health and Sexuality* 8 (5): 435–49.

– 2008. "Defiant Desire in Namibia: Female Sexual-Gender Transgression and the Making of Political Being." *American Ethnologist* 35 (1): 20–33.

– 2009. "Beyond Pseudo-Homosexuality: Corrective Rape, Transactional Sex and the Undoing of Lesbian Identities in Namibia." In *The Routledge*

Handbook of Sexuality, Health and Rights, edited by Peter Aggleton and Richard Parker. London: Routledge.

Lovekin, Adams, and H. Newton Maloney. 1977. "Religious Glossolalia: A Longitudial Study of Personality Changes." *Journal for the Scientific Study of Religion* 16 (4): 383–93.

Lugones, Maria. 2008. "The Coloniality of Gender." *Worlds & Knowledges Otherwise* Spring 2008: 1–17.

Lyons, Andrew P., and Harriet D. Lyons. 2004. *Irregular Connections: A History of Anthropology and Sexuality*. Lincoln: University of Nebraska Press.

MacDonald, Prince. 2004. "Same Sex Relations Remain a Crime in Ghana: LGBT in Ghana to Boycott December Polls." http://www.global gayz.com/ghana-news.html.

Machera, M. 2004. "Opening a Can of Worms: A Debate of Female Sexuality in the Lecture Theatre." In *Re-thinking Sexualities in Africa*, edited by Signe Arnfred. Uppsala: Nordiska Afrikainstitutet.

Macintosh Booth, Donald, Hart Cantelon, and Lisa McDermott. 1993. "The IOC and South Africa: A Lesson in Transnational Relations." *International Review for the Sociology of Sport* 28: 373–92.

Magubane, Zine. 2004. *Bringing the Empire Home: Race, Class, and Gender in Britain and Colonial South Africa*. Chicago: University of Chicago Press.

Mah, Timothy L., and Yusupha F. Dibba. 2008. HIV/AIDS *in The Gambia: A Qualitative Assessment of Most-at-Risk Populations*. Banjul: National AIDS Secretariat, UNAIDS, UNDP.

Majavu, Anna. 2009. "Parliament to Petition UN over 'Abuse'." *Sowetan*, 25 August. http://www.sowetanlive.co.za.

Makang, Jean-Marie. 1997. "Of the Good Use of Tradition: Keeping the Critical Perspective in African Philosophy." In *Postcolonial Philosophy: A Critical Reader*, edited by Emmanuel Chukwudi Eze, 324–38. Cambridge: Blackwell.

Mamdani, Mahmood. 1996. *Citizen and Subject: Contemporary Africa and the Legacy of Late Colonialism*. Princeton: Princeton University Press.

Manalansan, Martin F. 2003. *Global Divas: Filipino Gay Men in the Diaspora*. Durham: Duke University Press.

Mann, Jonathan M. 1995. *The Impact of Homophobia and Other Social Biases on AIDS*. San Francisco: Public Media Center.

Mansbridge, Jane. 1997. "Social and Cultural Causes of Dissafection with U.S. Government." In *Why People Don't Trust Government*, edited by Joseph Nye Jr, Philip Zelikow, and David King, 133–54. Cambridge: Harvard University Press.

Maquet, J. 1961. *The Premise of Inequality in Rwanda*. London: Oxford University Press.

Marcus, George E. 1980. "Rhetoric and the Ethnographic Genre in Anthropological Research." *Current Anthropology* 21 (4): 507–10.

Marcus, Sharon. 2007. *Between Women: Friendship, Desire, and Marriage in Victorian England*. Princeton: Princeton University Press.

Mardrus, J.C. 1900. *Le livre des mille nuits et d'une nuit*. Paris: Éditions de la Rue Blanche.

Marks, M. Suzanne. 2006. "Global Recognition of Human Rights for Lesbian, Gay, Bisexual, and Transgendered People." *Health and Human Rights* 9 (1): 33–42.

Marquardt, Niels. 2006. "Business Action Against Corruption in Cameroon: Joint Government-Private Sector Strategies." November 7. http://yaounde.usembassy.gov/ambassador_corruption_business.html.

Masquelier, Adeline. 2009. "Lessons from Rubi: Love, Poverty, and the Educational Value of Televised Dramas in Niger." In *Love in Africa*, edited by J. Cole and L.M. Thomas, 204–28. Chicago: University of Chicago Press.

Massad, Joseph A. 2002. "Re-Orienting Desire: The Gay International and the Arab World," *Public Culture* 14 (2): 361–85.

– 2007. *Desiring Arabs*. Chicago: University of Chicago Press.

Massaquoi, Notisha, and Njoki Wane. 2007. *Theorizing Empowerment: Canadian Perspectives on Black Thought*. Toronto: Inanna.

Matory, J. Lorand. 2005. *Black Atlantic Religion: Tradition, Transnationalism, and Matriarchy in the Afro-Brazilian Candomblé*. Princeton: Princeton University Press.

Maxwell, David. 1999. "Historicizing Christian Indepedency: The Southern African Pentecostal Movement C. 1908–60." *The Journal of African History* 40 (2): 243–64.

Maynard, Steven. 2004. "'Without Working?': Capitalism, Urban Culture, and Gay History." *Journal of Urban History* 30 (3): 378–98.

McFadden, Patricia. 1992. "Sex, Sexuality, and the Problem of AIDS in Africa." In *Gender in Southern Africa*, edited by Ruth Meena, 157–95. Harare: SAPES.

McLean, Hugh, and Linda Ngcobo. 1995. "Abangibhamayo Bathi Ngimnandi (Those Who Fuck Me Say I'm Tasty): Gay Sexuality in Reef Townships." In *Defiant Desire: Gay and Lesbian Lives in South Africa*, edited by Mark Gevisser and Edwin Cameron, 158–85. New York: Routledge.

Meguid, Bonnie. 2005. "Competition between Unequals: The Role of Mainstream Party Strategy in Niche Party Success." *American Political Science Review* 99 (3): 347–59.

Messner, Michael Allen. 2002. *Taking the Field: Women, Men, and Sports*. Minneapolis: University of Minnesota Press.

Mhlongo, Mongezi. 2009. "Another Blow for Gambian Homosexuals." *Behind the Mask*, 4 June. http://www.mask.org.za/article.php?cat= gambia&id=2154.

Miescher, Stephan F. 2005. *Making Men in Ghana*. Bloomington: Indiana University Press.

Miescher, Stephan F., Catherine M. Cole, and Takyiwaa Manuh. 2007. "Introduction: When Was Gender?" In *Africa After Gender?*, edited by C.M. Cole, T. Manuh, and S.F. Miescher, 1–16. Bloomington: Indiana University Press

Miescher, Stephan F., and Lisa A. Lindsay. 2003. "Introduction: Men and Masculinities in Modern African History." In *Men and Masculinities in Modern Africa*, edited by L.A. Lindsay and S.F. Miescher, 1–28. Portsmouth, NH: Heinemann.

Miguel-Alfonso, Ricardo, and Sylvia Caporale-Bizzini, eds. 1994. *Reconstructing Foucault: Essays in the Wake of the 80s*. Amsterdam: Rodopi.

Miller, A. 2005. "Gay Enough: Some Tensions in Seeking the Grant of Asylum and Protecting Global Sexual Diversity" In *Passing Lines: Sexuality and immigration*, edited by B. Epps, K. Valens, and B.J. Gonzalez, 137–88. Cambridge: Harvard University Press.

Miller, Christopher. 1985. *Blank Darkness: Africanist Discourse in French*. Chicago: University of Chicago Press.

Ministry of Finance. 2001. *Census Highlights*. Government of Ontario.

Mkhize, Nonhlanhla, Jane Bennett, Vasu Reddy, and Relebohile Moletsane. 2010. *The Country We Want to Live In: Hate Crimes and Homophobia in the Lives of Black Lesbian South Africans*. Cape Town: HSRC Press.

Moberly, Elizabeth R. 1983. *Homosexuality: A New Christian Ethic*. Cambridge: James Clarke and Company.

Moffett, Helen. 2008. "Gender." In *New South African Keywords*, edited by Nick Shepherd and Steven Robins, 104–15. Athens: Ohio University Press.

Molema, S.M. 1920. *The Bantu Past and Present: An Ethnographical andHistorical Study of the Native Races of South Africa*. Edinburgh: W. Green.

Monga, Celestin. 1997. "Cartoons in Cameroon: Anger and Political Derision Under Monocracy." In *The Word Behind Bars and the Paradox of Exile*, edited by Kofi Anyidoho. Evanston: Northwestern University Press.

– 1998. *The Anthropology of Anger: Civil Society and Democracy in Africa*. Translated by Linda Fleck and Celestin Monga. London: Lynne Rienner.

Moodie, T. Dunbar. 1975. *The Rise of Afrikanerdom: Power, Apartheid, and the Afrikaner Civil Religion*. Berkeley: University of California Press.

Moodie, T. Dunbar, with Vivienne Ndatshe. 1994. *Going for Gold: Men's Lives on the Mines*. Berkeley: University of California Press.

Moore, Mignon R. 2011. *Invisible Families: Gay Identities, Relationships, and Motherhood among Black Women*. Berkeley: University of California Press.

Morgan, Ruth, Charl Marais, and Joy Rosemary Wellbeloved. 2009. *Trans: Transgender Life Stories from South Africa*. Auckland Park, South Africa: Fanele.

Morgan, Ruth, and Saskia Wieringa, eds. 2005. *Tommy Boys, Lesbian Men and Ancestral Wives: Female Same-Sex Practices in Africa*. Johannesburg: Jacana Media.

Morrell, Robert. 2001. *Changing Men in Southern Africa*. Scottsville: University of Natal Press.

Morrish, Liz, and Helen Sauntson. 2007. *New Perspectives on Language and Sexualities*. London: Palgrave Macmillan.

Muhammad, Akbar. 1985. "The Image of Africans in Arabic Literature: Some Unpublished Manuscripts." In *Slaves and Slavery in Muslim Africa*, edited by John Ralph Willis, 1: 47–74. London: Frank Cass.

Muller, M. Alice. 2000. "Sexual but Not Reproductive: Exploring the Junctions and Disjunctions of Sexual and Reproductive Rights." *Health and Human Rights* 4 (2): 68–109.

Munro, Brenna. 2010. "Caster Semenya: Gods and Monsters." *Safundi: The Journal of South African and American Studies* 11 (4): 384.

Murray, Stephen O. 2000. *Homosexualities*. Chicago: University of Chicago Press.

– 2009. "Southern African Homosexualities and Denials." *Canadian Journal of African Studies/Revue Canadienne Des ÉtudesAfricaines* 43 (1): 168–73.

Murray, Stephen O., and Will Roscoe. 1998a. "Africa and African Homosexualities: An Introduction." In *Boy-Wives and Female Husbands: Studies in African Homosexualities*, edited by Stephen O. Murray and Will Roscoe, 1–18. New York: St Martin's Press.

– eds. 1998b. *Boy-Wives and Female Husbands: Studies in African Homosexualities*. New York: St Martin's Press

Muskin-Pierret. 2010. "Uganda's Anti-Homosexuality Bill." *The Young Idealist* 1 (1): 20–6, 31–3.

Nackenoff, Carol. 1994. *The Fictional Republic: Horatio Alger and American Political Discourse*. New York: Oxford University Press.

Nana, Joel. 2010. "If Not, Why Not? Doublespeak on LGBTI Rights at
   the African Commission." *Pambazuka News*, 506: Special Issue: African
   Commission blocks LBGTI Human Rights Edition. http://www.
   pambazuka.org/en/issue/506.

Ndashe, Sibongile. 2010. "The Battle for the Recognition of LGBTI
   Human Rights." *Perspectives: Political Analysis and Commentary from
   Africa* 4 (10): 4–9.

– 2011. "Seeking the Protection of LGBTI Rights at the African Commission for Human and People's Rights." *Feminist Africa* 15: 17–37.

– 2012. "SA's 'Betrayal' of the AU at UN." Soweta, 1 September 2012.
   http://www.sowetanlive.co.za/columnists/2012/03/23/sa-s-betrayal-of-
   au-at-un.

Nel, Juan A., and Melanie Judge. 2008. "Exploring Homophobic Discrimination in Gauteng, South Africa: Issues, Impacts, and Responses." *Acta-
   Criminologica* 21: 19–36.

Neustadt, Richard. 1997. "The Politics of Mistrust." In *Why People Don't
   Trust Government*, edited by Joseph Nye Jr, Philip Zelikow, and David
   King, 179–202. Cambridge: Harvard University Press.

Nguyen, Vinh-Kim. 2005. "Uses and Pleasures: Sexual Modernity, HIV/
   AIDS, and Confessional Technologies in a West African Metropolis." In
   *Sex in Development: Science, Sexuality, and Morality in Global Perspec-
   tive*, edited by Vincanne Adams and Stacy Leigh Pigg, 245–67. Durham:
   Duke University Press.

– 2009. "Therapeutic Evangelism – Confessional Technologies, Antiretro-
   virals and Biospiritual Transformation in the Fight against AIDS in
   West Africa." In *Aids and Religious Practice in Africa*, edited by Felicitas
   Becker and P. Wenzel Geissler, 359–78. Leiden: Brill.

– 2010. *The Republic of Therapy: Triage and Sovereignty in West Africa's
   Time of AIDS*. Durham, NC: Duke University Press.

Niang, Cheikh I. 2010. "Understanding Sex Between Men in Senegal:
   Beyond Current Linguistic and Discursive Categories." In *The Routledge
   Handbook of Sexuality, Health and Right*, edited by Peter Aggleton and
   Richard Parker. London: Routledge.

Niang, Cheikh I., Amadou Moreau, Codou Bop, Cyrille Compaore, Mou-
   stapha Diagne, Kees Kostermans, and Aissatou Diack. 2004. *Targeting
   Vulnerable Groups in National HIV/AIDS Programs: The Case of Men
   Who Have Sex with Men – Senegal, Burkina Faso and The Gambia*.
   New York: World Bank.

Niang, Cheikh I., Placide Tapsoba, Ellen Weiss, Moustapha Diagne, Yous-
   soupha Niang, Amadou Moreau, Dominique Gomis, Abdoulaye Sidibé
   Wade, Karim Seck, and Chris Castle. 2003. "'It's Raining Stones':

Stigma, Violence and HIV Vulnerability among Men Who Have Sex with Men in Dakar, Senegal." *Culture, Health and Sexuality* 5 (6): 499–512.

Nkabinde, Nkunzi Z. 2009. *Black Bull, Ancestors and Me: My Life as a Lesbian Sangoma*. Auckland Park, South Africa: Fanele; Jacana Media.

Nkoli, Simon. 1993. "This Strange Feeling." In *The Invisible Ghetto: Lesbian and Gay Writing from South Africa*, edited by Matthew Krouse and Kim Berman, 19–26. Johannesburg: COSAW.

– 1995. "Wardrobes: Coming out as a Black Gay Activist in South Africa." In *Defiant Desire: Gay and Lesbian Lives in South Africa*, edited by Mark Gevisser and Edwin Cameron, 249–57. New York: Routledge.

Noble, Bobby. 2004. *Masculinities Without Men? Female Masculinity in Twentieth-Century Fictions*. Vancouver: UBC Press.

Nsom, Kini. 2006. "Biya Castigates Journalists on Homosexuality Saga." *Post*, February 14. http://allafrica.com/stories/200602150319.html.

Nyanzi, Stella. 2008. "Negotiating Scripts for Meaningful Sexuality: An Ethnography of Youths in The Gambia." PhD thesis, University of London: London School of Hygiene and Tropical Medicine.

– 2012. "President Jammeh's HIV/AIDS Healing Saga in The Gambia." In *African Responses to HIV/AIDS: Between Speech and Action*, edited by S. Ige and T. Quinlan, 124–52. Durban: University of KwaZulu Natal Press.

Nyanzi, Stella, Ousman Rosenberg-Jallow, Ousman Bah, and Susan Nyanzi. 2005. "Bumsters, Bigblack Organs and Old White Gold: Embodied Racial Myths in Sexual Relationships of Gambian Beachboys." *Culture, Health and Sexuality* 7 (6): 557–69.

Nyeck, S.N. 2004. "(Homo)sexuality and Calixthe Beyala." *A Globe of Witnesses Magazine Online*. http://www.thewitness.org/agw/nyeck012904en.html.

– 2011. "The Autobiography of Things Left Undone: Politics of Literature, Hyphenation and Queered Friendship in Africa." *Transcript Journal* 1 (February): 171–200.

Nyong'o, Tavia. 2010. "The Unforgivable Transgression of Being Caster Semenya." *Women & Performance* 20: 95–100.

Nzegwu, Nkiru. 2004. "The Epistemological Challenge of Motherhood to Patriliny." *JENdA: A Journal of Culture and African Women Studies* 5.

O'Flaherty, Michael, and John Fisher. 2008. "Sexual Orientation, Gender Identity and International Human Rights Law: Contextualising the Yogyakarta Principles." *Human Rights Law Review* 8 (2): 207–48.

O'Mara, Kathleen. 1999. "Queers Performing on Campus: Concealment and Revelation by Students of Color in the 1990s." *Phoebe: Journal of Gender and Cultural Critiques* 11 (2): 43–50.

– 2007. "Homophobia and Building Queer Community in Urban Ghana." *Phoebe: Journal of Gender and Cultural Critiques* 19 (1): 35–46.

Okpewho, I. 2009. "Introduction: Can We 'Go Home Again?'" In *The New African Diaspora*, edited by I. Okpewho and N. Nzegwu, 1–30. Bloomington: Indiana University Press.

Ombolo, J.-P. 1990. *Sexe et société en Afrique noire*. Paris: l'Harmattan.

Ottoson, Daniel. 2008. *State-Sponsored Homophobia: A World Survey of Laws Prohibiting Same Sex between Consenting Adults*. ILGA. http://www.ilga.org/statehomophobia/ilga_State_Sponsored_Homophobia_2008.pdf.

Ottosson, Daniel. 2009a. *State-Sponsored Homophobia: A World Survey of Laws Prohibiting Same Sex Activity between Consenting Adults*. ILGA. http://www.ilga.org.

Ousmane, Dème. 2005. *Between Hope and Scepticism: Civil Society and the African Peer Review Mechanism*. Ottawa and Addis Ababa: Partnership Africa Canada.

Ouzgane, Lahoucine. 2003. "Islamic Masculinities: Introduction." *Men and Masculinities* 5 (3): 231–5.

Ouzgane, Lahoucine, and Robert Morrell, eds. 2005. *African Masculinities: Men in Africa from the Late Nineteenth Century to the Present*. London: Routledge.

Oyéwùmí, Oyèrónké. 1997. *The Invention of Women: Making an African Sense of Western Gender Discourses*. Minneapolis: University of Minnesota Press.

– 2004. "Conceptualising Gender: Eurocentric Foundations of Feminist Concepts and the Challenge of African Epistemologies." In *African Gender Scholarship: Concepts, Methodologies, and Paradigms*, edited by Signe Arnfred, 1–8. Dakar: CODESRIA.

Pateman, Carole. 1988. *The Sexual Contract*. Stanford: University of California Press.

Patton, C., and B. Sanchez-Eppler. 2000. *Queer Diasporas*. Durham: Duke University Press.

Payne, Leanne. 1995. *Crisis in Masculinity*. Grand Rapids, Michigan: Baker Books.

Pelak, Cynthia F. 2010. "Women and Gender in South African Soccer: A Brief History." *Soccer and Society* 11: 63–78.

Perfect, David. 2008. "Politics and Society in The Gambia since Independence." *History Compass* 6 (2): 426–38.

Petchesky, Rosalind P. 2000. "Sexual Rights: Inventing a Concept, Mapping and International Practice." In *Framing the Sexual Subject: The Politics of Gender, Sexuality and Power*, edited by Richard Parker,

Regina Maria Barbosa, and Peter Aggleton, 81–103. Berkeley: University of California Press.

Phillips, Oliver. 2000. "Constituting the Global Gay: Individual Subjectivity and Sexuality in Southern Africa." In *Sexuality in the Legal Arena*, edited by Carl Stychin and Didi Herman, 17–34. London: Athlone Press.

Pickering, Helen, Jim Todd, David Dunn, Jacques Pepin, and Andrew Wilkins. 1992. "Prostitutes and Their Clients: a Gambian Survey." *Social Science and Medicine* 34 (1): 75–88.

Pierce, Steven. 2007. "Identity, Performance and Secrecy: Gendered Life and the 'Modern' in Northern Nigeria." *Feminist Studies* 33 (3): 539–65.

Plummer, Ken. 2001. "The Square of Intimate Citizenship: Some Preliminary Proposals." *Citizenship Studies* 5: 237–48.

Polikoff, Nancy. 2008. *Beyond (Straight and Gay) Marriage: Valuing All Families under the Law*. Boston: Beacon Press.

Population Council. 2008. *Sexual and Gender-Based Violence: Key Issues for Programming*. Nairobi Population Council Sub-Saharan Africa Office. http://www.popcouncil.org/pdfs/AfricaSGBV_KeyIssues.pdf.

Posel, Deborah. 2001. "Race as Common Sense: Racial Classification in 21st Century South Africa." *African Studies Review* 44: 87–113.

– 2005. "'Baby Rape': Unmaking Secrets of Sexual Violence in Post-Apartheid South Africa." In *Men Behaving Differently: South African Men Since 1994*, edited by Graeme Reid and Liz Walker, 21–64. Cape Town: Double Storey Books.

– 2011. "'Getting the Nation Talking about Sex': Reflections on the Politics of Sexuality and Nation-Building in Post-Apartheid South Africa." In *African Sexualities: A Reader*, edited by Sylvia Tamale, 130–44. Cape Town: Pambazuka Press/Fahamu Books.

Povinelli, Elizabeth A, and George Chauncey. 1999. "Thinking Sexuality Transnationally: An Introduction." *GLQ: A Journal of Lesbian and Gay Studies* 5 (4): 439–49.

Price, Linda. 1989. "A Documentation of the Experiences of Military Conscripts in the South African Defence Force." Unpublished MA dissertation, Durban: University of Natal.

Puar, Jasbir K. 2008. "Homonationalism and Biopower." In *Out of Place: Interrogating Silences in Queerness/Raciality*, edited by Adi Kuntsman and Esperanza Miyake, 13–70. London: Raw Nerve Books.

Purchas, Samuel. 1613. *Purchas: His Pilgrims or Relations of the World and the Religions Observed in All Ages and Places Discovered from the Creation until This Present*. London: William Stansby for Henrie Fetherstone.

– 1905. *Hakluytus Posthumus or Purchas, His Pilgrimes*. Vol. VI. Glasgow: James MacLehose.

QAYN, Queer African Youth Networking Center. 2012. *Struggling Alone: The Lived Realities of Women Who Have Sex with Women in Burkina Faso, Ghana and Nigeria*. Ouagadougou: QAYN.

Quinn, T.C, J.M. Mann, J.W. Curran, and P. Piot. 1986. "AIDS in Africa: An Epidemiologic Paradigm." *Science* 234: 955–63.

Rachewiltz, Boris de. 1964. *Black Eros: Sexual Customs of Africa from Prehistory to the Present Day*. London: George Allen and Unwin.

Ratele, Kopano. 2004. "Kinky Politics." In *Re-thinking Sexualities in Africa*, edited by Signe Arnfred, 139–57. Uppsala: Nordiska Afrikainstitutet.

– 2011. "Male Sexualities and Masculinities." In *African Sexualities: A Reader*, edited by Sylvia Tamale, 399–419. Cape Town: Pambazuka Press.

Ray, Carina. 2009. "Caster Semenya: 21st Century 'Hottentot Venus'?" *New African*, November: 18–19.

Reber, Arthur S. 1995. *The Penguin Dictionary of Psychology*. 2nd edition. Hamondsworth Midds: Penguin.

Reeser, Jonathon C. 2005. "Gender Identity and Sport: Is the Playing Field Level?" *Br. J. Sports Med* 39: 695–9.

Reid, Graeme, and Teresa Dirsuweit. 2002. "Understanding Systemic Violence: Homophobic Attacks in Johannesburg and Its Surrounds." *Urban Forum* 13 (3): 99–126.

Reid, Graeme, and Liz Walker, eds. 2005. "Sex and Secrecy: A Focus on African Sexualities." *Culture, Health and Sexuality* 7 (3): 185–94.

Reifenstahl, Leni. 1976. *People of Kau*. New York: Harper and Row.

Richardson, Diane. 1998. "Sexuality and Citizenship." *Sociology* 32: 83–90.

– 2001. "Extending Citizenship: Cultural Citizenship and Sexuality." In *Culture and Citizenship*, edited by Nick Stevenson, 153–66. London: Sage Publications.

Richmond, Edmund. 1993. "Senegambia and the Confederation: History, Expectations and Disillusions." *Journal of Third World Studies* 10 (2): 176.

Riggs, Daniel. 2006. *Priscilla, (White) Queen of the Desert*. New York: Peter Lang.

Ritchie, Ian. 2003. "Sex Tested, Gender Verified: Controlling Female Sexuality in the Age of Containment." *Sport History Review* 34 (1): 80–9.

Ritchie, John F. 1943. *The African As Suckling and As Adult: A Psychological Study*. Livingstone: Rhodes-Livingstone Institute.

Roberts, Benjamin, and Vasu Reddy. 2008. *Pride and Prejudice: Public Attitudes Towards Homosexuality*. Cape Town: Human Sciences Research Council.

Roberts, Matthew. 1995. "Emergence of Gay Identity and Gay Social Movements in Developing Countries." *Alternatives* 20: 243–64.

Robins, Robert, and Jerrold M. Post. 1997. *Political Paranoia: The Psychopolitics of Hatred*. New Haven: Yale University Press.

Robins, Steven. 2005. *From "Medical Miracles" to Normal(ised) Medicine: AIDS Treatment, Activism and Citizenship in the UK and South Africa*. Brighton, England: Institute of Development Studies.

Rose, Nikolas S. 1999. *Governing the Soul: The Shaping of the Private Self*. 2nd edition. New York: Free Association Books.

Ross, Marc. 2007. *Cultural Contestation in Ethnic Conflict*. Cambridge: Cambridge University Press.

Ross, Marlon B. 2005. "Beyond the Closet as Raceless Paradigm." In *Black Queer Studies*, edited by E.P Johnson and M.G. Henderson, 161–89. Durham: Duke University Press.

Rubin, Edward. 2005. *Beyond Camelot: Rethinking Politics and Law for the Modern State*. Princeton: Princeton University Press.

Rupp, L. 2001. "Toward a Global History of Same-Sex Sexuality." *Journal of the History of Sexuality* 10 (2): 287–302.

Rushton, Phillippe. 1997. *Race, Evolution and Behavior: A Life History Perspective*. New Brunswick, NJ: Transaction.

Ryan, Orla. 2007. "Ghana's Secret Gay Community." *BBC News*, March 14. http://news.bbc.co.uk/2/hi/africa/6445337.stm.

Sachs, Wulf. 1937. *Black Hamlet: The Mind of the Black Negro Revealed by Psychoanalysis*. London: Geoffrey Bles.

Sade, D.A.F. 1990. "'Histoire de Sainville et de Léonore' (chapter XXXV of Aline et Valcour)." In *Sade: Œuvres*, edited by M. Delon. Vol. 1. Paris: Éditions Gallimard.

Sadgrove, Joanna, Robert M. Vanderbeck, Johan Andersson, Gill Valentine, and Kevin Ward. 2012. "Morality Plays and Money Matters: Towards a Situated Understanding of the Politics of Homosexuality in Uganda." *Journal of Modern African Studies* 50 (1): 103–29.

Said, Edward. 1979. *Orientalism*. New York: Vintage.

– 2003. *Orientalism: 25th Anniversary Edition*. New York: Vintage.

Saine, Abdoulaye. 2000. "The Gambia's Foreign Policy since the Coup, 1994–99." *Commonwealth and Comparative Politics* 38 (2): 73–88.

– 2002. "Post-Coup Politics in The Gambia." *Journal of Democracy* 13 (4): 167–72.

– 2008. "Presidential and National Assembly Elections, The Gambia 2006 and 2007." *Electoral Studies* 27: 165–70.

Sallah, Tijan M. 1990. "Economics and Politics in The Gambia." *The Journal of Modern African Studies* 28 (4): 621–48.

Salo, Elaine, and Pumla Dineo Gqola. 2006. "Editorial: Subaltern Sexualities." *Feminist Africa* 6 (September): 1–7.

Samuels, J. 1999. "Dangerous Liaisons: Queer Subjectivity, Liberalism and Race." *Cultural Studies* 13 (1): 91–109.

Sapienza, Paola, et al. 2007. "Understanding Trust." *National Bureau of Economic Research*. Working Paper 1338. http://www.nber.org/papers/w13387.

Saxonhouse, Arlene. 1992. *Fear of Diversity: The Birth of Political Science in Ancient Greek Thought*. Chicago: University of Chicago Press.

Schapera, Isaac. 1940. *Married Life in an African Tribe*. London: Faber and Faber.

Schlemmer, Lawrence. 2008. *Dormant Capital: Pentecostalism in South Africa and Its Potential Social and Economic Role*. CDE in Depth. Johannesburg: The Centre for Development and Enterprise.

Sedgwick, Eve K. 1994. *Epistemology of the Closet*. Harmondsworth: Penguin.

Setel, Phillip W. 1999. *A Plague of Paradoxes: AIDS, Culture, and Demography in Northern Tanzania*. Chicago: University of Chicago Press.

Setel, Phillip W., Milton Lewis, and Maryinez Lyons, eds. 1999. *History of Sexually Transmitted Diseases and HIV/AIDS in Sub-Saharan Africa*. Westport, Conn: Greenwood Press.

Sharpley, Richard. 2007. "Tourism in The Gambia – Ten Years On." In *Developments in Tourism Research*, edited by J. Tribe and D. Airey, 49–62. Oxford and Amsterdam: Elsevier.

Shepherd, Gill. 1987. "Rank, Gender, and Homosexuality: Mombasa as a Key to Understanding Sexual Options." In *The Cultural Construction of Sexuality*, edited by Pat Caplan, 240–70. London: Tavistock Publications.

Sircar, Oishik, and Dipika Jain, eds. 2012. "Law, Culture and Queer Politics in Neoliberal Times." *Jindal Global Law Review* 4 (1, special issue): 1–16.

Skramstad, Heidi. 1990. *Prostitute as Metaphor in Gender Construction: A Gambian Setting*. Bergen: Chr. Michelsen Institute.

Smith, Adrian, Placide Tapsoba, Norbert Peshu, Eduard J. Sanders, and Harold W. Jaffe. 2009. "Men Who Have Sex With Men and HIV/AIDS in Sub-Saharan Africa." *The Lancet* 380 (9,839): 367–77.

Smith, Maureen M. 2006. "Revisiting South Africa and the Olympic Movements: The Correspondence of Reginald S. Alexander and the International Olympic Committee: 1961–1986." *The International Journal of the History of Sport* 23: 1193–216.

Spivak, Chakravorty. 1999. *A Critique of the Postcolonial Reason: Toward a History of the Vanishing Present*. Cambridge: Harvard University Press.

Statistics Canada. 2006. *Immigration and Citizenship Highlight Tables, 2006 Census*. Statistics Canada.

Statistics South Africa. 2012. *Census 2011 Municipal Report: Western Cape*. Pretoria: Statistics South Africa.

Stillwaggon, Eileen. 2003. "Racial Metaphors: Interpreting Sex and AIDS in Africa." *Development and Change* 34 (5): 809–32.

"Stofile Threatens 'War' if IAAF Excludes Semenya." 2009. *Mail and Guardian*, September 11.

Stoler, Ann Laura. 2002. *Carnal Knowledge and Imperial Power: Race and the Intimate in Colonial Rule*. Berkeley: University of California Press.

– 2004. "Affective States." In *A Companion to the Anthropology of Politics*, edited by David Nugent and Joan Vincent, 4–20. Malden, MA: Blackwells.

Stratton, Florence. 1994. *Contemporary African Literature and the Politics of Gender*. London; New York: Routledge.

Stychin, Carl. 1996. "Constituting Sexuality: The Struggle for Sexual Orientation in the South African Bill of Rights." *Journal of Law and Society* 23 (4): 455–83.

– 2003. *Governing Sexuality: The Changing Politics of Citizenship and Law Reform*. Oxford: Hart.

Sullivan, Claire F. 2011. "Gender Verification and Gender Policies in Elite Sport: Eligibility and 'Fair Play'." *Journal of Sport and Social Issues* 35: 400–19.

Swarr, Amanda Lock. 2000. *The Aversion Project Interviews*. Johannesburg: NCGLE.

– 2009. "Stabane, Intersexuality, and Same-Sex Relationships in Soweto." *Feminist Studies* 35 (3): 524–48.

– 2012. "Paradoxes of Butchness: Sexual Violence and Lesbian Masculinities in Contemporary South Africa." *Signs* 37 (4): 961–86.

Swart, Sandra. 2001. "'Man, Gun and Horse': Hard Right Afrikaner Masculine Identity in Post-Apartheid South Africa." In *Changing Men in South Africa*, edited by Robert Morrell. London: Zed Books.

Sykes, Heather. 2006. "Transsexual and Transgender Policies in Sport." *Women in Sport and Physical Activity* 15: 3–13.

Sylla, Aliou, Amadigué Togo, Alou Dembélé, and Christophe Broqua.
    2007. *Analyse de la situation du groupe des hommes ayant des rapports
    sexuels avec d'autres hommes*. Bamako: Rapport de Recherche Arcad-
    sida/Onusida.

Tamagne, Florence. 2004. *A History of Homosexuality in Europe. Berlin,
    London, Paris, 1919–1939*. London: Algora Publishing.

Tamale, Sylvia. 2007a. "Out of the Closet: Unveiling Sexuality Discourses
    in Uganda." In *Africa After Gender?*, edited by C.M. Cole, T. Manuh,
    and S.F. Miescher, 17–29. Bloomington: Indiana University Press.

– 2007b. "Response to Martin Ssempa's Article, 'Homosexuality Is against
    Our Culture'." In *Homosexuality: Perspectives from Uganda*, edited by
    Sylvia Tamale, 62–64. Kampala: Sexual Minorities Uganda.

– ed. 2011. *African Sexualities: A Reader*. Cape Town: Pambazuka Press/
    Fahamu Books.

Tebbe, Nelson. 2007. *Witchcraft and Statecraft: Liberal Democracy in
    Africa*. Social Science Network Electronic Paper Collection. http://ssrn.
    com/abstract=1010148.

Teetzel, Sarah. "On Transgendered Athletes, Fairness, and Doping: An
    International Challenge." *Sport in Society* 9 (2006): 227–51.

Teunis, Niels. 1996. "Homosexuality in Dakar: Is the Bed the Heart of Sex-
    ual Subculture?" *Journal of Gay, Lesbian and Bisexual Identity* 1: 153–69.

– 2001. "Same-Sex Sexuality in Africa: A Case Study from Senegal." AIDS
    and Behaviour 5 (2): 173–82.

Thomas, Greg. 2007. *The Sexual Demon of Colonial Power*. Bloomington:
    Indiana University Press.

Thomas, Lynn M. 2009. "Love, Sex, and the Modern Girl in 1930s
    Southern Africa." In *Love in Africa*, edited by Jennifer Cole and Lynn
    M. Thomas, 31–57. Chicago: University of Chicago Press.

Thompson, Paul. 2000. *The Voice of the Past: Oral History*. 3rd ed.
    Oxford: Oxford University Press.

Thoreson, Ryan, and Sam Cook, eds. 2011. *Nowhere to Turn: Blackmail
    and Extortion of* LGBT *People in Sub-Saharan Africa*. New York: Inter-
    national Gay and Lesbian Human Rights Commission.

Thornberry, Patrick. 1991. *Minorities and Human Rights Law*. London:
    Minorities Rights Group.

Tilly, Charles. 2002. *Stories, Identity, and Political Change*. New York:
    Rowman & Littefield.

– 2008. *Contentious Performances*. Cambridge: University of Cambridge
    Press.

Touray, Isatou. 2006. "Sexuality and Women's Sexual Rights in The Gambia."
    IDS Bulletin 37 (5): 77–83.

Towle, Evan B., and Lynn M. Morgan. 2002. "Romancing the Transgender Native: Rethinking the Use of the 'Third Gender' Concept." *GLQ: A Journal of Gay and Lesbian Studies* 8 (4): 469–97.

Travers, Ann. 2008. "The Sport Nexus and Gender Injustice." *Studies in Social Justice* 2: 79–101.

Truth and Reconciliation Commission (Department of Justice). 1998. *Truth and Reconciliation Commission of South Africa Report*. Vol. 4. Cape Town: TRC.

The Truth and Reconciliation Commission of South Africa. 1999. *Volume One: The Truth and Reconciliation Commission of South Africa Report*. London: MacMillan References Limited.

Tucker, Andrew. 2009. *Queer Visibilities: Space, Identity and Interaction in Cape Town*. Chichester: Wiley-Blackwell.

Tutu, Desmond. 1999. *No Future Without Forgiveness*. New York: Doubleday.

Umozurike, U.O. 1992. *The African Charter on Human and Peoples' Rights*. Lagos: Nigerian Advanced Institute of Legal Studies.

UN High Commissioner for Human Rights. 2011. *Discriminatory Laws and Practices against Individuals Based on Sexual Orientation and Gender Identity*. UNHCR. http://www2.ohchr.org/english/bodies/ hrcouncil/docs/19session/A.HRC.19.41_English.pdf.

UNAIDS. 2007. *Gambia Country Profile*. http://data.unaids.org/pub/ Report/2008/gambia_2008_country_progress_report_en.pdf.

Undie, Chi-Chi, and Kabwe Benaya. 2006. "The State of Knowledge on Sexuality in Sub-Saharan Africa: A Synthesis of the Literature." *JENdA: A Journal of Culture and African Women's Studies* 8. http://www. jendajournal.com/issue8/undie-benaya.html.

UNFPA. 2004. "Key Concepts and Definitions: Population and Reproductive Health." *United Nations Populations Fund*. http://www.lao.unfpa. org/defcon.htm.

UNHCR. *Ghana Treatment of Homosexuals by Society and Authorities and Availability of State Protection; Names and Activities of Groups or Associations Promoting Homosexual Rights*. UNHCR. http://www. unhcr.org/refworld/type, queryresponse,gha,45fl1473820,0.

Valdes, F. 2002. "Mapping the Patterns of Particularities: Queering the Geographies of Identities." *Antipode: A Radical Journal of Geography* 34 (5): 974–87.

Vannini, April, and Barbara Fornssler. 2011. "Girl, Interrupted: Interpreting Semenya's Body, Gender Verification Testing and Public Discourse." *Cultural Studies & Cultural Methodologies* 11 (3): 243–57.

le Vay, Simon. 1996. *Queer Science: The Use and Abuse of Research into Homosexuality*. Massachusetts: MIT Press.

Vilakazi, Fikile, and Sibongile Ndashe. 2010. "The Day the African Commission Disavowed Humanity." *Pambazuka News*, 506: Special Issue:
African Commission blocks LBGTI Human Rights Edition. http://www.
pambazuka.org/en/issue/506.

Vincent, Louise, and Bianca Camminga. 2009. "Putting the 'T' into South
African Human Rights: Transsexuality in the Post-Apartheid Order."
Sexualities 12 (6): 678–700.

la Violette, N. 1997. "The Immutable Refugees: Sexual Orientation in
Canada (A.G.) v. Ward." *University of Toronto Faculty of Law Review*
55 (1): 1–41.

de Vos, Piere. 2000. "The Constitution Made Us Queer: The Sexual Orien-
tation Clause in the South African Constitution and the Emergence of
Gay and Lesbian Identity." In *Sexuality in the Legal Arena*, edited by
Carl Stychin and Didi Herman, 194–202. London: Athlone Press.

Wackwitz, Laura A. 2003. "Verifying the Myth: Olympic Sex Testing and
the Category of 'Woman'." *Women's Studies International Forum* 26:
553–60.

Walcott, R. 2005. "Outside in Black Studies: Reading from a Queer Place
in the Diaspora." In *Black Queer Studies: A Critical Anthology*, edited
by E. Johnson and M. Henderson.

Walgrave, Stefaan, and Jan Manssens. 2000. "The Making of the White
March: The Mass Media as a Mobilizing Alternative to Movement
Organization." *Mobilization: An International Journal* 5: 217–39.

Wanner, Catherine. 2003. "Advocating New Moralities: Conversion to
Evangelicalism in Ukraine." *Religion, State & Society* 31 (3): 273–87.

Warhol, Robyn R. 2002. "The Rhetoric of Addiction: From Victorian
Novels to AA." In *High Anxieties: Cultural Studies in Addiction*, edited
by Janet Farrell Brodie and Marc Redfield, 97–109. Berkeley: University
of California Press.

Warner, M. 2002. *Publics and Counterpublics*. New York: Zone Books.

Weeks, Jeffrey. 1977. *Coming Out: Homosexual Politics in Britain from
the Nineteenth Century to the Present*. London: Quartet Books.

Wenden, Anita. 2008. "Discourses on Poverty: Emerging Perspectives on a
Caring Economy." *Third World Quarterly* 29 (6): 1051–67.

Wenger, Etienne. 1998. *Communities of Practice: Learning , Meaning, and
Identity*. Cambridge: Cambridge University Press.

White, Luise. 2000. *Speaking with Vampires: Rumor and History in Colonial Africa*. Los Angeles: University of California Press.

– 1990. *The Comforts of Home: Prostitution in Colonial Nairobi*.
Chicago: University of Chicago Press.

Wieringa, Saskia. ed. 2011. *Women-Loving-Women in Africa and Asia:
Trans/Sign Report Findings*. Amsterdam: Riek Stienstra Fund et al.

Wieringa, Saskia, and Evelyn Blackwood, eds. 2007. *Women's Masculinities in a Globalizing Asia*. New York: Palgrave Macmillan.

Wilson, Sherryl. 2003. *Oprah, Celebrity, and Formations of Self*. New York: Palgrave Macmillan.

Wiseman, John A. 1997. "Letting Yahya Jammeh off Lightly?" *Review of African Political Economy* 24 (72): 265–9.

– 1998. "The Gambia: From Coup to Elections." *Journal of Democracy* 9: 64–75.

Woodford-Berger, Prudence. 1997. "Associating Women: Female Linkages, Collective Identities, and Political Ideology in Ghana." In *Transforming Female Identities: Women's Organizational Forms in West Africa*, edited by E.E. Rosander, 37–51. Uppsala: Nordiska Africa Institute.

World Bank. 2004. "Ghana Key Trends." http://info.worldbank.org/etools/docs/library/211239/Ghana_KeyTrends-and_%20Policy_Issues.pdf.

– 2012. *Gender Equality*. Washington: IBRD.

Xaba, Thokozani. 2001. "Masculinity and Its Malcontents: The Confrontation between 'Struggle Masculinity' and 'Post-Struggle Masculinity' (1990–1997)." In *Changing Men in South Africa*, edited by Robert Morrell, 105–24. London: Zed Books.

Yankah, Kwesi. 1991. "Power and the Circuit of Formal Talk." *Journal of Folklore Research* 28 (1): 1–22.

– 1995. *Speaking for the Chief: Okyeame and the Politics of Akan Royal Oratory*. Bloomington: Indiana University Press.

Young, Crawford. 1994. *The African Colonial State in Comparative Perspective*. New Haven: Yale University Press.

Youth With a Mission. 2012. http://www.ywam.org.

van Zyl, Mikki, Jeanelle de Gruchy, Sheila Lapinsky, Simon Lewin, and Graeme Reid. 1999. *The Aversion Project: Human Rights Abuses of Gays and Lesbians in the South African Defence Force by Health Workers During the Apartheid Era*. Cape Town: Simply Said and Done (on behalf of Gay and Lesbian Archives, Health and Human Rights Project, Medical Research Council and the National Coalition for Gay and Lesbian Equality).

Index